"Dr. Margaret J. Meeker has written an excellent description of what young boys experience growing up in our overtly secular culture. To both parents and especially to fathers, she gives sound advice as to how they can meet the specific emotional needs of their young sons."

—**Armand M. Nicholi, Jr., M.D.**, professor of psychiatry, Harvard Medical School

"*Boys Should Be Boys* is another great installment from Dr. Meeker. It's a must-have for parents and anyone else concerned about the impact of today's culture on young people and families. In her no-nonsense, direct style, Meg cuts through the clutter and the conflicting messages coming at us from Hollywood, the mass media, the education establishment, and society in general, and provides clear advice on how to help boys grow up to be healthy, happy, and productive men."

—**Teresa Tomeo**, author, motivational speaker, and nationally syndicated radio show host

"This book should be read by every woman who wishes to love the boys in her care, and by every man who desires a greater understanding of the boy he once was, and the son to whom he is a father. A real page-turner filled with stories, facts, and inspiration that will bring a smile to your face, and a renewed confidence that God knew what he was doing when he created us male and female (boys and girls are *not* the same). I highly recommend it."

—**Chris Godfrey**, former professional football player, president and founder of Life Athletes, and inspirational family speaker

BOYS SHOULD BE BOYS

BOYS SHOULD BE BOYS

7 Secrets to Raising Healthy Sons

Meg Meeker, M.D.

Since 1947
REGNERY
PUBLISHING, INC.
An Eagle Publishing Company • Washington, DC

Cataloging-in-Publication data on file with the Library of Congress

ISBN 978-1-59698-057-0

Published in the United States by
Regnery Publishing, Inc.
One Massachusetts Avenue, NW
Washington, DC 20001
www.regnery.com

Manufactured in the United States of America

10 9 8 7 6 5 4 3 2 1

Books are available in quantity for promotional or premium use. Write to Director of Special Sales, Regnery Publishing, Inc., One Massachusetts Avenue NW, Washington, DC 20001, for information on discounts and terms or call (202) 216-0600.

To "T"—
*I am so very proud
of the man you are becoming*

CONTENTS

The Seven Secrets to Raising Healthy Boys

I THINK OF THIS BOOK AS sort of *The Dangerous Book for Parents*. The bestselling *The Dangerous Book for Boys* was full of fun information and projects that boys love but that too many of us have tried to deny them. Tree houses? Too dangerous. The boys might fall and break their arms. Insects and spiders? Yuck. And you want to teach them about hunting, how to make a bow and arrow, and great battles of history? Are you crazy?

Actually, these are all things boys like, and there is no harm in them. As a pediatrician, I've seen plenty of boys with broken arms, spider bites, or who have scraped a knee playing soldier in the woods. But these are just part of growing up. Too many of us parents obsess about healthy diversions that active boys like to do, while not recognizing what is truly dangerous for our boys—like popular music, television, and video games that deaden their sensibilities, shut them off from real human interaction, impede the process of maturation, prevent them from burning up energy in useful outdoor exercise, divorce them from parents, and lower their expectations of life.

In this book I mean to cut through a lot of the misapprehensions, misinformation, and misleading assumptions that too many parents have. It's a book of practical advice based on my clinical experience, relevant scientific data, and the sort of common sense that too many of us managed to misplace from reading too many politically correct "parenting" books. My concern is not with what is politically correct, but with what is true and what is best for our boys. I've seen, and I've learned, that when it comes to raising sons, what is politically correct and what is true are often at opposite ends of the spectrum. I think it's time we put our sons first.

In this book you will learn how to raise healthy and happy boys—boys who are honest, courageous, humble, meek (in the sense of willingly withholding their power), and kind. There are secrets to raising such boys. Among these secrets are the big seven. I can mention them in passing here, but we'll look at what they mean and how to use them in the chapters that follow.

- Know how to encourage your son. One fault is babying and spoiling him. But another is being so harsh that you lose communication with your son and destroy his sense of self-worth. We'll look at how to strike the right balance.
- Understand what your boys need. Guess what? It's not another computer game; it's you. We'll look at how to get the most of your time with your son.
- Recognize that boys were made for the outdoors. Boys love being outside. A healthy boy needs that sense of adventure—and the reality check that the outdoors gives him.
- Remember that boys need rules. Boys instinctively have a boy code. If you don't set rules, however, they feel lost.

- Acknowledge that virtue is not just for girls. Boys should, indeed, be boys—but boys who drink, take drugs, and have sex outside of marriage aren't "normal" teenagers, they have been abnormally socialized by our unfortunately toxic culture. Today, my practice as a pediatrician has to deal with an epidemic of serious, even life-threatening, problems—physical and psychological—that were of comparatively minor concern only forty years ago. A healthy boy strives after virtues like integrity and self-control. In fact, it is virtues like these that make a boy's transition to manhood possible. They are *necessary* virtues, and he needs your help to acquire them. I'll show you how.
- Learn how to teach your son about the big questions in life. Many parents shy away from this, either because they are uncomfortable with these questions themselves, or want to dismiss them as unimportant or even pernicious, or because they don't want to "impose" their views on their children. But whatever one's personal view, your son wants to know— and needs to know—why he's here, what his purpose in life is, why he is important. Boys who don't have a well-grounded understanding on these big questions are the most vulnerable to being led astray into self-destructive behaviors.
- Remember, always, that the most important person in your son's life is you.

Being a parent can often seem a daunting task. But I'm here to tell you that almost every parent has what it takes to raise healthy sons. You have the intuition, the heart, and, yes, the responsibility to change the life of your son for the better. This book is a step toward showing you how.

CHAPTER ONE

Boyhood under Siege

WE ALL KNOW WHAT BOYHOOD SHOULD BE. We carry the iconic images of Huck Finn, of boys trading baseball cards and carrying slingshots in their back pockets, of tree houses and "no girls allowed." If we're parents of sons we know what it's like to see a boy with the instincts to be a leader, a protector, a provider; to be a hero and thwart the villains. Toddler boys don't need any prompting to pick up twigs and use them as swords.

As a mother and pediatrician, I've seen iconic boyhood come to life both at home and in my clinical practice. But for too long, we've tried to kid ourselves in the name of equality that boys and girls are the same, or that we need to push girls to be more aggressive, competitive, and focused on math and science. We think we need to temper boisterous boys to be more submissive, cooperative, and quiet. Of course, as a woman and a doctor, I encourage girls to improve their science scores, but what is *wrong*, and what can be seen in too many social indicators, is social engineering that tries to change our children into something they were never meant to be. My previous book, *Strong Fathers, Strong Daughters*, discusses the challenges facing our daughters. But if anything, the challenges facing today's boys are even greater, because we've been shortchanging the needs and attributes of boys.

Boys and girls bring different gifts to the world. We need to let boys be boys, to recognize the value of boyhood, and to understand how parents can help guide their young sons—yes, the ones with frogs in their pockets, dirt in their hair, and a guilty past of breaking windows with baseballs—into mature, confident, and thoughtful men.

Boys do things that girls, or women, would never do—or think of doing—but that have a value all their own. Consider eight-year-old Seth. He taught me something after more than twenty years of practicing medicine that was finally worth knowing: how to build a bear trap.

"First Dr. Meeker, you dig a really big hole. It has to be big enough for you to jump into," he spread his arms wide, showing me just how enormous the hole needed to be. "Then you fill the hole with some really sharp sticks. And then you can cover it with lots of other sticks that you break off of branches." By this time, his arms were moving furiously, breaking imaginary branches and spreading the sticks.

"Timmy and me put lots of leaves and branches on the top, see. That way the bears won't know the trap is there."

Seth was full of excitement and pride at telling me about how to make a bear trap. So I asked him, had he ever seen a bear? Only a few times, he said: maybe eight or ten.

His mother rolled her eyes as Seth added that, of course, those sightings only occurred at night. Bears needed to sleep a lot during the day while the boys were making traps; besides, he had only a few trees in his back yard, and the bears usually stayed in the bigger forests.

Second-grade boys build bear traps in the woods. They turn couches into the flight decks of aircraft carriers, using shaving cream to outline the launch paths. Fourth-grade boys blow up two-liter pop bottles with Drano and aluminum foil. They shoot light bulbs out with pellet guns. Sixth-grade boys experiment making rockets. They race their bikes until they collapse, exhausted and laughing with their friends. And why? Because rambunctious, healthy, young boys like testing the limits of their physical and mental powers; it simply feels good. They love to wrestle and play football. They like the challenge of making things, blowing things up, fixing things, figuring out how things work; they like becoming experts on anything from bear traps to baseball statistics.

OUR BOYS AT RISK

But today that natural, healthy boyhood is under attack. It is threatened not only by an educational establishment that devalues masculinity and boyishness, and not only by widely remarked social changes including widespread divorce and the rise of single-parent households that deprive boys of the responsible fathers they need, but by a noxious popular culture that is as degrading to boys as it is dangerous to girls.

As parents, we know that boyhood has been changing—for the worse. We want our boys to be like Seth, building tree forts and bear traps, not shooting aliens in video games. We remember when boys use to go trout fishing, sitting under a tree while daydreaming about the future, and now we fear that our boys are cutting themselves off from us with iPods, ear buds, and computer porn. When we grew up in the '60s, '70s, and even in the '80s for the most part, it was safe for boys to flip on the TV, because the networks still upheld a general moral consensus; but now we grimace as our boys are inundated with cheap, nasty dialogue and

graphic images that reflect cheap, nasty values and an impover-
ished imagination. Even when they watch a football game we feel
a gnawing in our stomach because commercials will educate them
about Viagra, erectile dysfunction, and most certainly about
voluptuous older women. Outwardly we go about our work but
inwardly we hold our breath. During the past decade, psychologists have written about the emotional troubles our boys endure.
Educators have sounded alarms because elementary school and
high school boys are performing much more poorly than girls.
Their SAT scores are too low; fewer are graduating from high
school and college. In my own profession of medicine, medical
school applications from young men have dropped.

The American Academy of Pediatrics warns pediatricians like
me about the importance of early diagnosis of autism because it is
on the rise in boys. Then we have Attention Deficit Hyperactivity
Disorder (ADHD) which has skyrocketed in boys over the last
decade. It isn't affecting girls nearly as much as it affects our boys.
In my more than twenty years of medical practice, I have never
seen so many boys struggling with learning issues, hyperactivity,
boredom, and depression as I have over the last five years.

Sociologists, meanwhile, produce reams of data on the social
implications of "gender equality," single-parent households (usually headed by women), astonishingly high divorce rates, the rise
of deadbeat dads, and gang violence, as well as the enormous
risks to young men, particularly African American men, who
grow up without a father's influence.

We become numb to the statistics, while worrying that our
sons will join them. Will our son be the one to drop out of high
school, start drinking, or take drugs? Will he seriously consider
suicide this year (the shocking statistic is that almost one in ten
boys do)? Or God forbid, will he be walking down the hall of his
high school and hear gunfire in a classroom? And what about car
accidents? We know that any teen boy (even a good kid) might

act recklessly behind the wheel of a car, and that accidents are the leading cause of death for teen boys. All it takes is a couple of misguided friends and a few beers.

I am neither a psychologist nor a teacher nor a social scientist. I am a pediatrician and mother who has listened to and observed thousands of boys. I have sat with parents of boys who have committed suicide and seen others leave a world of drugs and violence to move into highly successful professions and lead wonderful lives. I have loved and watched a multitude of boys in good times and bad over the years, and I believe that I am their advocate.

Are our boys in trouble? If so, are they in more danger than past generations? Yes, and most definitely yes. But unlike some psychologists, sociologists, and educators, I believe that the troubles hurting our boys stem from three major sources: lack of close relationships with men (particularly fathers), lack of religious education, and aggressive exposure to a toxic media that teaches boys that the keys to a great life are sex, sex, and a bit more sex—and a whole lot of money and fame.

Educators and political scientists blame the education system and want it corrected. Sociologists blame drugs, alcohol, and poverty, and they want tougher laws, more welfare, and more job opportunities. Many psychologists argue that we have suppressed male emotions and that we need to be more sensitive to our boys, teaching them how to express anger and other emotions constructively.

Certainly these are all valid points. But they miss something very large. They miss *the boy,* the whole boy, the entire sum of his life and being. Too often we deal with pieces of the boy. If he has attention problems we get him a prescription. If he has learning issues, we hire a tutor to correct them. If he is athletically unskilled, we find him a trainer. We attend so meticulously to the individual parts of boys that we miss who they really are.

We must be willing to see that what our boys need isn't simply more education, more prescriptions, more money, or more activities. What they need is *us*. You and me. They need parents who are willing to take a good hard look at what their sons think and what they are doing. They need fathers who will embrace their sons and watch them with the eyes of schooled hawks.

The world of our sons is not the world we lived in when we were young. Most boys can't ride their bikes until sunset without worrying about being abducted. The world has grown sad for our boys. But the good news is: we can bring them back. We can reinstitute some of the joy of boyhood for them, and we can ease their pressures (even the ones we think are beneficial for them, like earning good grades to get into an Ivy League school) by giving them the freedom to be boys: to simply enjoy pick-up games of basketball in their neighborhoods, to find that safe acreage of woods where they can hike and imagine, and to have that home library where classic adventure books await.

Your boys need a refuge, because it's a harsh world out there. Here is an overview of the current state of boyhood in America:

EDUCATION

- 21 percent of boys in grades one through five are identified as having a learning "disability" (including speech impediments and emotional problems)[1]
- ADHD is diagnosed seven times as often in boys as in girls (8 to 10 percent of school-aged children are diagnosed with ADHD)[2]
- 65 percent of boys graduate from high school compared to 72 percent of girls[3]
- Fewer than half (46 percent) of black and half (52 percent) of Hispanic boys graduate from high school[4]
- 56 percent of college undergraduates are women, 44 percent are men[5]

- 58 percent of graduate school students are women[6]

DEPRESSION

- 12 percent of boys have seriously considered suicide[7]

ALCOHOL

- 11 percent of boys admit to drinking and driving[8]
- 27 percent of boys admit to heavy drinking (more than five drinks in a row)[9]
- 29 percent of boys drank alcohol before the age of thirteen[10]

TOBACCO

- 31 percent of boys use tobacco[11]
- 18 percent of boys smoked before they were thirteen[12]

WEAPONS

- 29 percent of boys admit carrying a weapon (gun, knife, or a club)[13]
- 10 percent carried a weapon to school[14]
- 43 percent of boys have been in a fight recently[15]

SEXUAL ACTIVITY

- 42 percent of white boys, 57 percent of Hispanic boys, and 74 percent of black boys have been sexually active before they graduate from high school[16]
- 8 percent of boys admit to having had intercourse before they were thirteen years old[17]
- 16.5 percent have had intercourse with more than four partners[18]

PHYSICAL HEALTH

- 16 percent of American boys are overweight[19]
- 40 percent of boys do not attend PE class regularly in school[20]

Seeing these numbers is disturbing. And there are many more such numbers. Within my lifetime doctors have gone from having to worry about only two major types of sexually transmitted diseases to worrying about more than thirty; and we now find them in epidemic numbers of patients, and increasingly in younger patients. For example, one in five Americans, (the number soars to nearly half of African Americans), over the age of twelve is Herpes 2 positive;[21] nine out of ten men who have genital herpes don't know it; and the costs of such an epidemic are counted not only in my waiting room, not only in depression (which afflicts 20 percent of high school students),[22] but in the havoc it wreaks on our young men's character, which in turn leads to all sorts of other pathologies.

HOW TO TURN THINGS AROUND

The foundation of any boy's life is built on three things: his relationships with his parents, his relationship with God, and his relationship with his siblings and close friends.

If these three are strong, any boy can thrive in the midst of academic and athletic challenges, a toxic culture, and harmful peer pressure. So set aside for the moment thinking of your son in terms of his grades or his athletic performance. Think of him as a person, complete and whole. He has, like any of us, deep needs that have to be met, and if we as parents don't meet them, his character and the decisions he makes will be up for grabs; they'll be shaped by the people who do. The most important people in a boy's life are his parents. You should never feel powerless with your son. No one is more important to him than you are.

Your son needs more time with you: time to talk and time to play. He needs less Internet time, more outdoor time. He needs to know that God exists and that his life is no accident. He needs—and wants—the benefit of your wisdom, life experience, and maturity. Let's look at a few places where you can begin.

KEEP FIRST THINGS FIRST

Boys need strong relationships with their parents. Period. Every boy, without exception, wants a better relationship with his mother and his father because his physical and emotional survival depends on you.

Boys spend far too little time with parents and they suffer because of it. And we all know it. In one survey, 21 percent of kids said that they needed more time with their parents. But when the parents of these kids were polled, only 8 percent responded that they needed more time with their children.[23] We become so absorbed with keeping up with our daily lives that we miss seeing what our boys really need, which is simply more of us: our time and our attention.

In our earnestness to make up for lost time, to help our boys, we give them all the wrong things. But our boys don't need *things*, they need us, even just being around us, watching how we handle life, how we talk, listen, help others, and make our decisions. Every son is his father's apprentice, studying not his dad's profession but his way of living, thinking, and behaving.

Boys need to see fathers who behave as good men so that they can mimic that behavior. They need to see men at work. They need men who set standards—and if you don't give them standards to live by, they'll pick them up where they find them: MySpace, YouTube, or the wrong kids at school. A father needs to give his son the model of a man to measure up to. That's what a son wants from his dad; he wants to admire him and be like him. That's a lot of pressure to put on a father, but that's what being a dad is all about; and the good news is that all dad really needs to do is to be available for his sons; to share time with them and let them watch him and learn from him.

When Jason was ten he came in to see me for his annual physical. I have become so convinced of the central role that healthy parental relationships play in a child's overall health, that I began asking questions about life with his father early on in his appointment.

"How's your dad?" I asked as I peeked into his ear.

"Good," he said, succinct as only ten-year-old boys can be.

"What do you like to do together?"

"Anything. Just stuff I guess. Problem is, dad's got a new job and he's really, really busy. . . . " Jason's voice grew quieter as his sentence trailed off.

"I'm sorry," I said. "I bet his new job is hard for you. I bet you miss him a lot."

"Oh, he's not gone. That's the good part. He's home more. But he's just busy with his work while he's at home. He's on his laptop all the time. I hate it. So does my mom. She complains a lot. She shouldn't, you know; he's just doing what he needs to do."

Then, in his wonderful boyish wisdom, Jason said something quite extraordinary.

"Here's the thing: you know, Dr. Meeker, dad and I used to do a lot of chores outside when he was home. Like chop wood and stuff. He doesn't have much time for that anymore but I guess it's okay. The thing is, I can still be with him. When he goes into the living room to work on his computer, I go in too. I do my homework or read whenever he's in there because, well, it just feels so good to be in the same room with my dad."

That's a ten-year-old boy who understands his dad has a very demanding job, and a dad who understands that letting his son sit with him as he works is one of the best things he could do for his son. What Jason needed from his father, he got. He had his presence. He worked alongside his father. They were, in a way, a team.

I can guarantee that nights doing homework beside his father made Jason a better student. Would their shared time have been more meaningful, more enriching, if his father had set his work aside and helped Jason do his homework or shot hoops with him in the driveway? Perhaps. But his father didn't have much choice. Shooting baskets would certainly have been more fun, but the thing that matters is that Jason had his dad.

By the time their sons become teenagers, many parents feel intimidated at the prospect of spending time with them, or have unrealistic expectations about what that time requires. As a result, they often avoid their teen sons altogether, thinking they don't need time with mom or dad any more. Don't do this. Your teenage son needs you more now than he did when he was six. He just doesn't want you to know it.

It's also important that you don't set yourself up to fail by treating time with your son as "teaching time" where you set him straight about his friends and his tastes. That almost always leads to nothing but frustration. So does expecting time with your sons to be consistently fun and light. Divorced fathers fall into this trap routinely. They want to create positive memories for their sons. They try too hard and when something inevitably goes wrong, or there is a conflict, life feels as though it is falling apart. But it isn't. The reality is that stronger relationships are forged in painful times as well as joyful ones and parents must be willing to persevere. Stay with sons in the midst of battles. Resolve the battle, leave it behind, move forward, and create more enjoyment ahead.

The key thing is the simple thing: just resolve to spend more time with your sons, whether that time is filled with tension, argument, laughter, or silence. All of it is important. Nothing replaces life lived alongside of you, his mother or father, *nothing*. And don't be fooled into believing that you can be substituted, because you can't.

He doesn't want you to buy him stuff, haul him to hockey games, or work longer hours to buy a nicer home (though he might try to convince you of all these things). He needs to see you smile when you are proud, see how you work through problems, and how you deal with tension and frustration. And most important, he needs to know that you will be there when he needs you. Once he knows this, the center of his world will feel tight and secure. Give him that security, and he will feel free to work hard at school, pay attention during his piano lessons, and enjoy all the good things that can be a part of boyhood.

Your son will also want you to teach him about God, and you should. It's a fact of life that children and teenagers with a strong religious faith do better in school, are at less risk of dangerous behaviors, and are more likely to be happy and well-adjusted. It's worth reiterating here that research has consistently shown that religion:

- Helps kids stay away from drugs[24]
- Helps keep kids away from sexual activity[25]
- Helps keep kids away from smoking[26]
- Gives kids moral guidance[27]
- Gives them significantly higher self-esteem and more positive attitudes[28]
- Contributes to their growing maturity as they pass from childhood through adolescence[29]
- Helps them set boundaries and stay out of trouble[30]
- Helps teens keep a good perspective on life[31]
- Helps teens feel good and to be happy[32]
- Helps teens experience fewer depressive symptoms[33]
- Helps most teens get through their problems and troubles[34]
- Helps kids feel better about their bodies and physical appearance[35]
- Helps increase "learned competence" in leadership skills, coping skills and cultural capital[36]

Some parents are uncomfortable with the subject of religion, but religious belief and practice is one of the best protections you can give your children. God matters to boys, as it matters to many people, because it provides an anchor, an ultimate authority to whom they can turn, a sense of purpose, a way to place themselves in the cosmos. As such, faith in God builds confidence, is a powerful guard against depression, and provides moral instruction. Having a moral framework is extremely important for boys. As we will discuss in later chapters, boys intuitively have a moral code. Even at age three boys know what is right and wrong. They gain security by having that moral code defended and enforced.

Spending time with your son and teaching him about God are two vital steps to putting first things first. But there's one more. Your job as a parent also entails maintaining a stable home with a minimum of sibling rivalries. Of course, all boys fight with their siblings. Normal sibling rivalry is part of the maturation process and can actually strengthen a boy's character. But whether it helps or harms him depends in large part on how his parents handle the rivalry. If mom or dad acknowledges it, deals with it in a simple, non-threatening way as normal competition, that's one thing. But if parents fuel the competition between siblings or ignore it when a son is consistently bullied by his brother or chided by his sister, the results can be devastating. Your son shouldn't have to compete for a place in your heart; his hold on you shouldn't feel tenuous and frail. If it does, he won't enjoy school, his playtime will suffer, and his personality will become more brittle and fragile.

Boys must learn how to negotiate healthy relationships within a family. This experience sets the ground rules for his future relationships. Boys who feel rejected by their siblings, grandparents, and parents, will expect to be rejected by others. But if they grow up in a family where there is mutual trust and respect, where they feel like they fit in, they will grow into confident young men.

More important than succeeding at work is succeeding with your family. Of course, life is a balance between competing priorities, but mothers and fathers who want strong, healthy children should always put their family first.

Throughout a boy's life, from preschool to high school, the most important things are keeping a healthy relationship with mom and dad, having faith in God, and having a solid family life. If we want to truly give our sons the best boyhood, the best preparation to become a man, this is it; these are the building blocks on which all else depends.

CHAPTER TWO

Bucking Peer Pressure

WE PARENTS ROUTINELY BLAME PEER PRESSURE for our sons' behaviors. If Johnny didn't mouth off at the kindergarten teacher, then our Sam wouldn't. From the time our boys enter elementary school we fret about bad influences.

But there is one pressure far more important in a boy's life than his peers' behavior. That is, the pressure we experience as parents from our own peers.

How many fathers have watched their friend's son make the varsity basketball team and succumb to the temptation to encourage their own son to practice more? How many mothers have signed sons up for one more tae kwon do session, or one more round of piano lessons, because their friend's sons are busier than theirs? We all have.

We hyper-conscientious parents reel with a constant thought stream regarding what else we should be doing. We should get him a tutor, we should make him have a job at fourteen, we should.... You fill in the blank. This is what we do best—fret over what else we can do for our sons. But that is exactly the wrong way to look at it. It's far more important for parents to *be*, as in be around, and far less important for them to *do*, and certainly to buy, anything. In fact, what we should usually do is schedule *fewer* activities for our children (and fret less as well).

Take a critical inventory of what you do for your son and why. How many sports is he in? Does he enjoy them? Or are they really a way for you to assuage your inner restlessness that he isn't "involved enough"?

The primary areas in which adult peer pressure really gets at boys are athletics, academics, and the arts. If Tom's eleven-year-old son lifts weights for soccer, then we want our ten-year-old son to start lifting weights, because our son is tougher. If Paul's son is in the top 10 percent of his class, we want our son to be in the top 5 percent. If Jim's son is a concert level pianist, we book our son for extra lessons to catch up.

In my experience, every good parent intuitively knows what is good and not good for his sons. The problem is, we ignore our intuitions and jump on the train loaded with mothers and fathers pushing their sons to outshine the others. *Get off of that train.*

Take a hard look at what you want your son's character to look like when he is twenty-five and focus on helping him build that character. Do you really want your son to be a pro-baseball player first and a man of integrity second? Or do you want the order reversed?

Once we identify our motives and our goals, we are half way home in keeping boys on track. The pressure for parents is intense. And I will say that parents of affluence have a terribly difficult time refraining from over-scheduling and over-buying. Resist the temptation. Remember, more than anything else, your son wants *you*, and it is counterproductive to keep him scheduled in activities that take him away from you.

FIVE PARTS LOVE, ONE PART DISCIPLINE

Parents consistently lament that sons won't listen and behave. Their discipline falls on deaf ears and stony hearts. Well, there is a secret to disciplining boys. *Boys will do virtually anything their fathers want them to do.* Even at three years old, every boy wants to feel loved, accepted, and valued. The quickest way he knows to get there is by seeing mom or dad happy with him. That doesn't change. A parent's job is to understand this need and meet it. It gets hard because most parents get exhausted. And when the teen years hit, and our boys are home less, we feel pressured to get our points across quickly and emphatically.

In short, we speak (or lecture) too soon, too frequently to our sons and fail to give them an ear. No boy listens to a parent who lectures before he listens. No son wants his father's advice if he is repeatedly interrupted or criticized. The truth is most sons know already the point a mother or father wants to drive home. Sons know what you like, dislike, want, or expect from them. That's why, when dealing with a teenager, it's less important to talk than to listen.

Many have heard the adage that for every criticism made to a child, seven compliments must follow. In the teen years, it is equally important that your son has seven times as much positive time with you (listening to him) as he has negative time (criticizing or correcting him).

Sons listen to people (parents) whom they respect, like, admire, or fear (in a healthy way). They reject words from adults who only criticize, deride, or push them. If you are a parent who compulsively criticizes and rides your son, stop. For one month stop doing it. You are wasting your energy, pulling your son down, and harming yourself as well. Chances are excellent that the way you communicate to your son is exactly the way your parents communicated to you as a child. Parents act out what is familiar, not what they want.

Fifteen-year-old Lincoln and his father, Brent, came into my office because Brent was concerned about Lincoln's behavior. He was mouthing off at his father, sneaking out of the house at night and dabbling with drugs. His grades were plummeting. What, he wondered, was he to do with "this boy," as he called him.

For the first ten minutes I let Brent talk. Clearly he needed to vent.

"I just don't get it" he said. "I give the boy everything. He takes driver's ed, plays hockey, and goes to a private school. He just won't step up to the plate and work hard. He's running around with a bad group of kids and lies. I never would have lied to my dad. I would have been much more respectful."

Then Lincoln spoke. He was hesitant and quiet. His father refused to look at him as he started, acting frustrated and disgusted.

"My dad—he just doesn't get it. I mean, I'm a good kid. He doesn't give me a chance. He never believes me...." His father interrupted him.

"Why should I? All you do is lie!"

I made him stop.

"See what I mean? He hates me. He's on me all the time. Nothing I do is right. I'm not smart enough. I'm back-up goalie and he even fought with my coach about making me first goalie on my team. How embarrassing is that?" Lincoln paused.

I flashed the palm of my hand toward his father, motioning him not to interrupt. "What do you want from your dad?" I asked.

He dropped his head and paused longer.

"Nothing, just nothing." he mumbled.

Brent's face went ashen.

"Brent," I asked, "how did your father talk to you?"

"My dad—let me tell you—my dad was not one to take any nonsense from any kid. Not like I do from this boy."

"That's not what I asked. How did your father speak to you?"

His eyes widened and he looked frightened. He stared at me, ignoring Lincoln. The tone in the room changed. Somehow it softened. Lincoln looked up at his dad to see his response. Suddenly he was interested to hear about what his dad had to say.

"Pretty bad, actually. Pretty bad. He criticized me constantly. He wanted me to be tough and strong and he never stopped letting me know. I guess he thought that by pointing out my faults that I would get better. It didn't work. It made me stop trying— at anything I guess."

Surprise and sadness swept over Lincoln's face. As Brent and I talked, it became apparent to all of us that he was doing to Lincoln what his father had done to him. He realized now how he was sabotaging Lincoln, and he apologized.

Was he responsible for Lincoln's dishonesty, his drug use, or his failing grades? No, not completely. But his constant criticism most certainly set Lincoln up for failure by making him feel alienated, deadening his interest in anything his father said, and leaving him vulnerable to finding other sources of affirmation (in drugs and bad company). Brent made two enormous changes after he realized what he was doing. Rather than drift in guilt, he challenged himself. He checked his anger and knee-jerk responses. He made a point of listening, and then listening more, before he spoke. And when he spoke, he offered sage advice— advice he expected himself to follow—rather than simply criticizing. He also committed himself to spending more time with Lincoln (with his son's agreement) and purposely avoided lecturing him. Instead, they tried to spend time together doing things they enjoyed. They camped, fished, and occasionally skied or snow-shoed. The times weren't long, but they were fun. In fact, about a year later, Lincoln told me he gave up a few hockey practices so the two of them could go off alone together.

The best news was that Lincoln stopped lying. He stopped sneaking out of the house at night. He made efforts to improve.

Time, attention, affection, and approval: they are what every boy needs in abundance from his parents. I can guarantee that if the majority of parent-son interactions are focused around these four things, then correction and discipline will work when they are required. Sons try to please their parents when they know they *can* please their parents. Without balancing love and discipline, boys are lost.

DON'T LET HIM BE SOMEONE'S DUMPING GROUND

Boys love fun, pleasure-seeking, and risk-taking. They are fun to be around because they embrace mischief and excitement. In response to their propensity toward fun, we American parents indulge them in order to fuel that fun. We do so because we want our boys to be happy. Ask any parent of an eight- or eighteen-year-old son what he hopes for his son's future, and chances are excellent that he will respond by saying that he simply wants his son to be happy.

The question is, however, is happiness enough? Is aspiring to raise a son to be happy more important than raising a boy to be *good*?

In an effort to help our boys be happy, we provide for them. We give them toys, clothes, money, and entertainment. We inadvertently teach them that it is better to receive than to give. And gadget-producing corporations have our number; they play on our guilt, fears, and pocketbooks. But we forget that the happiness that comes from receiving things is fleeting, and worse, it fuels a desire to get more. In very short order, boys who have $100 basketball shoes want $120 basketball shoes. More begets more, and we become obsessed with possessing. As parents, we have had enough shoes to know that they are only shoes. But when it comes to our sons, we allowed ourselves to be fooled. Maybe this Wii game, that soccer jersey, or that skateboard will bring him happiness, at least temporarily.

Be very, very careful. There is nothing wrong with boys being entertained, but the question is how they're entertained. A laptop allows a son access to wonderful articles and research, but it also brings pornography into his bedroom. And pornography seriously endangers boys.

Many boys plead for televisions in their bedrooms. Teens want space, privacy, and a chance to make some decisions about what to watch. Is there a problem with a boy watching football on television in his bedroom? Of course not, but football is not all that's broadcast into his bedroom. Who can watch an hour of television (particularly a sports event) without numerous doses of tawdry, soft porn? A boy sees breasts flashed, ugly language, sexual banter targeting twelve-year-olds, and he leaves his viewing ever so slightly different than he was before he watched. Any teen will insist that television has no impact on his thinking but let's not be fools. Television is a dumping ground where callous advertisers and pop culture pimps pour their trash, hoping your son will find a few pieces appetizing.

When it comes to televisions and computers and phones, you need to be a diligent and fastidious filter for him. You need to set ground rules. Keep televisions and computers out of his room; they need to be used communally, for the family; that's safer. There are many influences you can't prevent, but what comes into your home you most certainly can.

Remember, watching more and being exposed to more demeaning conversations and almost adolescent sexual behavior through media won't make him happier. And it most certainly won't help him become good.

Restraint will accomplish both. Limiting excess television, games, shoes, you name it will indeed help him become happier *and better*. Too much is too much for boys. He doesn't need more of anything but you.

YOU ARE NOT THE ENEMY

Contrary to popular belief, boys are not born to rebel against their parents at any age. To a very large degree, this boy-hating-his-parents phenomenon has been contrived by popular media with the aid of some psychologists. Sadly, many of us simply hold our breath until we sense the first snarls, the back talk, and the rejection from our boys.

But boys don't naturally hate their parents at six or at sixteen. Certainly as he matures he will desire more independence, but obnoxious behavior or rebellion is not natural or healthy.

Part of the problem, again, comes from popular culture, where rude sons and stupid fathers are a rule of almost every sitcom, where entire industries (including much of the pop music world) are devoted to inciting teenagers against their parents, and where the traditional values that parents provide boys as guardrails are derided.

As parents we need to recognize that in this regard popular culture is our enemy; it's competing for our sons, and it's up to us to defeat it. Don't ever forget that in your son's eyes you are huge. Every statistic we have affirms that no one is more important in a son's life and in the decisions he makes about drinking, drugs, and sex, than his father. Don't abdicate your authority. Don't become the cool, stupid dad you think he wants, because he doesn't—and once you cross that line, it's hard to step back. Every boy hates it when his father becomes funny, dumb, or acts too much like his adolescent peers. He wants to respect you—and that means looking up to you.

You might have seen young boys, even toddlers, say rude things to their parents and been appalled—perhaps a third-grader yelling at his father. And what did the father do? Did he shrug his shoulders or pretend to ignore the child? Most likely he did. And if he did, it's because our perspectives regarding normal child-parent behaviors have been re-worked. Our media has normalized aberrant behavior for so long that we have come to live with it. But we shouldn't. And the way to stop it is not only to limit your child's exposure to the media waste bin, but to always make sure your son knows that you're his ally. Musicians, screenwriters, and movie producers sidle up beside adolescent boys and try to convince them that parents are the foe, that they, the pop culture pimps, understand your son better than you do—they understand his thinking and feelings; and they have just the CD or DVD that he should buy.

Realize that this is happening, that it is unnatural, and that even if your son embraces it, he knows it's unnatural too. Deep down he knows that life is not supposed to be this way. He knows that his mother is the person who cares about him more than anyone else in the world, that his father is what a man should be, and that he himself should be a young man of character and moral strength.

Let's bring our boys back. They are waiting for us to champion their masculinity and challenge them to be sound boys who are ready to grow into men of great virtue. But they can't get there alone. They're kids. So let's get to work and help them.

CHAPTER THREE

Bullfrogs and Racecars

"MY HUSBAND IS THE MISSING LINK," Annie blurted, shaking her head in exasperation and wonder. "I just don't *get* men and woods. Stan can't stay out of them. He comes inside, then after ten minutes, he's out again, back in the dirt. During the summer he floats for hours in his tiny boat on top of the water waiting for a fish to take a bite out of the worm. And in the winter, he tromps around the woods for hours on his snowshoes."

She had an epiphany. "That's it!" she said. "Water. He must have some anthropologic connection with moving or frozen water. He loves to be on it, in it, around it. Maybe he was a whale in a former life."

Annie's frustration with her husband's disappearances out onto the lake or into the woods was compounded by the fact that she genuinely couldn't grasp his fascination. What impulses drove him outside? They had a good marriage, she insisted, but she often found herself jealous of snow and water! Living in a northern climate, white Christmases weren't on her wish list.

But the call of the wild is heard by many men—often with odd if instructive effect.

A PORCH AND A PUMPKIN

At fifteen, Eli wasn't so much rebellious as he was, well, peculiar. He had just returned home after canoeing for six weeks with his camp mates. In that time, he'd decided that living indoors was for sissies. Who needs beds, pillows, and carpeted bedrooms? How much better to breathe fresh air and sleep soundly beneath the stars in the black sky.

So Eli announced to his family that he had no further use for his bedroom. He was going to make a room for himself in the small area of grass in the back yard.

His mother told him it was a ridiculous idea, and that it was too dangerous for him to be out alone all night. Eli devised a back-up plan. On the second floor, beneath his sister's bedroom window was balcony. Eli saw it as his makeshift, open-topped tent. He could sleep there, outside and unnoticed, just as if he were camping. And better yet, he wouldn't have to tell his mom. The balcony was, after all, part of the house, so technically he was sleeping inside.

When bedtime came, Eli collected his sleeping bag and a flashlight. He crept through his sister's room after she fell asleep, carefully opened her bedroom window, and slipped out onto the small balcony. He needed to step gingerly on the wood platform. He imagined he was on a cliff high above a rock-packed stream. He felt free. He unzipped his sleeping bag, wriggled his body into the down, and pulled the drawstring tight. He was secure. In his cocoon, he was alone with the stars, with the tree branches and the coal-black sky. He felt wonderful.

The next morning, when his mother opened his bedroom door to awaken him, she screamed. His bed was made and his room was too neat. She thought he had run away. She woke up his younger sister and they ran down the stairs calling his name. Perhaps he had fallen asleep on the couch in the living room. No, he wasn't anywhere downstairs.

His mother told his sister to go upstairs and get ready for school. She was going to call the police. When his sister walked into her room, Eli was there at the window, tapping to be let inside.

Somehow, after calming his mother, Eli convinced her to let him continue to sleep on the balcony. He would be safe, and besides, he reassured her, no one could see him behind the railing. For the ensuing two months, Eli claimed the tiny porch as his own. He didn't have to sneak through his sister's room; she welcomed him. Eli thought she actually liked him sleeping there because it made her feel safe. He was her security guard.

In late October, Eli's mother put up her outdoor Halloween decorations. Eli loved Halloween and decorated his balcony with pumpkins. He found a few small ones and placed them along the top of the balcony railing.

Several days before Halloween, Eli crawled through the bedroom window onto the porch to get ready for bed. The night air was getting colder, to the point that he could see his breath, so he quickly crawled into the sleeping bag and zipped the hood tightly around his face. Because he was so acclimated to the cool night air, he fell asleep easily.

During the dark hours of the early morning, Eli awoke to a peculiar noise. He heard scratching and faint groaning. Someone was near him, but he couldn't see anyone. He lay still on his back, his heart pounding in his chest. He breathed downward into his bag, in order to keep his misty breath hidden from the prowler.

Again, he heard a grunt and gentle banging. Someone was right below him. The noise grew louder. He wanted to get inside the house, but he didn't dare unzip his bag. Suddenly Eli's plan to live outside seemed dumb. What was he thinking? This wasn't Canada, where he'd gone camping, this was his neighborhood. Pretend was fun, but at this very moment it was highly impractical.

He lay as still as he could. He thought he felt something move to his right, level with his head. From the corner of his eye he saw a hand grabbing the porch banister. It was coming to get him!

Before he could think what to do, he bolted upright in his bag. His head was enveloped by the hood of the bag and when he turned towards the banister he stared face to face at another man whose features where indistinguishable in the darkness. Eli screamed and the prowler, viewing the black, faceless, upright mummy screamed back.

For what seemed like minutes rather than seconds, the two stared at one another screaming. The prowler dropped the pumpkin he was apparently trying to steal, and fell off the balcony onto the ground. Eli heard a thud and the snap of branches. He pushed the sleeping bag off of his head and rolled his body towards the edge of the railing. He saw a figure wrenching himself from the bushes below. The thief grabbed a bike (newspapers were bundled to the back of it) and sped away.

When Eli arrived at school, he told his best friend about the thief trying to steal a pumpkin from the balcony. Eli said that if he found that thief, boy, he would beat the crap out of him.

The first morning bell rang and Eli went to math class. As the other students filed in, Eli noticed something wrong with Pinky Watts. (He was dubbed Pinky after wearing a pink button-down shirt frequently in the second grade.) He looked down in the mouth, and then Eli noticed that Pinky's right arm was in a cast.

Eli couldn't contain himself. He ran to Pinky's desk and blurted, "How'd you break your arm, Pinky, huh?"

"I fell off my bike this morning riding to school." His words sounded rehearsed. "Sure you did," Eli shot back. He wanted to taunt him, to prove him wrong, but something stopped him. Eli realized that Pinky had lost, he had broken his arm. And he realized, at fifteen, that Pinky had endured enough humiliation. Pinky knew that Eli knew and his eyes pleaded with Eli not to tell anyone. Suddenly, Eli felt sorry for him. He looked quite pathetic. Eli assured Pinky with a nod that the secret would stay quiet between the two of them.

During his years in college and graduate school, Eli spent his summers in the Wyoming mountains as an instructor at an outdoor survival school. On the morning of his wedding day, his fiancée couldn't find him. His bed was still made. Had he got cold feet and bolted? But then she found him outside, asleep under an enormous maple. Today, he usually sleeps indoors in their four-bedroom home.

Eli's sleeping on the balcony might have been unusual, but there was nothing harmful in it. In fact, there was something very good in it. It expressed a boy's love for the freedom of the outdoors. It gave Eli a sense of independence, of hardiness amidst the elements. And his confrontation with Pinky taught him about how to deal with people.

THE SCIENCE OF OUTDOOR LIFE

Some scholars say that the male brain is wired to enjoy the outdoors, starting with the fact that boys are visually more attracted to movement—including, presumably, the movement of game through the woods—than girls are.

Other psychologists attribute the male fascination with nature to a desire for, a memory of, freedom—boys see nature as a larger arena where they can roam and daydream, and men feel that in the outdoors they can safely express their aggressive tendencies in sports or hunting.

Anthropologists relate a boy's fascination with the outdoors to his evolutionary roots, when men were hunters who provided for the tribe, and boys were apprentices who proved themselves in rights of initiation that required courage and developing hunting skills.

Whatever the reason, most boys simply love to be outside. They like to romp in nature because it feels good. In my experience, a boy's fascination with tree bark, snakes, bullfrogs, and insects stems from an outworking of his physiological and his psychological needs, which is a scientific way of saying that boys like nature because it offers them a physical and imaginative testing ground.

A PIECE OF CABLE, A BACKPACK, AND ONE PVC PIPE

It was the woods that brought Billy, Tyler, and Ethan together, because their houses backed onto a small forest. The boys loved the woods because they were private. No one could see them amidst the trees and pine needles. The woods belonged to them.

After school or on Saturday mornings the three convened in the woods. Occasionally a few other boys, like their friends Timmy and Mike, joined them, but visitors had to agree to keep the woods—and everything that happened there—secret.

Shortly after claiming ownership of the forest, Tyler and Billy made plans for a fort. They pounded broken boards, pieces of plywood, and yards of rope between two trees. They found a large piece of PVC piping and decided this would sit at the center of the fort floor and drop straight to the ground; it would serve as their toilet. One final touch, Tyler insisted, was to nail a dead salmon to a tree right below the fort. The dead fish was a warning to all who trespassed. This fort was theirs.

And once they built their fort what did they do? They let their imaginations run wild, and imagined they saw men in camouflage circling their patch of forest. The invaders knelt at the perimeter, spying on the boys through binoculars, cutting off all possible escape routes for the boys. The boys' hearts pounded. They needed a plan and quickly. Billy suggested that they climb as high as they could in the pine trees supporting the fort. That way, when their enemies stormed the fort, the boys could drop rocks, branches, and leftover food on their heads. If they could kill one, the others might get frightened and run away.

Tyler thought Billy's scheme was stupid. He had a much smarter idea. All five of them could parachute out of the woods. They would stay high, float quietly. They were, after all, skilled paratroopers (or aspired to be) and skirting past the camouflaged enemy would be a cinch. But they needed a few more items to make parachutes.

It was brilliant, Ethan, Timmy, and Mike agreed. Billy wasn't happy but since he was out-voted, but he decided to cooperate.

Swiftly and quietly they ran a piece of cable from the highest board of their fort to the trunk of a nearby pine tree, anchoring the cable about two feet off the ground.

Ethan grew impatient. What if the enemy stormed the fort before they were finished? If he or his friends were hurt or killed, what would his mother say? She'd never let him go to the fort again.

They heard leaves crackling all around them, crunching beneath the steel-toed boots of the men. Tyler spied a rifle barrel. The enemy was closing in. They had to move fast.

Finally the cable was secured. The five scampered up into the fort and planned their next move. Ethan would parachute out first. He was the youngest and the lightest; the lightest boy had to go first—just in case.

Ethan didn't want to be first. He was terrified but didn't want the others to know. Instead, he argued that because parachuting down the cable would be so much fun, the older boys should go first, and he should go last. That was ridiculous, the others shouted. Ethan had to go first, he was the lightest.

They strapped Tyler's backpack to Ethan's shoulders and began filling it with fort paraphernalia. The backpack would be his weighted parachute. They put plastic cups, a jar of peanut butter, and two half-drunk bottles of Sprite into the pack.

Listen, Timmy whispered. He thought he heard voices. Did the camouflaged men see them? Ethan started to cry as Mike, Billy and Tyler affirmed that they could see hundreds of the men tucked behind trees, just waiting to grab the boys. Ethan was petrified that they would get him. Tyler pulled a carabineer from his pocket and clipped it to a loop at the top of Ethan's backpack. But Ethan flailed his arms in front of him, protesting that he wasn't ready. The others told him there was no time for delay; he had to go now. Tyler and Billy hoisted Ethan to the roof of the fort, while Timmy and Mike kept watch. Tyler clipped the carabineer to the cable. The aluminum clasp was all that held Ethan fifteen feet high in the air—but it worked. Ethan was on, ready to fly.

They gave him a push. His whole body lurched forward, parallel to the ground, but he wasn't moving. He was swimming in the air, trying to propel himself forward by grabbing the air with alternating strokes of his arms.

The enemy saw him. The other four boys confirmed this. Billy had an epiphany. He broke a thick branch from the pine tree and stripped the bark off. Its flesh was green and shiny. Surely it would fly. Just to be sure, Billy grabbed a tub of margarine left over from lunch and slathered the yellow stuff generously over the middle of the branch. Then he buttered the carabineer.

He told Ethan to grab the ends of the branch and hold it across the top of the cable. This would help him slide to safety.

With a new handle in place and a freshly buttered clip, Ethan nodded that he was ready. On the whispered count of three, all four boys pushed him forward.

And he flew! With his scrawny frame hanging from the cable, he held a firm grip to the pine branch and headed straight toward the ground. Suddenly, the pine branch snapped and the backpack jerked him to a halt. Seven feet in the air, dangling by a tiny clip attached to a cable, Ethan hung. He squealed. He hurled his feet wildly behind him trying to make his body move. But he couldn't. He was stuck. And he was frightened. He looked at the dirt beneath him. On the tree in front of him he saw the salmon, their trademark, nailed to the tree that anchored the cable, and in a moment of maturity born of crisis, he at once thought it was the stupidest thing he had ever seen.

Before he realized it, the other four boys had climbed down the ladder of the fort and were standing beneath him, wondering how to get him down. One tried to pull him down by his feet. But the others stopped him, saying it was too dangerous. Tyler had a different idea. He needed a baseball bat, or something like it. He looked for a long, thick branch on the ground. He found one, grabbed it, and ran back to rescue Ethan. Ethan was a sitting duck and would die quickly if he didn't act.

Tyler shouted at the others to grab rocks. For a moment they looked at him quizzically and then like the obedient, well-trained junior paratroopers they were, they grabbed small rocks and filled their pockets. The big rocks wouldn't fit inside, so they carried them in their arms.

Tyler explained his idea: they were going to knock Ethan free. He ordered his troop to aim for the top of the backpack. Those who had excellent aim could shoot for the carabineer. Make it move. With enough force against the backpack, Ethan could finish his jump, they could unclip him, and then they would have to sprint away from the surrounding enemy. Tyler batted the backpack with his branch. The others threw rocks and Ethan screamed. Their aim wasn't as good as they thought. Billy hurled a good-sized stone, which hit Ethan in the kidney. Then came another. Stones smacked against his wrists, his knees. He could feel the welts erupting over his body and he yelled at them to stop.

With a final blow, Tyler swung his branch at Ethan and clipped the carabineer. It opened and Ethan thudded belly first onto the ground. One of the pop bottles in his backpack burst and he felt liquid soaking through the canvas onto his shirt.

The boys unstrapped Ethan from the backpack, dropping it behind them, and then grabbed their injured buddy and ran, past the enemy, past their rifles pointing at them through the bushes, past the bullets buzzing by their heads. When they reached Billy's yard, they collapsed on the grass. They lay on their backs, breathing hard, their chests pounding. None of them spoke for a good ten minutes.

They were victorious! Ethan had almost died and Tyler had wrenched his ankle during the escape but they were alive. The boys of Fort Salmon, the paratroopers, had won. They had proved their courage, tenacity, and skill. They were men.

After several moments of quiet, Tyler rolled on his side to face the other four. "So," he said, "what do you want to do now?"

Today, Tyler is a pilot for a company that charters jets. Occasionally he flies his buddies to Michigan's Upper Peninsula to camp and hike. He still likes the woods, but hasn't tried gliding down a cable greased by margarine in a long time.

Nature was important to Tyler, as it is for all boys, because boyhood is meant to be lived between a boy's imagination and his feet. He needs to move his feet in order to keep up with his sense of wonder. That is why boys are so physical, so rough. Life is a continual experiment to see what can happen if....

As we watch these fort-building, parachute-jumping boys, we see threads of essential boyhood and why nature brings it alive: the desire to create, build, and imagine; the desire to live by a code of conduct (emphasizing independence, friendship, and courage); the desire to test and prove one's abilities.

Of course, for each of the boys, the fort offered something different. It could be a fort, but it could also be a castle harboring knights, the deck of a ship, or a club where retired officers smoked cigars. But whatever adventures they dreamt there, the place was always theirs—and that sense of ownership and privacy is important to boys. The fact that boys like to isolate themselves from girls, or even, when they're playing, from their parents, is not unhealthy or antisocial or dangerous. Boys like to be in charge among their peers; they like to be free to let their thoughts and their games run wild—and being outdoors lets them do that; it's where they can play cowboys and Indians, whittle sticks, have adventures tramping through the forest, and laugh about boy things.

Boys need forts to play in and asphalt for street hockey games with their buddies. It's in those places that they learn confidence and decision-making. It's playing in forts and in pick-up, sandlot football games that boys find a healthy venue for growing into men. Boys actually thrive more when they're not forced into organized activities—or shuttled from one organized sport to another—but when they organize games and adventures and projects on their own, when they're outside with their buddies. They need that time on the fort and in the sandlot, to mix it up with their peers, with kids from different grades, to feel what it's like to be the runt (like poor Ethan) and to grow into a leader (like Tyler).

It's important, as I've emphasized, for parents to be there for their kids; but it's also important that we not micromanage our kids. When boys play in their tree fort, it's not necessary for mom and dad to be crouching down inside. In fact, they shouldn't be. When adults supervise and set the rules for every outdoor game, boys don't learn how to assert themselves in their unique, individual ways.

When boys play in organized sports, they always play with boys their own age, when what young boys need—and what they can get when they play on their own in the neighborhood, is a mixture of older boys and younger boys. When parents run the show, no one can be king; no one can be the ball boy; no one can be the ghost runner between the bases. We all, as parents, want our son to be the pitcher, but that isn't real life. Boys who begin on top and who stay on top because a parent is always two steps ahead of him clearing his way and talking to coaches (or being the coach) robs him of opportunities to learn to navigate his own way—to take some bumps and learn to get back up again.

In their fort in the woods, Tyler learned how to take charge. Ethan was forced to overcome his fears. And most of all, the boys worked together; no one went solo; they were a band of warriors, depending upon one another for "survival." At the fort, they formed their own social circle; they had fun and tested their inventiveness; and when they left the fort, they felt better about themselves, not from a hollow "self-esteem" pumped into them by parents and teachers, but from a real sense of accomplishment earned on their own.

When given a patch of trees and a bit of lumber, boys make life work. Between pounding the boards and wounding their shins, they fight imaginary wars and send little boys flying down a cable. There's nothing like watching uninterrupted play amongst a pack of boys to highlight the dramatic differences between the sexes. Show me six girls who traipse into the woods Saturday after Saturday to fight battles and build tree-forts with dead fish nailed to the front. You won't. But boys do, and should be allowed to. It's what their dreams are made of.

THE RED SQUIRREL

Nature is where boys of all ages, grown men included, can enter and be challenged, where their wits can be sharpened, where they can learn about themselves and about life. That was especially true for Josh.

In a patch of woods, on an unusually chilly but beautiful fall day in Yarmouth, Maine, seven-year-old Josh's life was changed.

In Maine, fall ushers in a very important time: deer hunting season. Herds of pickup trucks, filled with men of all ages, find their way up north. The hunters are looking for the Big One: the granddaddy of all bucks. Josh wanted to learn to hunt and go deer hunting with his dad. His father told him that he was too young to handle a gun. Not even a pellet gun. What he could do, however, was learn to shoot a bow and arrow. His father had a compound bow and he told Josh that if he decreased the tension on it then Josh would be able to shoot it.

Josh was thrilled. This was going to be the best fall of his life. But then his dad added that, no, he couldn't hunt deer. And no, he couldn't hunt ducks, pheasants, or any other living thing. What he could do was practice shooting at a target mounted on bales of straw in the back yard.

On weekends Josh and his dad took to the patch of woods at the end of their yard and practiced shooting the bow and arrow. Pulling the bowstring hurt his arm, but he didn't want to say anything to his dad. And sometimes when he released it, it snapped against his forearm, stinging his skin.

Josh loved the discipline of shooting the bow. He liked the fact that he could shoot it when dad and mom were there to watch and that it was off limits when they weren't.

But October in Yarmouth was tempting, sometimes too tempting. After school one day Josh decided to cut through the garage to the trampoline in the backyard. But then he saw his dad's compound bow hanging on the garage wall. He thought for a minute that he shouldn't touch it. His dad was at work. But his mom was home. She was in the kitchen. She could watch him in the woods when she looked out the window. That counted.

Reasoning was over and off he trotted with the bow and a quiver full of arrows. He strode past the trampoline and the swing set into the patch of orange and red woods behind. The leaves crunched beneath his sneakers and he quickly altered his pace. He didn't want any deer or squirrels to hear him in the woods.

Josh made his way towards a big pine tree and sat down at its base. He watched quietly as birds flew above him and squirrels darted by preparing their nest for the hearty winter.

He was chilly because he had no jacket on. He had purposely left it in the house, thinking it would make him sweaty while he was jumping on his trampoline. He stood up, rubbed his arms to get warm, and walked deeper into the woods. He took an arrow out of the quiver, just to be ready in case the granddaddy of all bucks came by. And what if he got the buck? What would his dad think then?

One day, he was certain, he and his dad would hunt together. They would camp way up north and track the Big One for days—and the days would be hard. No deer baiting for them. They would eat cold hot dogs, and baked bean sandwiches, and raw potatoes, because that's what serious hunters do when they hunt. At night it would rain and he would get up early and start a fire. He could almost smell the smoke from his damp fire. And he would learn to make coffee with grounds and water in a tin pot over the flames.

Something moved to his right. Josh stood still and waited. Another movement. He turned forty-five degrees very slowly, very carefully. He slipped his arrow onto his bow, wrapping his index finger around its shaft to secure it in place.

A big red squirrel sat on a dead log gnawing on an acorn just twenty-five feet away. He felt his heart pound in his throat, and knew this was his chance to be a real hunter. What would his dad say? Boy, would he be proud.

He deliberately raised his bow and drew the bowstring taut, though he had difficulty holding it steady. He aligned the arrow

tip with the squirrel and before he could make a conscious decision to let the arrow fly, the string was released and he saw the
arrow pierce the squirrel.

Josh was stunned. He had never shot anything before in his
life. Suddenly he was hot and cold at the same time. He dropped
the bow and to his amazement, the squirrel began to move. Then
he saw a terrible sight. The red squirrel was running with the
arrow stuck through its belly. Josh felt sick. What should he do
now? He didn't want to hit it again with another arrow. What if
he missed? What if he didn't?

He chased the squirrel through the woods and caught up with
it. He grabbed one end of the arrow shaft. It felt oozy and creepy
with squirrel blood, and Josh felt afraid. The squirrel was still
struggling for life. Not knowing what else to do, he decided to
take it home and ask his mother. He walked across the yard, the
red squirrel hanging upside down, suspended in mid-air like a
giant cooked marshmallow on a stick. He walked into the garage
and the moment he opened the back door he burst into tears. He
saw his mother and he cried harder.

"Joshua, what's the matter?"

"Mom, come here. A squirrel—I shot a squirrel."

Josh led his mother to the garage and she saw the speared
squirrel, still alive, lying on the cement. She was angry but didn't
want to make Josh feel worse. So she did what most upset mothers do. She blamed his dad.

"This is your father's fault. He's the one who got you into this
with all this hunting stuff! What are we going to do now?" she
yelled.

Josh's mother hated hunting. She tolerated it because that's
what most wives and mothers do who live in hunting territory.

"Call your father. No, I'll call your father, right now—he's got
to fix this problem. Someone has to kill the poor squirrel to put
him out of his misery and I'm not going to do it," she insisted.

The phone rang in Josh's father's office at Maine Medical Center. As head of a large department, he usually let his secretary answer, but this time he happened to pick up the phone.

"Michael, you need to get home right now. We have a problem on our hands. Your son just shot a squirrel in the back woods and it isn't dead. The arrow is sticking out of his body and something needs to be done now. And I'm not going to touch it."

Michael's response irritated her. "Whoa. He hit a squirrel with a bow and arrow? How far away was he?"

"What difference does it make? Just get home and do something."

As his parents talked, Josh realized what he had to do. His mother put him on the line with his father. His dad couldn't come home just now. He told Josh that if he was going to hunt with his bow and arrow he had to see his actions through. He couldn't stop halfway and let the little squirrel suffer.

So Josh took the squirrel into the back yard and crying with each breath killed the squirrel with a stone, and then he buried it.

When Michael came home that night, he didn't scold Josh for using his bow alone (which he was forbidden to do), but praised his accuracy. A squirrel on a log at twenty-five feet—that was hard even for him. But mostly, he praised Josh for taking responsibility for the squirrel.

"I'm proud of you because you respected the squirrel. If you ever come to a point where you don't feel sad about hunting an animal, it's time to stop," his dad told him.

Josh admired his dad and admired his dad's manliness. His dad set the standard he wanted to reach, but at seven, he wasn't quite ready. The red squirrel taught him that.

Today, having graduated from an elite New England college (he wrote about the red squirrel in his admissions essay), Josh works at an investment firm in Boston and is highly successful. His co-workers regard him as a man of integrity and sensitivity;

and that experience in the woods when he was a boy is a part of that. Boys learn lessons about themselves, about nature, and about life when they're out in the wilderness. Josh's experience with the red squirrel was one of the most important of his life. He still loves the outdoors but has since exchanged hunting for fly fishing (catch and release, of course).

WHAT NATURE TEACHES

Boys, like men, tend to hide many emotions and lock them inside. Rather than cry openly or talk out their problems with siblings and friends, the ways girls do, boys often turn in on themselves; they need somewhere to go when they can be alone and think—and nature provides that refuge.

It provides many other lessons to a growing boy as well, helping him to come to terms, for example, with his growing physical strength and aggressiveness, qualities that can be unsettling for parents, especially mothers. When we watch boys wrestle in the hallway at school or bang one another into walls, we see their emerging strength and we fear it; we fear that someone will get hurt, that things will get out of control. We want them to stop wrestling and be polite; we don't want our son, or someone else's son, to get physically or emotionally hurt.

But boys need to press their strength, to test their power, and even to assert it. Of course they must learn self control, temperance, and compassion for others. But one of the great things about nature, as with the story of the red squirrel, is that it's where boys can be a hunter—and learn his discipline and skill—while also learning about the inevitable tragedy of the hunt. It's also where boys can learn a lot about unyielding reality. Trees and boulders aren't moved by wishes, arguments, complaints, or desires; a shot arrow can't be called back, it can't be erased by a delete button; the hunt can't be started over by a computer command. Whether a boy's play in the woods is partly imaginary—as with Tyler and his tree fort paratroopers—or as real as shooting an arrow, the play is three-dimensional, real, and instructive in a way that no computer game can ever be. Boys need to get their hands dirty and try to knock life around or at least pretend to knock it around.

RISK-TAKING

The teenage boy's bent towards risk-taking gives his parents gray hairs—and his parents are frightened for good reason. Adolescent boys haven't completed their cognitive maturity. While they think more abstractly than fifth graders, they can't think like a twenty-five-year-old, and this inability to weigh risks and consequences accurately (or at all) supercharges their risk-taking. They never or rarely think that driving a hundred miles an hour down a country road is anything more than fun. If they hit a tree, they'll just walk away from the demolished car and go home and eat supper. They can imagine other people dying but never themselves.

Many teenage boys live in what psychologists refer to as "personal fable." This is the belief that they can do anything they want to—they have a distorted sense of their own power to change other people's minds. This is one of the reasons young teen boys suffer so greatly after a parent's divorce. At fifteen, a son believes that he could have prevented his father from walking out. He could have reversed his mother's depression or saved a friend from drowning. In short, he feels overly responsible for much of life because he genuinely believes he has the power to change the immediate destiny of himself, his loved ones, and his friends.

All of these levels of psychological immaturity—his difficulty connecting present actions with future consequences, his belief in his invincibility, and the personal fable—prime a boy for risk-taking adventure.

He has felt power emerging within him and he wants to define it further in order to feel more like a man. He doesn't want to destroy, over-power, manipulate, or harm others. He wants to feel the exhilaration of his own power. And a very enticing place for this to happen is in cars. Racecars, in particular.

Look at the millions of young and older men alike who are enthralled with racecars. The machines are sleek, they are fast, and they are very masculine—almost as masculine as the drivers themselves. The appeal of racecars to boys makes complete sense because it is the epitome of a man's test of his own masculine power. How fast can he make a car move? How many other cars can he leave behind in his dust? How effectively can his personal power as a driver and the power of the car become one?

This experience, I believe, is wholly male. A very large portion of a man's masculine identity is defined by his understanding of his power. This is not true with women whose femininity is defined by many more emotional and intellectual factors, and none so overwhelming, as power is for men.

So should we let our sixteen-year-old boys loose on the highways in snappy little cars? Absolutely not, but we do need to recognize that boys look for outlets to define their power. Understanding this gives us a better way of understanding how to protect them. Most parents believe their teen sons are more cognitively, psychologically, and emotionally mature than they really are; they don't understand that when their son gets behind the wheel of car, he might think of testing his limits. We can't afford to be so deceived by our teenage sons' long legs and stubbly faces. You won't be able to reason with a sixteen-year-old boy or talk him out of taking risks. His mind thinks completely differently from yours. His development is at a very different stage from yours. When he wants to take risks, don't criticize him, but instead of letting him drive like a madman, pay for him to go parachuting a few times. Let him feel the thrill but re-channel it into an activity that feels risky to him, but is in reality a lot safer. Ty told me about a three-week backpacking trip he took to the Canadian Rockies to photograph the big-horned Dall sheep. He was excited to be away from home, to live outdoors where he wouldn't be able to shower, shave, or even eat decent food. Ty, his brother, and his father joined two other friends who knew the mountain terrain well and acted as their guides. They trekked to their base camp on horseback. The camp was set up in a valley between two mountains. From there, they traveled on foot. One day, after a long hike, they returned to camp, and were so tired that they all fell asleep early from exhaustion. Four hours later, Ty was awakened by a peculiar smell. It was smoke.

He leaped from his sleeping bag and ran out of his tent. From the backside of one of the mountains he saw enormous billows of black smoke. He couldn't see the flames. He woke his brother, dad, and friends and the five conferred about what to do. Ty wanted to run the mile down the valley to where the horses were kept, saddle them up, and get out of there. That wouldn't work, his friends said, because the horses were too near the fire. His brother insisted that they run away from the smoke. This meant that they would travel up the other mountain and down its backside. But one friend said that the backside was too dangerous to navigate.

The more options the men conceived and discounted, the more frightened Ty became. After ten or fifteen minutes of bantering with one another, Ty became terrified, more frightened than he had ever been in his life. The five concluded that they could neither outrun, nor out-ride, nor out-hike the fire. They had no means of containing the fire or putting it out. The only option they had was to sit together in the middle of the large valley between the two mountains and wait; and hope and pray that the fire would turn in the opposite direction.

It did. After three hours of terror, the men realized that billows of smoke were shrinking. The fire was receding and even the smell of smoke grew fainter.

Ty and the men came face to face with their own powerlessness. The emotional, intellectual, and physical strengths of each of the men bumped up against nature and they, the men, lost. They didn't burn to death, but they knew that nature was stronger than they were.

Ty left his adventure with a deeper understanding of himself as a man. He learned the realities of his own strengths—and also of his limits. In short, he learned humility. When we talk about the cognitive, emotional, and psychological immaturity of teenagers, we are talking about a simple scientific fact. But it is also true that experiences like Ty's help teenagers mature faster. It is experiences like these that boys take from testing themselves against nature and each other.

It is extremely important for young men to learn the limits of their power. It's a challenge they feel bound to confront, and it's why they climb mountains, race cars, and wrestle. It is about understanding what they have inside and how far they can take it. It's when they hit the wall that humility begins to set in.

Sometimes the challenges are solitary, but usually boys make sense of their power by comparing themselves to others. Boys are naturally competitive, and one of the first comparisons they make is how strong they are compared with other kids; first it's strength in muscles, later it might be strength in brains: qualities they like not only to test but to quantify. They also learn, through competition, a deeper appreciation for other's abilities as well as their own.

This last point is especially important because boys need to learn to apply their skills, their power, to helping others. Boys need to serve; it is good for them; it directs their energies and helps them define the useful purposes of power; it tempers power with responsibility. They need to find a widow who needs her yard mowed or a friend with a physical disability who needs help or a group like Special Olympics that could use young mentors for disabled athletes. Such service is one of the best ways to keep teenagers from feeling separated and isolated. It is always good for boys to be reminded that there is far more to life than just themselves. Parents, if you want to strengthen your son's character, help him find activities where he can develop his sense of service. It will help him to recognize how valuable his gifts are, and that all people, including the people who need his help, are valuable.

CHAPTER FOUR

Electronic Matters

MOST OF US ENJOY A PECULIAR RELATIONSHIP with our laptops, iPods, and televisions. Make no mistake—that is exactly what we have with these inanimate machines: relationships. We love them, we hate them. Electronic media has made our lives more organized, brought more entertainment to us, made research for us and our kids easier, and opened a floodgate of information that can feel overwhelming. For those of us who lived a large part of our lives without the Internet, video games, and all the rest, we have a different appreciation for the benefits as well as the ills that electronic media bring. Our boys, however, don't have this perspective. We have read enough books with black and white pages to understand what it feels like to read without a message from a friend popping into view. We learned to savor movies because we couldn't watch them seventeen times in a row. We bought stationery at the store, wrote messages to friends and relatives in our own handwriting, and actually sat down and thought before we wrote. Sometimes we threw the letters away because either we didn't express ourselves succinctly or we said things that we didn't really mean to say. Perhaps we were too harsh or too sentimental, so we scrapped the letter and started again; letters that merely vented our feelings ended up in waste paper basket. Our parents taught us to think about the person we were writing to, and what that person wanted to hear. Then we sent the letter and waited. Was our handwriting neat enough for grandma and grandpa to read? What did they think about what we said? Would they write back?

Before the days of electronic media, we had to work at communication, and much more of it was face to face. But who writes handwritten letters anymore (even though they're far more personal than e-mail)? We had to work at researching (which meant going to the library) and using typewriters or pens to write papers for school (remember brushing Wite-Out across letters?). We didn't play games against a computer; we played games with our friends. One thing we've lost with the rise of electronic media is a sense of permanence. Who among us saves e-mails? What boy saves all of his text messages? Very few. But what do we do with handwritten letters? Even the cynics among us stash them in a special box, or a folder in the closet.

When I get a hand-addressed Christmas card, I can tell who sent it even before opening the envelope, because our handwriting identifies us. My sister-in-law's handwriting is exquisite. It is upright, formal, and very neat. So is she. She loves to read and when she writes a note, I know that she has put a lot of thought into it. I will never forget a note that my father wrote me after the birth of my son. His handwriting was horrible. I was one of the few in our family who could decipher it accurately.

Dear Meg, it started. *I am so very proud of you and all of your accomplishments. Especially this one. I love you, Dad.*

He wrote it sixteen years ago and I still tear up when I read it. The words move me, but seeing his handwriting makes me cry because today he has Alzheimer's and can no longer write even his own name. How glad I am that he didn't have a computer to write the note on.

No one wrote the word *Dad* like he did. Think about the handwriting of someone you love. You recognize it immediately. Read a few words and you know his mood. Handwriting is deeply personal. Words on a computer screen can never have the same impact.

Boys need handwritten notes. They need letters to remind them that deeper communication exists than what can be found through computers or cell phones. They don't understand the value of paper and pen or the texture of a note card, or the heartfelt words of a father sharing his wisdom on paper. But they should.

Electronics have changed more than simply the way we write and communicate. Yes, we are now able to stay in "contact" with more friends and family than ever before, but the connection is different. It is done through an impersonal filter. We have gained and we have lost—and we need to compensate for the losses. Our sons need to be guided through the electronic landscape. They might understand the technicalities of it better than we do, but they shouldn't be left to navigate it on their own. I know from clinical practice that much electronic media is not only lurid and frightening, but it can suck the mind and heart out of a boy. And extricating him from that lurid, frightening world can be extremely difficult.

Of course, electronic media is here stay, and our boys are going to use it and be changed by it no matter what. Even their vocabulary is different. Instant Messaging is their language.

The other day I asked my sixteen-year-old son what he felt like eating for dinner. We were driving in the car and he was looking at his cell phone. His response to me? "IDK, mom."

He wasn't trying to be rude, though at first I thought he was. (For those without teens, IDK means I don't know.) Text language isn't an English language, it is a series of abbreviations that shortcut responses.

I took the opportunity to have fun with him. "Great," I said. "Now you have a foreign language all your own. But when talking to your mother, dear heart, I like wonderful, complete words strung together with excellent syntax. How about it, hmm? Find me a word tonight that neither of us knows. I bet you can't." He took the challenge and ran with it.

Specifically, electronic venues such as the Internet (with its chat rooms, Web sites, e-mail, iTunes, etc,) television, electronic video games, and music paraphernalia (iPods, etc.) bring fun to our boys, but also carry some very serious risks. Let's look at them.

The American Academy of Pediatrics recently announced yet again that television violence is bad for our kids. But, we already knew that. Who amongst us hasn't held our breath watching TV during prime time when our ten-year-old sees a graphic scene of a man getting shot in the street? Violence on TV these days isn't like it was when we watched *Gunsmoke*. And when we were growing up we didn't have computer games where the object is to go around shooting people. The American Academy continues to heighten the sense of urgency regarding boys and violence in the media for three reasons, I believe. First, the violence is getting more frequent and more graphic because pushing the envelope sells better. Boys become desensitized to specific levels of violence and then they become bored. So, to keep the sales up, producers of the games and programs up the ante.

Second, we in the medical and educational worlds continue to see boys acting more aggressively and becoming more violent. Many times the violence and aggression seems random. Boys yell at passersby, hit girlfriends, and use more graphic language in their conversations.

Third, we know that something has to be done. On the one hand, we can't just pull the plug. One the other hand we know if we don't, we run grave risks—some of which today are more than risks; they're realities. One very big reality is that we have become desensitized to the point that much of the garbage no longer makes us flinch. It seduces us. And, just like our boys, we feel pressure from our peers. Popular shows, even ones with vile content, creep into our living room, so we can talk about what everyone else is talking about. Because Sam's parents let their son play the latest video game, we feel pressured to let ours do the same.

But we have an abundance of evidence that substantiates our intuition that the terrible TV and the violent computer games are bad for our sons. We need to stand up and do what is right, because if we don't act on behalf of our son's best interests, no one will. We can't get steamrolled by marketers and computer programmers and television producers and trendy parents. As a pediatrician I can tell you that disconnecting, or strictly limiting and strictly supervising your son's access to electronic media is one of the best things you can do for his emotional, mental, and physical health. Boys are suffering from some serious problems from using the wrong electronic media. And it starts not in their teenage years, but long before, when busy parents use the television as a babysitter. Just as parents use the television to keep younger children occupied, they'll let their sixteen-year-old son play computer games in his room to keep him out of their hair for a few hours. Don't get me wrong. Parents *do* need a bit of rest, because so many of us are so very tired. Flipping on the TV or allowing a computer game does seem to make life so much easier; it keeps the kids entertained and we can have some quiet time to relax or get some chores done. But unless that TV is locked onto some classic kid's show or that computer game is something you're entirely at peace with, it isn't worth the cost.

The physicians in my medical practice frequently teach medical students and residents in training. Recently, we had a medical student interested in pediatrics. When I arrived at work he was reading a textbook and ready to go; he saw me and quickly introduced himself. I had a very busy day scheduled, and while I normally love having students accompany me as I see patients, I was hoping one of the other doctors might take him. But now I was caught.

I told him that I was sorry that I wouldn't have much time to talk to him today, but that he was welcome to watch as I examined my patients.

After three or four patients something began to gnaw deep inside me. It is true that doctors today are busier than ever. Because insurance companies continue to cut reimbursements we have to see more patients per hour. Because computers have taken over our lives, we sit staring at computer screens, clicking away at laptops in the examination room, rather than browsing through a patient's manila folder before the examination. But twenty-five years ago, a doctor took the time to show me how to examine a live patient. I learned things from that doctor that can never be learned from a screen or a page. A doctor taught me how to watch a baby's movements to be sure that he didn't have early cerebral palsy. A doctor made me examine a baby's heart and pulses to make sure there was no coarctation of the aorta. A doctor showed me how to look into a baby's eyes for signs of a tumor that would need immediate attention. I needed to do the same for this student. But if I took that much time I couldn't keep to my schedule, and if I couldn't keep to my schedule I'd be late to pick up my son from soccer practice, and then. . . .

My scenario is yours. We all have to get through the day, and on time. And because we live like this, we like electronic gadgetry—both because we think it makes us more efficient, and because it becomes a way to keep our kids entertained while we work or recover from working. The danger is that we're creating bigger problems for ourselves. A mother who buys off a toddler's or a teen's temper tantrums with television or a video game clearly has a problem on her hands. She needs to learn to deal with her toddler or teenager—and the sooner the better. He will develop wretched habits if he learns it's that easy to manipulate his mother.

As parents we all need to reinvigorate ourselves so we can corral some serious energy to deal with our sons. Whether our son is three or eighteen, he needs our help. The great news is that not only do our sons benefit from the energy we invest in them; so do we.

WHAT BOYS SEE

Children and teens between the ages of eight and eighteen spend about six and a half hours a day with various forms of media. Three hours, on average, are spent watching television, approximately two hours are spent with a radio, CD, or MP3 player, and another hour or more is spent on the computer outside of schoolwork.[1] Boys of all ages are drawn to electronic media, particularly interactive video games, much more feverishly than girls are, so for boys these numbers could actually go higher.

But taking these numbers as given—they come from the Kaiser Family Foundation, which has done one of the most extensive studies on media use by kids—it means that in an average week, a boy spends forty-five and a half hours, or more time than he would spend at a full-time job, with either television, computer, music, or MP3.[2]

It's even more startling to compare media time against other activities in a boy's week. Typically, a boy spends forty-three minutes a day reading, a bit over two hours per day with his parents, an hour and a half doing some sort of physical activity, and half an hour per day on chores.[3] Over the course of a week he'll spend less than sixteen hours with his parents (or well less than half the time he'll spend with electronics) and a measly five and a quarter hours doing homework. His weekly total for physical activity at ten and a half hours a week is roughly one quarter of the time he'll spend behind a computer screen, watching television, or listening to an iPod, which is one very big reason why we have an epidemic of obesity in our kids.

MEDIA AND ITS IMPACT ON A BOY'S MIND

But the physical ramifications are just the beginning. The American Academy of Pediatrics warned in their journal, Pediatrics, that boys who watch violent television or play violent video games are much more aggressive than boys who don't.[4] In another sophisticated study published by the Mind Science Foundation, researchers studied brain activity in children who viewed nonviolent videos versus children who watched violent videos. The differences between the brain patterns of the two groups was remarkable. Specifically, certain portions of the childrens' right brains were stimulated only when the children viewed violence on the screen. The study also found that viewing violence on television recruited a network of brain regions involved in regulating emotions, arousal, attention and memory coding. They concluded that since children who watch media violence frequently are more likely to behave aggressively, that this phenomenon may be explained by the brain's ability to store violent scripts in the child's long-term memory.[5] Indeed, over the last fifteen years the amount evidence tying heavy electronic media use to aggressive behavior in boys has become overwhelming and irrefutable.

Violence

A 2005 report in the *Lancet* medical journal states, "Violent imagery on television, film, and video and competitive games has substantial short-term effects on arousal, thought and emotions, increasing he likelihood of aggressive or fearful behavior in younger children" especially in boys.[6] The majority of television programs (more than 60 percent) contain violence, and that violence is both rarely condemned and often ambiguous in its morality. The perpetrators of violence are often treated as glamorous and worthy of emulation.

Boys are much more attracted to violent media than girls are. Girls are more likely to listen to music; boys are more likely to play a violent video game or watch a violent movie. There are many reasons for this. We know that infant boys respond to moving objects, while infant girls respond to stationary faces. As they develop, we know that boys are physically more rambunctious than girls. But, additionally, as boys mature they perceive violence as manly; and certainly the media deserves some of the blame for this. We've already discussed the need for boys to come to terms with their own power. It is very important that when they see power being used, that they see it being used morally, within constraints. But movies today rarely fit into the Gary Cooper, Jimmy Stewart mold. Today, what psychiatrists would consider anti-social behavior—such as ridiculing, insulting, lying, or exhibiting aggression with our without weapons—is the norm for men in movies. When boys repeatedly see men they admire ridiculing others, lying, and acting aggressively, they attach these qualities to the actor's manliness, and they will think that adopting such behaviors will make them manlier. When the images are bombarded on an eight-year-old brain, a boy can easily shift from believing that a man is supposed to be trustworthy and self-controlled (as you, his father, might have taught him) to believing that real men are cruel and aggressive. In this way, through continual media reinforcement of this theme—and sometimes its reinforcement by classmates and bullies and gangs and violent adults—ugliness is thrust upon a boy, and many boys are pushed into being boys they would rather not be. Certainly many boys are seduced into aggressive behaviors that we as parents, and as a society, would rather they did not have.

Developmental psychology studies tell us that in the first two years of life, boys show more emotional reactivity and expressiveness than girls do, but that this changes over time. Between the ages of two and six, boys becomes less verbally and facially expressive. This emotional shutting down leads to what some researchers call normative male alexitymia, or the inability of boys to put their emotions into words. Right around this age (four to six years old), boys often begin exhibiting more antisocial behaviors than girls. These behaviors can be aggressive as well as non-aggressive.

In other words, the aggressive behavior in boys begins to increase as this emotional shutting down intensifies. If at the same time a boy is increasingly exposed to violent media, the results can be very harmful. We know from the data, we can even chart on a graph, that boys become more aggressive, at least in the short term, after watching violent media.[7] Even brief exposure can be harmful, and it gets worse with heavier doses. It also gets worse if the violence is not a television show or a movie but an interactive video game. Psychology researchers stand at odds with the video game industry over the issue of whether or not violent games cause violent behavior in boys, but the scientific data appears irrefutable. One recent meta-analytic review of the scientific research on video games revealed crystal clear results. Concerning aggressive behavior, it concluded that high video violence was definitely associated with heightened aggression. Furthermore, the research concluded that "exposure to violent video games is correlated with aggression in the real world."[8]

But exposure to violence affects boys on other different levels. Studies also clearly show that violent video games are "negatively correlated with helpers in the real world."[9] They increase aggressive thoughts, can increase feelings of anger or hostility, and can raise a boy's blood pressure and heart rate.[10]

In sum, exposure to media violence harms boys. Whether they view it on television, on computer screens, or interact with violent video games, the best medical literature clearly shows that media violence affects boys at all developmental stages and increases their tendencies towards anti-social aggression. Why take that risk with your son? No violent video game is something he has to have. And while there is likely little harm in letting him watch old Westerns like *Bonanza*, there is no R-rated movie or violent prime time television crime show he has to see. Rather than using violent media as a babysitter, even doing something as simple as playing checkers, chess, or Scrabble with your son will provide better stress relief for you and better, healthier, and happier time for him.

Boys and Sex in the Media

Every boy over the age of eight in the United States is under sexual assault. From the early elementary school years on, many boys begin seeing PG-13 movies. And what is the hook in these movies that captures the interest of the pre-teen crowd? Sex, of course. Not allusions to romantic sex between husband and wife but sex between teens and unmarried young adults. And studies show that in the media, high contents of sex and violence go together.

Then there are music videos. Even the milder ones imply casual sex between teens. Sometimes sex is depicted as part of romance; sometimes it isn't. But we have all seen the music videos where sex is depicted as dark, violent, and either angry or emotionless.

Chat rooms, frequented by millions of young boys, center around sexual talk. If you're a parent and have never visited one and your child has, you need to visit one. The language is abominable. It is abusive, pornographic, and debasing.

Patricia Greenfield, director of the Children's Medical Center of UCLA, has investigated Web sites that cater to adolescents. Here is what she found:

> I continued past the personal information form into this free web portal, clicked on "teens" and got into the portal's teen site. The site's motto was "be seen, be heard, be you." I was quite shocked to see what was being seen and heard. First, I clicked on "teen chat" and found a personal ad there. Clearly this ad would expose a teenager to a not-so-virtual sexual come-on which the teen may not have been seeking and may not be developmentally or psychologically prepared for. This could be a rather scary experience for adolescents just starting to develop romantic and sexual relationships. The developmental issue is, at what age are you able to cope with initiatives, especially sexual initiatives, taken by others, particularly strangers?

Language used by electronic media is notoriously dirty. It isn't simply sexual—it is filthy. Ten- and eleven-year-old boys use sexual vocabulary that they don't even understand. Consider this brief conversation as recorded by Greenfield:

Person A: A proctologist, eh?

Person B: I'm a sexologist.

Person C: Maybe he should pay more attention to his wife and baby than to me.

Person D: The Ass! Harmless eat my cum and be happy.

Harmless 2: You started by calling me a whore which was like soooo MATURE.[11]

By the last sentence we can glean that the writers were quite immature. This exchange is a very mild one; I have visited chat rooms where the "f" word is used continually, and the conversation seems to center on demeaning references to each other's anatomy. In my experience, IM (instant messaging) language can be similar in its sexual offensiveness. Because of the relative or complete anonymity of the writers, the electronic exchanges are replete with shock value and insults. For boys, it is a form of showing off without being seen. It is a sexual testing ground. The problem is, it leads boys into a dark, perverse, and self-denigrating hole.

According to a report from the Kaiser Foundation that examined television viewing habits and frequency of sex and violence in programs, the average "family hour" of television (8pm to 9pm) contains eight sexual incidences. In addition, in 1,300 shows analyzed, "50 percent of the shows and 66 percent of prime time shows contain sexual content." Only 11 percent referred to the risks or responsibilities associated with sexual activity. The Kaiser report also found that 76 percent of teenagers surveyed said that one reason that young people have sex is "because television shows and movies make it seem more normal for teenagers."[12]

Take a look at some of the report's other findings:

- In 1998, 56 percent of shows contained sexual content[13]
- In 2005, 77 percent contained sexual content[14]
- Of the top twenty shows teens like, 70 percent have sexual content and 45 percent show sexual behavior[15]
- 75 percent of teenagers aged fifteen to seventeen say that sex on television influences the sexual behavior of their peers[16]
- When sexual intercourse is depicted or implied on television, the characters involved have usually just met[17]

When we look at television trends in sexual content, we see that not only has the frequency of sexual content increased, but the intensity of it has increased as well. Intercourse is depicted more graphically and oral sex is frequently implied.[18] In my experience parents and other adults are more worried about violence in the media than they are about sex in the media. Hating violence in the media is politically correct, but when it comes to sexually explicit media, parents tend to shrug their shoulders and civil liberties activists raise their hackles. Somehow we've convinced ourselves that it is more reasonable to expel violence than it is sex—that sex, after all, is "natural" and harmless. But the medical truth is that both violent behavior *and* sexual activity are high-risk actions for teenage boys. And no, it is not natural for teenage boys to be sexually promiscuous. Rates of sexual activity outside of marriage have changed so dramatically over the last seventy years that it would almost be fair to say that normalcy has been turned on its head. Undoubtedly there are many factors that have played into this, but with regard to teenagers we know that they are heavily influenced by the media they watch and use; and we know that while violent and sexually explicit media can lead to subsequent aggressive behaviors, we also know that children and teens imitate what they see, and so it is reasonable to conclude that if they were fed a media diet of positive behaviors, such behaviors would be reinforced. Several years ago I participated in a *Dateline* TV special on teens and sex. The host and I spent hours listening to teen girls and boys and their parents. The teens were picked from diverse backgrounds, but all had conscientious, hardworking, involved parents. What absolutely astonished me, however, was that so many of the adults had no clue as to why teens are sexually active earlier and with more partners now than ever before. They had, apparently, never stopped to think through an average day in their son's or daughter's life, during which that child is barraged with sexual lyrics, images, and references continuously in virtually every hour of media time they have. And what they see, they do—they consider it "normal." The results, however, are any-thing but normal. Boys who are violent or sexually active have a much higher risk of depression. We've already seen some of the data about the epidemic of sexually transmitted diseases among young people in this country. Not coincidentally, this explosion of new STDs correlates with changes in what we consider normal and appropriate sexual behavior. What used to be considered normal and appropriate meant that in 1960 doctors only had to worry about two sexually transmitted diseases and only in small high-risk populations. Today, doctors—and pediatricians—have to worry about more than thirty sexually transmitted diseases that threaten *every single one* of our teenagers who become sex-ually active.[19]

Pornography and Boys

Before the advent of the Internet and sexual videos, pre-adolescent and adolescent boys plotted a secret acquisition of *Playboy* mag-azines. They snuck peeks while adults weren't watching and hid magazines under beds, in tree forts, and buried them in closets. Adolescent boys have always been fascinated with sex and nudity because curiosity is a part of their emerging sexuality. Such behavior is understandable, if not to be encouraged. But what might have titillated teenage boys when we were young is tame compared to what is available to them now. Women in *Playboy* magazines twenty or thirty years ago were alone. While they stared seductively at the viewer, they were not engaged in a sex-ual act. But *Playboy* over last few decades has been nudged aside by more graphic magazines and other media. In 1985, 92 percent of adult males had a *Playboy* magazine by age fifteen. Today the average age of a boy's first exposure to pornography is eleven,[20] and where he might once only have seen a naked woman, now he is much more likely to view sex acts between partners. Nearly half of boys between the third and the eighth grade have visited Internet sites with "adult content."[21] The more graphic the content, the more severe the trauma it inflicts on our boys. And we shouldn't fool ourselves into thinking that it is not traumatic. Pornography warps the natural development of sexuality in boys. It can lead them down paths of perversity that, in their normal development, they would never have otherwise considered. Young boys who view pornography are having their morality, their sense of what is acceptable, shaped by it. And the Internet is full of seducers ready to prey on them, including sexual predators. The problem isn't that many young boys seek pornography out of curiosity, but that pornography pops up at them unawares and drags them in. When we look at why boys watch sexual media, we find that they often end up watching such material because someone else, an older sibling or friend, wanted to. In congressional testimony regarding children's exposure to pornography on the Internet, Dr. Patricia Greenfield concluded: "Peer-to-peer file sharing networks [a way to download and share files without going through the World Wide Web, often used to download music that would otherwise be restricted by copyright laws] are part of an all pervasive sexualized media environment. This total environment, including file sharing networks, leads to a tremendous amount of inadvertent and unintentional exposure of children and young people to pornography and other adult media."[22]

Research has shown that viewing pornography can be quite disturbing to boys and that viewing explicit sex changes the way boys behave sexually. For example, viewing sexual material (not just pornography) has been shown to make male college students significantly more accepting of the use of aggression against women, both in a sexual and non-sexual manner. And, contrary to what one might think, studies have shown that when college students recall memories of sexual media their memories are overwhelmingly negative. Their responses include (from most common to least common): disgust, shock, embarrassment, anger, fear, and sadness. Interestingly, sexual response to those viewings was very low.[23]

The Big Deal about Boys and Sex

An overwhelming majority of parents I encounter shake their heads and smirk when discussing boys and sexual media. "Come on," they quip, "it's just sex after all. They're all interested; they're all going to try it."

Such comments, I'm afraid, reveal a profound ignorance about sex and boys. If we were truly interested in letting boys be boys, we would let them be just that—boys, not voyeurs lured into a dark underworld of pornography. If pornography did not exist, boys would not be out there creating it. It is adults who thrust it upon them.

Sex is a big deal for boys. They are not naturally emotionally dull human beings. Boys are feeling, thinking, and spiritual beings, and a healthy sexuality is one that grows within that well-rounded framework. A healthy sexuality is not exercised too young, it is not artificially aroused and diverted, and it is not promiscuous. And deep down our boys know this, but we allow them to be pressured by the pornographers and pimps of pop culture. We shouldn't.

I travel across the country speaking to groups of teenagers about sex and its medical risks. I've noticed that junior and senior boys lean forward in their seats not when I describe the dangers of sexually transmitted diseases, but when I talk about the emotional costs associated with unmarried sexual intercourse. What I've discovered is that while girls are vocal about this sense of loss, boys are not—but feel it just as deeply. But what's more, the emotional costs of sexual intercourse are something boys didn't expect. Boys feel they were never told that sex can bring emotional hurt. In fact, pornography would have taught them exactly the opposite. The bottom line is, we allow electronic media to lie to our sons about sex—and our boys pay the price.

OUR TV, OURSELVES

One interesting fact about teenage boys and television is that they often watch television with their parents. So for many parents the question is not monitoring what our teens watch in their bedrooms, but monitoring what *we* choose to watch with our teens. We can, however, view it as something else: wasted time. Our teenagers are with us for a surprisingly brief period of their lives. How many meaningful conversations can you have with your sons during a television program? It might be nice watching a baseball game on TV with your son, but how much better, how much more would you talk, if you took him to a real baseball game—major league, minor league, college, or high school.

Certainly if you watch TV, parental participation is extremely important, *if* you put your child's viewing needs above your own. If a father chooses a program that is age-appropriate for his son, if he pops a bag of popcorn and pulls out a classic comedy DVD with Abbott and Costello or Bob Hope, they can have fun. If, on the other hand, a parent chooses to watch a show more to his or her liking rather than the child's, harm can be done to him. Here's why.

If a young boy watches sex or violence before he can handle either one—and we should ask ourselves why *we* want to handle it, that's part of the problem—he can be traumatized. Furthermore, if he is traumatized with his parents' approval, the boy becomes confused. He associates his parents with giving him good things, and now they have given him something that makes him feel unsettled, uneasy, depressed, or even angry. Young boys, because they are developmentally self-centered, blame themselves when they feel discomfort rather than blaming another person—particularly a parent.

Many parents rationalize exposing their kids to R-rated movies. They say that some of these films are very good, or that they can discuss the disturbing aspects of the films, or that they can use them to teach their sons what is right and wrong in films.

Don't do this. Scenes of graphic sex and violence scar your son's mind and heart. Don't be a part of that, and do everything you can to prevent it.

E-Relationships

When you and I were growing up we didn't have e-relationships. We might consider ourselves lucky, because for every benefit electronics have given us they've given us new worries too. Consider cell phones. While it is true that with cell phones boys can let parents know where they are (that is, if they tell the truth), they also give parents a false sense of security. Knowing that they can always call a teen on his cell phone, parents sometimes let teens wander too far. But more important is the way that for many young people cell phones, instant messaging, and the other gimmicks of e-communications don't strengthen relationships—they distort them. Behind a computer screen or even on a cell phone, people write or say things they otherwise would not. Instant messaging is deeply impersonal and what it actually does is cheapen communication, reducing it to abbreviations, just as chat rooms don't help people to mingle and make new friends the way parties do, but rather encourage teens to try on different personas, to push the envelope of what they're willing to say, and sometimes to launch into darker territory.

George's mother called my office three times one Monday morning. My secretary alerted me that Sara sounded panicked. I called her as soon as I had a break in my schedule. "What's the problem?" I asked. "It's George," she said. "I think he's got an addiction problem."

My stomach sank. I had watched George grow up. As a young boy, he had been delightful, quiet, and very shy. As a teenager, he had gone through his high school years without any significant problems. What could have gone wrong now? Was it drugs or alcohol or pornography?

No, his mother said, it was something else.

Over the next thirty minutes, Sara described to me a very disturbing pattern that had evolved in George's behavior. He had dropped out of college after a year because, he told his parents, the "kids were stuck up." His parents were disappointed, but felt that perhaps he simply needed more time to mature. George lived at home, got a job in a coffee shop, and enrolled in a few courses at a nearby community college. Over the ensuing months, he dropped one class, then another. He spent more and more time alone in his room. He left his job at the coffee shop and got another waiting tables at a nice restaurant. That lasted about two months before he was onto another job.

"Now," his mother told me, "he doesn't work at all. He's not a lazy kid. He just has one excuse after another. All he wants to do is sit in his room and play interactive video games."

I dug further and found out that George played an online war game where he could be any person he chose. He could create his personality, height, and physique. He could "dialogue" with others online. They didn't dialogue as themselves, but as the characters they had created. George lived for long hours every day in this fabricated online community. When his parents insisted that he stop, he became belligerent, even violent. But they persisted. Once, Sara told me, he broke down sobbing, saying that he couldn't stop. The people in this online world, he said, were the only ones who accepted and loved him for who he was. He felt totally safe with them.

His parents were stunned and didn't know what to do.

I want to clarify that George never had a history of mental illness. From a psychiatric standpoint, he knew the difference between reality and non-reality. He was not, and had never been, truly delusional or psychotic.

For his mother, trying to get George to limit his time online was like to trying to take heroin away from an addict.

George's story is not uncommon. He was always a shy, introverted boy who felt socially awkward. But he always forced himself to talk to friends at school and interact with other boys on various sports teams. When his friends left and he went to college, he tried to establish new friendships, but felt more awkward than before. He had been pulled off of the waiting list in order to get into the college and always felt that he wasn't as smart as the other kids at school. When he arrived in his dorm, a friend on his hall introduced him to the war game and immediately, he told his parents later, he was hooked. He told them that when he was in the online world, he felt he was "home."

George indeed had an addiction. His game acted as a mood-altering substance. It became his "friend," just like alcohol becomes the "friend" of the alcoholic and drugs become an addict's best "friend." Playing the game gave George a sense of freedom and escape from the troubles of his life. It made him feel that life wasn't as bad as it really felt—at least for the hours he played. When George was completely honest, though, he admitted that the feeling of freedom he got wasn't completely satisfying—it often made him feel a bit nauseated—particularly after he had played for a long time.

George's parents took him to an addiction specialist. The first thing that George needed, they all agreed, was to confront his addiction. This was a real stumbling block for George. He wasn't doing anyone any harm, he insisted. Nor, he argued, was he even harming himself. But of course, he was.

The next step, the counselor told his parents, was to get rid of his laptop. At first they squirmed. It seemed a ridiculously harsh move. After all, they said, George was twenty. But finally they did as the counselor advised.

George threw a fit, left home, and found a friend to live with. But he was back home after only a month, saying that he had fought with his roommate constantly. Over the ensuing months at home, the tension level was high, but George agreed to get help from the addiction counselor so that he could "square away his life." Thanks to his parents' stubborn refusal to allow him to keep a laptop at home, or otherwise to indulge his unhealthy lifestyle, he realized that the game was interfering with his life. He took a step closer to seeing his addiction.

Ultimately George learned that playing the game was an easy way of avoiding life and avoiding himself, in particular his social awkwardness. He felt shy, insecure, and terribly lonely. He genuinely believed that no other men his age would want his company because, he said, he was a loser. So when the game offered him friends, albeit, "virtual" friends, he jumped for it.

I can happily say that George feels much better about life today. He has a profound respect for the power of electronics and avoids them unless absolutely necessary, much like an alcoholic avoids alcohol. When he feels the urge to play, he constructively calls a friend and joins him to watch a football game or play hockey.

Boys need emotional connections. They need them with parents and friends. And, for healthy emotional development, the relationships have to be face-to-face, not "virtual" and electronic. Electronic media entice boys in part because the boy feels in complete control of it. If he doesn't like what someone in a chat room is saying, he logs off. If he loses a video game, he shuts it off and tries again. He calls the shots.

But with real friends, he is not in complete control. Friends laugh, argue, and disagree. A boy is forced to confront difficulties and find resolutions; he is forced, in a word, to mature. Boys need this friendly give and take, and they need the support of loving parents, siblings, and friends. If they don't have it, their emotional and even mental life will wither. Don't let that happen. Be sure your son spends more time with you, with nature, and with the real world, than he does in front of a glass computer or television screen.

CHAPTER FIVE

Does Testosterone Drive Cars?

AMERICA HAS A PERVASIVE AND OVERWHELMING animosity towards teenagers—particularly teenage boys. Even the words "teenage" and "adolescent" have come to be synonymous with obnoxious, uncontrollable, surly, and anti-parent. Listen to adults around you when they talk about your son and his friends. Many will roll their eyes and groan, purposely watching you for the anticipated response which says, "I know, teens are impossible. We parents must stick together in order to endure them."

We see billboards with sour-faced fifteen-year-old boys who rarely smile. Sometimes the billboards are selling jeans, and the boy is meant to represent a sort of menacing sexuality. Sometimes the billboards are exhorting us to keep him from taking drugs. In other cases the message is that teenage boys spell trouble. Popular culture caters to what it assumes are the debased tastes of teenagers (while doing everything it can to debase them itself). We know that popular culture is beating up on our kids, but we don't feel we can do anything about it. After all, we tell ourselves, adolescence is an ugly time of life when boys in particular get out of control. The best that we can do is to wait it out. We will love them, try to talk to them, and exercise patience until the poison leaves (and it may take years), until the brain tissue develops, and they return to normal. When they finally grow up, when they mature, maybe when they graduate from college or hold down their first real full-time job, we will be able to like them again. But for the moment we must simply endure them.

Pretend now for a moment that you are a teenage boy. You see those billboards with surly looking teenagers and the warning to parents to keep you away from drugs. You pick up the ever-present message that teenage boys are rebellious, that they're troublesome, that together they can be a pack of wolves. How do you feel about yourself? Are you in the same frame of mind? Should you be? Do you sit in class daydreaming of beating up kids in the hallway, or of your next drug deal, or of the weekend's party where you can get drunk? Probably not, but you realize you are a suspect because you are a teen and especially because you are male.

Or perhaps you're a different sort of teenager. Perhaps your parents aren't worried about drugs and alcohol; they don't expect you to get into trouble. But they're putting pressure on you to get ahead in life by being a star: the fastest and youngest quarterback on the varsity team, the smartest at math, the most accomplished pianist, the president of your class. You feel suffocated, confused, and anxious. Then you see the boy on the billboard who looks like he lives in a foreign world (the bad world) and you know that acting like him would really tick your dad off. That might at least get him to realize that you want some choices.

You quickly decide that, no, being like that billboard guy wouldn't help. It would prove to your dad, your mother, and your teachers what they already know, and you don't want them to have that satisfaction. Teenage boys are out of control. They're barely tolerable. They need to be constantly restrained from smoking, beating people up, having sex, or taking drugs. You don't want to be like that guy because you don't want to see them gloat about being right all along.

Parents blame peer pressure for almost all of the dangerous behaviors that teenage boys try. We do so because that's what we are told: that pressure from the pack, the group, or even just one bad friend can cause our boys to try just about anything. We believe this because we understand that teen boys want to establish an identity, that they want to be accepted by their peers, and that they are boiling over with hormones. Our job is to teach our sons to be assertive enough and strong enough to be different from the rest. They must walk away from the party where their friends are drunk. They need to have the strength to say no to their girlfriends (who are increasingly sexually aggressive).

The problem with this reasoning is that it is only partly true. Of course we all want our boys to walk away from the dangerous stuff and stay on the high road, to have a strong, unique identity, and to be young men of character, and we should teach them that. The problem is that we're dead wrong about why boys get into trouble in the first place. It isn't primarily peer pressure that's driving boys towards drugs, drinking, or depression, or that is causing them to fall behind academically or drop out of school.

The real reason is that *we have lowered our expectations* about teenage boys. We simply accept the idea that they are sexually out of control—and then allow them to be bombarded by sex-saturated media. We simply accept that they are likely to be surly, sullen, and aggressive—and then allow them to spend dozens of hours a week with media (from rap music to violent video games to obnoxious sitcoms) that reinforce surly, sullen, and aggressive behavior. We simply accept that testosterone will triumph over all moral beliefs—and then don't bother to teach them about morality or religion at all, either because we're uncomfortable talking about it, or because we "don't want to force our ideas on them," or because we find that life is too busy to go to church or synagogue. The truth is that much of the moodiness, the temper tantrums, and the defiance against parents that we assume is simply part of adolescence is *not* normal.

Many of the world's foremost authorities on adolescent psychology and psychiatry contend that this period that we call "adolescence" is an American phenomenon.[1] It exists only in a few other affluent, industrialized countries. Too few parents know that the eminent child psychologist Dr. Bruno Bettelheim taught us that "adolescence is neither a God-given stage of development, nor one that comes with our very nature—it is the consequence of recent social conditions."[2]

Certainly boys experience significant physiological, emotional, and cognitive changes during puberty. These changes unquestionably thrust young men into a period of tumult and anxiety. But relative to his age, the same occurs during the toddler years. In fact, the two-year-old boy's temper tantrums stem from his burgeoning intellectual and emotional desires to do things which his young body will not allow him to do. This exact phenomenon is responsible for much of the frustrations and anger in sixteen-year-old boys. One might argue that the feelings within the adolescent boy are more sophisticated and stronger. This is probably true but relative to his age and ability, the frustration and reasons for these frustrations remain the same as a two-year-old. In fact, according to education expert Dr. Tom Lickona, many adults get into more trouble than teens. In a lecture he gave at an international education conference in Manila, he said, "In fact, statistics show that, compared to teens, American adults age thirty-five to fifty-four are much more likely to engage in a wide range of risky behaviors. Middle-aged adults are much more likely to have fatal car accidents, commit suicide, engage in binge-drinking, and require hospital treatment for overdosing on drugs."[3]

The psychological and medical research on adolescents has grown tremendously over the last forty years. Here's some of what it has taught us.

THE MOODY TEEN

Mood is hard to quantify and even harder to express. But we do know that while the rates of depression among boys are higher than they were twenty or thirty years ago, boys experience depression at a far lower rate than girls do.[4] And there is a suspicious parallel between the rise of depression amongst teens and the skyrocketing STDs. Now, studies clearly show that sexual activity during the teen years puts them at higher risk for developing depression.[5] So while most boys (and girls) still survive adolescence quite well, depression in teens is a serious problem. Unfortunately, it is often overlooked or misdiagnosed by parents and even physicians. In order to recognize what it is, we must be able to differentiate it from other problem behaviors, as well as normal teen behaviors in boys. There is, for example, a medical condition known as dysthymia, which is a category of mood disorder, as well as one known as Oppositional Defiance Disorder. We can distinguish these from major clinical depression and normal teen behavior in the following ways:

MAJOR DEPRESSIVE DISORDER

Longer than two weeks of
and at least 5 symptoms of:

Depressed or irritable mood
Change in appetite or weight
Change in sleep pattern

Change in motor activity

Fatigue or loss of energy

Trouble concentrating

Thoughts of worthlessness or guilt

Recurring thoughts about death or suicide[6]

DYSTHYMIA

Greater than two months of and at least two of:

Feeling down, profound sadness

Decreased interest in activities that a person usually likes

Appetite disturbance

Increased irritability

Increased argumentativeness

Decreased energy, fatigue

Sleep disturbance

Poor concentration

Feelings of hopelessness

Periodic thoughts of worthlessness or guilt

Difficulty making decisions[7]

OPPOSITIONAL DEFIANT DISORDER

Negativistic, defiant, and hostile behavior longer than six months
and at least four of the following symptoms are present:

Frequent arguments with adults

Often loses temper

Often deliberately annoys people

Often blames others for his mistakes, misbehaviors

Often touchy or easily annoyed by others

Often angry and resentful

Often actively defies or refuses to comply with adults

Often spiteful or vindictive

Often angry and resentful

Persistent lying

Presence of a communication disorder

Physical aggression

Concomitant depression or ADHD[8]

NORMAL TEEN BEHAVIOR

Frequent arguments over independence issues

Occasional temper tantrums

Moodiness

Sulkiness

Increased fatigue (usually due to lack of adequate sleep)

More interested in spending time with friends than with family

I offer these charts not to provide a short cut to diagnosing depression—only a doctor performing a full examination of a patient can do that—but to point out that much of what we accept as normal teen behavior is in fact not normal at all; and that so much of what we simply accept as popular culture is in fact so toxic that it is pushing teens into pathological behavior and conditions.

If your child does suffer from depression, please seek help, because it is a serious illness, and boys who suffer from depression are at much higher risk of killing themselves and others. In my experience, teen boys balk at receiving help for depression; and fathers are more likely to block needed treatment of their son's depression. Anti-depressant drugs can be abused and over-prescribed but they do have their place; and if your son needs help, don't let his pride and ego—or yours—stand in the way of his being treated.

But for most parents, thankfully, the risk is less that their teen is a victim of clinical depression than it is accepting that disordered behavior is normal behavior. It is *not* normal for teenage boys to lie, hide away for hours in their rooms, and be hostile and even physically aggressive to friends and family. These behaviors have certainly become more prevalent, but they continue to be red flags that something is disturbing the boys who exhibit them. These behaviors are cries for help and we do a great disservice to boys when we pass them off as "normal."

COGNITIVE MATURITY

Many parents and educators have found great relief in recent discoveries of the teenage brain, most especially the confirmation that many boys don't have full cognitive maturity until they are in their twenties. According to Dr. Jay Giedd of the National Institute of Mental Health, teens may actually be able to influence how their brains are "wired" during the teen years, because the brain is undergoing so many developmental changes. By learning to order their thoughts, understand abstract concepts, and control their impulses, they exercise their brains, and this might influence their neural foundations. Dr. Giedd states: "You are hard-wiring your brain in adolescence. Do you want to hard-wire it for sports and playing music and doing mathematics—or for lying on the couch in front of the television?"

Specifically, scientists are finding different rates of maturity between different parts of the brain. For instance, the front part of the brain is called the frontal cortex. This part of the brain controls judgment, emotional regulation, and self-control. We now know that this doesn't develop completely until the early twenties in many boys.

Another part of the brain, the corpus collosum, connects the two halves of the brain. It controls intelligence, self-awareness and consciousness and, like the frontal cortex, still undergoes maturation into the twenties in most boys. The temporal lobes are the side portions of the brain (near the temples) and these deal with emotional maturity. In boys, they are well developed by the time they are sixteen, but continue to reach full development in the early adult years.

Much of the new brain research encourages parents and educators to recognize that teen boys are very much a work in progress, that they are still learning how to make mature decisions and control impulses, and that it is during the teen years that we can have the most decisive effect on helping them to shape these aspects of their character

But first a warning: the discoveries that we can make through neuro-imagery have their limits. We will never explain—and should never base our expectations about—our son's behavior on the basis of these pictures of the teenage brain. Educators who follow brain research are well aware of this danger and use the term "brain-based education" to describe it. The danger is that we tell ourselves: "Now we understand why boys are impulsive, argumentative, immature, and out of control. Their neurodevelopment is in such a stage that it prevents them from controlling their impulses, staying quiet instead of yelling, and making poor immature decisions." This a dangerous mental leap, and wrong because it equates the brain with the mind of a boy. The brain is a vital organ but the mind is a mysterious malleable part of a boy that is influenced by feelings, life experiences, personal beliefs, and the opinions and behaviors of loved ones.

Dr. Kurt Fisher from Harvard University's Mind, Brain and Education Program has wisely cautioned educators and parents to keep our newfound knowledge of the teenage boy's brain in perspective. He cautions that at the beginning of the twenty-first century, our understanding of neuroscience has its limitations.[9] And they are limitations that every parent should easily recognize. Do you think your son is a puppet controlled by the wiring of his brain—or do you think that while his brain, like his body, develops and matures, he is more than his neural wiring—he is a whole boy with a character and personality of his own? As both a mother and a practicing pediatrician I know that brain wiring isn't everything.

It is tempting for some people to cling tenaciously to biological discoveries about the brain because for some people science is supposed to explain everything—they want to put aside philosophy and religion, and dissolve morality into atoms. Science, they think, is the remaining bastion of truth and it is irrefutable. But this is an extremist position, and most boys, parents, educators, doctors, and scientists know that there is more to a boy's brain than tissue and neurons. Testosterone, estrogen, and neurochemicals bathe the teenage boy's brain, but somewhere between the confines of the skull and the human heart emerges the mind, which can be changed, influenced, guarded, and controlled. And therein lies the hardest truth of all. Who amongst us dares to enter its inner workings? After all, the real reason some of us want neuroscience to account for a boy's behavior is that it lets us off the hook. It makes life easier for us. Who are we to help a teenage boy focus and control himself when his brain won't allow it?

The beauty for our boys and for us is that we can embrace and influence his mind, we can help him decide what to do, what to think, and how to feel. We can do this because his mind is greater than his brain. He knows it and we know it. And the scientific data reveals it. Wiring does not explain everything.

What is it that keeps a boy's impulses restrained so that he doesn't get involved in high-risk behaviors? Parents, teachers, priests, pastors, rabbis, coaches, adults who can see a boy as a fully rounded human being with an abundance of emotional, intellectual, spiritual, and physical potential.

So the question remains: When your son gets behind the wheel of your brand new Honda, is he in charge, or isn't he? Is the level of testosterone circulating in his bloodstream and brain fluid going to cause him to race out of the driveway and drive like a crazy person? Certainly testosterone gives him energy and surges of aggression. When he is mad, testosterone can make him feel madder—even furious. But that isn't the issue. The real issue is, with all of the complexities of his brain development, shifts in his testosterone levels, and psychological needs, who's really in charge behind the wheel? Them or him... or you?

Given what neuroscience teaches us about the teen boy's brain, we know that while he is not fully capable of behaving like an adult, his brain needs constant training. It needs hard-wiring and that process depends upon what influences he receives to help the process along. He can learn to be responsible for his behaviors, his impulses, his thoughts and even his moods to a certain degree. But he can't do it alone, precisely because he is so limited. Which behaviors can he learn to control? The answer is many more than we sometimes believe possible. And it's our job to show him the way.

CHAPTER SIX

Encouragement, Mastery, and Competition

EVERY BOY NEEDS MORE ENCOURAGEMENT. He doesn't need false praise. He doesn't need pressure to perform better. What he needs is parental support as he matures through each developmental phase, physical and psychological, that all boys go through.

One wonderful aspect of young boys, even toddlers, is that they have an uncanny ability to read their parents' moods. If a father tells his son that he did a good job and he doesn't mean it, even the two-year-old boy knows that he isn't being truthful. Young boys can often tell better than a spouse if a parent is telling the truth or is lying.

The reason young boys read parents sincerity so well is that they *need* to know what a parent really thinks about them. A three-year-old boy who builds a tower of blocks higher than he did the last time feels proud of his accomplishment. But he needs to know what his father thinks, as well, to measure just how high of an accomplishment it is. (This is why young boys always want to show their mothers and fathers the drawing they made, the project they've built, the battle panorama they've set up with toy soldiers, and so on.) If a father smiles proudly at the block tower, the boy confirms his own estimate of himself as a good builder. If his father nods in approval but isn't really paying attention, the young boy unconsciously doubts his achievement, and thus his ability.

Toddlers are testers. A toddler will diligently watch his parents to see how they respond to his various actions, whether they elicit approval, punishment, or nothing at all. This is obvious in very young boys, but the principle, with modifications, remains true through their teenage years. Young boys are always internally questioning themselves. At their earliest stages, even before they can talk, you can see their mental processes at work. They ask: "Am I able to do this on my own? Am I able to do this well enough to win approval? Am I able to do this better than I did this the last time?"

Watch a preschool boy play. He builds things constantly. He makes towers and walls and random structures with blocks. Sometimes he wrecks them just to start again or he takes things apart to see if he can put them back the same way. Other times he invents projects you wish he hadn't: he smears shaving cream over bathroom walls and mops the garage floor with paint. When someone tries to interfere with his projects, he swats them away. Is he showing signs of meanness or disrespect? No, he is testing his capabilities in his play. What is he good at? What pictures emerge in the shaving cream? Sometimes (many times) when boys make enormous messes, they are pretending that their creations aren't as they appear. The shaving cream all over the bathroom walls are clouds in the forest. The red paint all over the garage floor is a carpet in his own private fort. It isn't in your garage, it is in his play space because now he imagines he owns that space.

While no three-year-old boy needs encouragement in destroying homes or garages, what he does need encouragement in is learning his own abilities. While his play projects might appear destructive, messy, and a pain for you to clean up later, for your son they are quite constructive. He isn't simply building and smashing, he is trying to figure out what his physical abilities are; and when he repeats these activities day after day he's trying to see if he can build something better than he did the last time.

Very often parents become disturbed when young boys play war. But they shouldn't. On the other hand, I remember one father telling me that he had set aside special time to be together with his son so that they could bond. I asked him what they did, and he said, "We play *Mortal Kombat* together—it's a blast!" Frankly, rather than playing a violent video game with his son, the two of them would have been better off with paint guns in the woods. Why? Because the woods are real and tangible, because the father and his son would actually be playing together rather than staring at graphic violence on a video screen together, and because in the woods a boy's imagination is not bombarded by violent images but can be creative. He can enjoy that confluence where the trees, birds, and squirrels become more than nature—they become enchanted with imagination, even imaginary armies.

The fact is all boys, if they're allowed to be boys, play at war. Boys need to feel challenged, they need to compete, and playing at war for them is like playing football, though with more imagination involved. Winning—which of course he won't always do—validates his masculine identity; it actually helps build his self-esteem and maturity. Playing at war serves another purpose for boys. Boys have an inherent moral code; and war, with its good guys and bad guys, reinforces his sense of moral order. The bad guys need to be beaten, and in his imaginary play he teaches himself that the bad can be overcome by the good. Certainly by the time he goes to school he's seen bullies and bad things happen. He needs to assert the fact that bad things can be overcome. Playing at war is one way boys do this. For boys, playing at war is a sort of morality play. Playing at war accomplishes far more in helping a boy resolve good over evil than simply watching a film or playing a videogame that touches on the same themes, because he is a participant; and a participant in the real world of the backyard or the woods or the basement, not tapping buttons and watching a screen. A boy needs to experience the thrill of victory himself.

The famous child psychologist Dr. Bruno Bettelheim summarized a boy's need to shape his moral order through battle games by saying, "a child will have a much easier time succeeding in life if the final identity he chooses is that of those who uphold the moral order.... Whoever the 'good' guys are, the child must finally adopt their identity as his own."[1] Playing war games where the good guys win, where he wins, helps a boy grow in confidence and optimism. As Bettelheim writes in his book *The Uses of Enchantment*, "If a child is for some reason unable to imagine his future optimistically, arrest of development sets in."[2] Good triumphing over evil when he plays at war helps a boy imagine his future optimistically and so advances his maturity.

As part of their internal moral order, boys know that evil exists. They know that they themselves can have ugly feelings and do bad things. Therefore, every good parent must provide a means for the boy to deal with the problem of evil and not simply ignore it. Religious instruction (in the Judeo-Christian tradition, with its emphasis on sin and repentance) is one way to do this. But playing at war is another. With proper moral instruction a boy can become not only a victor over evil but a chivalrous one. As Bettelheim says, "Serving the good becomes reinforced by the motivating force of a higher purpose.... He begins to appreciate a lesson which cannot be taught to him convincingly in a purely didactic fashion: that to fight evil is not enough; one must do so in honor of a higher cause and with knightly valor—that is, according to the rules of the game, the highest of which then has become to act with virtue. This, in turn, will promote self-esteem, a potent spur... to become more civilized."[3]

A MOTHER'S ROLE IN ENCOURAGEMENT

Mothers encourage their sons in very different ways than do fathers. Typically, a mother offers emotional warmth and security; she offers compassion, patience, and kindness. Since she is not male and therefore feels no competition with her son, she can embrace his individuality more easily than his father can.

Boys usually form stronger emotional bonds with their mothers during the early boyhood years, and it is important not to sever those bonds unnaturally or too soon. Mothers can encourage sons in areas where fathers typically don't. Being more emotionally attuned than fathers, they can see their sons' feelings and motivations more readily, and try to understand and direct them. Since many boys feel emotionally safer with their mothers, they feel less inhibited in front of them. That also mean boys will "act out" more in front of their mothers—yelling, having temper tantrums, and crying—than they do with their fathers. Boys feel less anxious about pleasing their mothers because they feel they already have their mother's approval and undying love; things they feel they have to earn from their father.

Because of these differences, mothers are in a wonderful position to help their sons sift their feelings and learn what to do with them. For instance, six-year-old Jack comes home from school and finds that his sister has smashed his Playmobil airplane. He erupts in anger and screams at his sister and hits her. He cries and runs into her bedroom and tears the head off one of her dolls.

Where dad might pick Jack up, spank him, and send him to his room, his mother would probably approach him differently.

Jack's mother might empathize with his frustration and anger and be upset at her daughter (because she probably feels a stronger emotional connection to Jack than does his father). She would put Jack in his room, let him calm down, and then help him realize that while his frustration and anger were understandable, hitting his sister and ripping the head off of his sister's doll was not an appropriate reaction.

By acknowledging Jack's anger, a mother helps lessen its intensity (boys can actually frighten themselves with their own anger). Then, by establishing rules for when he is mad—no hitting, no destroying things, no calling bad names—she instructs him about what to do with his anger.

When mothers do this repeatedly—month after month—it works not only to help a boy deal with feelings, but it builds his self-esteem. He feels less intimidated by his emotions and learns that, to at least some degree, he can control them. By helping her son deal with these emotions, a mother lends great encouragement to her son's masculinity.

Because of this bond between mother and son, mothers are very well placed to openly admire their sons when they exhibit good character, or achieve physical or intellectual goals. And most of all, mothers can make their sons feel that they are loved just for being themselves.

A FATHER'S ENCOURAGEMENT

Sadly for all of us, our culture does little to encourage boys to become great men. Television depicts men as stupid, or as sex addicts, and almost always intellectually and emotionally shallow. Men don't seem to care about these depictions, merely laughing them off. But I care about them, because our sons need good role models and given the amount of time boys spend with electronic media they need good role models on television. And of course, there is a bigger cultural fallout from the depreciation of masculinity and fatherhood, which is lower marriage rates, higher divorce rates, and the reality that many boys grow up in fatherless homes.

This is a national tragedy, because boys need healthy encouragement from their fathers more than they need it from anyone else. In a boy's eyes, his father's words are sacred. They hold enormous power. His words can crush a boy or piece him back together after a fall. If a father is not there at all, it is a huge void in a boy's life—and as the depressing statistics remind us, boys who grow up without fathers are at a dramatically greater risk of drug abuse, alcohol abuse, sexually transmitted diseases, and ending up in prison.

Encouragement from a father changes a boy's life. His words can ignite furious passion in a boy that will help him achieve any goal he sets out to accomplish. To a son, a dad's words are the final truth. If they are positive, a boy feels that he cannot be beaten, if they are negative, however, a son feels that he could never win.

If you are a son reading this, you know exactly what I mean.

Unfortunately, many fathers fail to realize the power of their words in their son's eyes. Just as a six-year-old boy brings home artwork from school to show his mother, he longs for his father to see the work and nod his approval. Then, he will want to draw again. A ten-year-old boy up to bat doesn't look into the stands for his mother as intently as he looks for his father. He waits for the "thumbs up" from his dad's expression to know that, of course he can hit a home run.

Fathers also tend to discipline boys more than mothers do; and they tend to be tougher on their sons than mothers are. This is both good and bad.

It is good because a father knows the heart and mind of a boy in the way a mother doesn't. He gets why his son wants to jump off the roof with a parachute made from trash bags. A father understands the antics, the energy, and a boy's need to settle questions about his masculinity. He also acts as an instructor. Fathers are famous for telling their sons to "toughen up and act like a man." No discussion about how a son feels; just do it. I have watched my own husband talk very differently to our son than to our daughter.

Fathers encourage masculine behaviors. Boys need this encouragement, but caution must be used. For many fathers, "encouragement" slips into berating, putting down, and accusing sons of being unmanly if they're not up to the mark. Don't do this. It can be devastating for sons; and unfortunately it is a mistake often passed down through generations. Many fathers were themselves raised in an atmosphere of fatherly criticism and negativity, of fathers who were pretty adept at telling their sons what they weren't very good at.

But young boys need positive words from their fathers. They don't need discouragement. Eight-year-old boys are not men—they are still boys trying to find their way. Sometimes well-intentioned fathers shut their boys up and disconnect them from themselves by criticizing them. Occasionally this happens by accident, through what a dad perceives as playful teasing.

Remember, a father's words are always huge in a boy's eyes. So if a father tells a ten-year-old son while they are wrestling on the ground that the boy is fighting like a girl—the boy might slough it off, or he might not. In his young boy's mind the son may hear "you aren't very strong and you never will be" or "you are unmasculine and a weakling."

What a father says and what a boy hears can be completely different. In teasing, by its very nature, there is always an underlying bite. Usually boys hear that bite and the impression magnifies in their mind when it comes from a father

When a father trains himself to drop positive words of encouragement periodically to his son, I cannot exaggerate the positive impact that this will have over a boy's self-esteem and the out-come of his life. In fact, for girls, the greatest predictor of good self-esteem is the physical affection her father shows her. Similarly, when a father encourages his son, whether through words or physical affection, the boy's life always changes for the better.

THE IMPORTANCE OF SPORTS

Boys like to watch games and participate in games because they want to see if they can win. Then they can know what winning feels like. Athletic games offer opportunities for boys to engage their physical (and masculine) energies in a safe and controlled way in order to beat the other guy. Then a boy can know that he is stronger, more skilled, and more capable.

Interestingly, to the boy competing in an athletic game, it isn't even as much about winning over the competitor as it is figuring out how good he is himself. Is he fast or slow, compared to his competition? Is he weak or tough? He emerges from the game, not just a winner or loser, he emerges more knowledgeable about himself.

THE IMPORTANCE OF WINNING

Imagine your fourteen-year-old son after he wins a hockey game against a team that he knows was a weaker team. Your son will come off the ice delighted at his victory even though he knows that it wasn't a grand accomplishment.

Now suppose your son plays another hockey team that is far better than his team. As expected, your son's team loses. But your son and his teammates played their hearts out and the coach rallies the boys in the locker room by telling them that he is proud of them and that they played an excellent game, better than they had the week before when they beat the weaker team.

The boys stomp out of the locker room. Your son tells you it doesn't matter that they tried hard; they still lost. Deep down, he knows he played well and he takes some consolation and pride in that, but to a fourteen-year-old boy, competition isn't as simple as doing his best. Winning, even against a bad team, is concrete evidence in his mind that he is a good hockey player. It isn't simply someone's perspective—it is a win on the scoreboard, not a loss. Seeing the win makes him readily believe that he is good at hockey. He can perform. He is strong, he is competitive, he can make his body excel at a sport he loves. By knowing this and experiencing this, he can believe in his heart that he is actually becoming a man.

Competition for a boy is more about building his identity and self-perception than it is about beating others. Winning elevates his mood precisely because it offers clear evidence that what he wants to feel about himself—that he is manly—is occurring.

COMPETITION: MASTERY OVER THE BODY

Competitive sports offer boys an excellent venue to burn off lots of energy and to gain control over their bodies. Boys can train their legs to sprint faster and kick balls more accurately. They can hone their hand-eye coordination by shooting hockey pucks or hitting tennis or golf balls.

Boys learn important lessons about themselves and life in general through competitive sports. Two-year-old boys scream frantically when they can't get their bodies to accomplish for them what they want. They throw themselves on the ground in frustration. Eight-year-old boys feel tough and strong when they whap a tee-ball and watch it whiz past the first basemen's head. But when he runs the bases and is tagged, the same eight-year-old boy walks off the field frustrated because his skinny legs wouldn't let him run fast enough.

A thirteen-year-old boy, experiencing fluctuating testosterone levels, finds dribbling a soccer ball a bit more difficult—he feels clumsy and awkward. His legs are longer, his gait feels uneven. He needs to correct this, to ease his frustration, and he needs encouragement from his parents to do so until puberty has served him better. He needs more testosterone, larger muscles, and better coordination. This will come, but he must keep going and stay in the game. Competition keeps him working harder to gain control over his shooting, dribbling, and his speed. Having others challenge his ability keeps him sharper, motivating him to push himself at practice, to increase his speed or lengthen his stride.

One of the first and longest lasting struggles a boy feels is mastery over his body. Getting his body to perform the way he wants it to is a monumental task for boys (and men) of all ages. But the desire to master it is a masculine desire and as such should be encouraged in boys.

This doesn't mean that boys need to lift weights at age ten or push themselves too hard. Boys need to exercise, but they need to rest too. Their bodies are growing, changing, developing, and you don't want to put too much stress on a too young body. Remember, as far as a boy is concerned, what he ultimately needs is not a string of victories in varsity sports; he doesn't need to be a star, but he needs to know that he has mastered his body, that he can make it do what he wants it to do, and that with it he can, in some sport or activity, at some level (including the sandlot or backyard level), achieve victories.

MASTERY OVER EMOTIONS

All boys need to learn to control their emotions as they mature. This does not mean that boys shouldn't feel. On the contrary, as a boy moves through elementary school to junior high and on into high school, his emotional life will intensify and become more complex. By the time he reaches adolescence, it will be harder for him both to understand and to compartmentalize his feelings for this very reason. There is a marked and very important difference for boys between ignoring his feelings and mastering them. The first is rooted in fear, the second in masculine maturity. Boys should not be encouraged to disengage emotionally or to avoid all feeling. Boys who shut down their emotions to the point of becoming emotionally dead are dangerous—indeed pathological and need treatment. They have not mastered their emotions; they have tried to bury them alive. A healthy mastering of feelings involves two components. The first is simply recognizing an emotion for what it is. The second is knowing what to do with that emotion. The goal of maturity is learning how to behave as a boy knows he should regardless of where his emotions want to take him. The goal is self-control. And just as a boy feels pride, achievement, and manliness in being able to control his body, he will have similar sense of accomplishment when he learns to control his feelings.

Competition can serve boys well in achieving this. Certainly athletic competition provides an outlet for aggression, but it also requires that aggression be controlled. In sports, a boy learns how to master and direct his aggression. He learns when to turn it on and when to turn it off. As he gains this control, his self-esteem rises and his maturity as a man proceeds. He learns that he is in charge—both of his abilities and his emotions.

MASTERY OVER ENERGIES

When I opened the door to the exam room, Sue leaped from her chair like she was going to tackle me. Sue was a (usually) delightful woman in her mid-forties. Her first child, a five-year-old daughter named Ellie, was with her. Ellie was all dressed up as if for church and sat quietly coloring a picture. Also with Sue was her eighteen-month-old son Aaron, who was here for his checkup. "You have to help me with this child," Sue blurted. "He's wild, I mean wild. He's going to kill himself, Dr. Meeker. He won't sit, walk, or stand. He runs, climbs, and swings." She didn't take a breath.

"In our store we have a display of Coke cans. They're stacked up like a pyramid. The other day, Aaron tried to hurdle them and they came flying down. Look at him—he's all bruises!"

Sue and her husband were great parents. They had, Sue had told me before, trouble conceiving a child, and so came to parenthood later in life. But they were absolutely devoted to their kids, and took turns between working—they ran a campground with a store at the front—and watching their children. The only babysitters they allowed were family, and they had plenty of family nearby. Sue's mother lived at the campground, as did her grandmother, and her sister with her family. Each of them agreed that Aaron was no ordinary child.

As Sue talked, I looked at Aaron. He had pulled a stool over to the window and was opening and shutting the shades. Then he crawled up on the stool and hoisted himself onto my exam table, which was almost four feet high. Once on top, he stood erect and prepared to jump. Sue didn't notice, but I did. I ran over and grabbed him from the table and held him on my hip. He twisted his small frame like a corkscrew and wiggled free, bouncing down to the floor.

Aaron was happy and funny, but also extremely hard to handle because of his energy. In fact, he was, medically speaking, hyperactive.

Sue and I agreed that Aaron's dad needed to spend a lot of time with him, giving him a very structured day with order and repetition, and consistent, straightforward rules to follow, with consequences if he broke those rules. Sue and her husband did all that. But Aaron remained an extremely active boy. When he was three-and-a-half, Aaron learned to ride a two-wheeler without training wheels. By four, he was swimming in the campground pool without floaties. By five his parents had to take the swing set in the back yard down because he took to climbing on top of the monkey bars and walking across them, until he fell down and broke his arm. Sue and her husband were truly afraid that someday he was going to have a fatal accident.

When Aaron was six, his mother and I discussed sports for him. She was afraid his restless energy would get him kicked off the team. But when he was seven, she threw up her hands and agreed to enroll him in a basketball league. He loved it. She encouraged his coach to make him run more than the other kids. He complied. Then she put him in soccer. Soon she realized that he benefited from "warming up" for soccer by playing for a good hour or two before he joined his team. Aaron loved sports, so his parents let him continue to play as much as he liked, but it was never enough to burn off all his excess energy.

When he was in the third grade, his father introduced him to chess. His dad loved the game and Aaron begged to be taught. Somewhat to his surprise Aaron fell in love with the game too, and he and his father played as often as they could. No one believed that the boy could sit still that long to finish a game.

But he did. He loved the competition. He was a smart boy and enjoyed the challenge. Although he had great difficulty concentrating, and would at times get frustrated, his competitiveness kept bringing him back to the board.

At twelve, Aaron will tell you that he still struggles with endless energy, sometimes feeling as if he's going to burst. He continues to play Pop Warner football, basketball, and, of course, chess.

Competitive sports gave Aaron an outlet for his physical energy, but equally important was the challenge of competition. Wanting to win helped him aim his energies and focus. It harnessed his aggressions and frustrations, and pointed them in a very specific direction so that they could be released. Boys with hyperactivity don't struggle with simple physical energy. They feel internal chaos erupting from frustration, anger, and disappointment, because they know they feel so different from other kids.

Chess allowed Aaron a venue for harnessing mental energy and expending it. And it forced him to pressure order into that intellectual energy. It forced him to think, then to re-think strategy so that he could try to be beat his father. Chess also taught to him concentrate and sit still to the best of his ability, and gave him valuable time with his dad.

Boys with extraordinary energy need outlets for that energy. But we mustn't forget that physical energy is only one part of the equation. Many boys are also brimming over with emotional and intellectual energy that needs to be properly directed. Competitive sports work beautifully for many boys. Competitive games, such as chess, work better for others.

Many boys who aren't interested in athletics find release through the arts—piano, French horn, painting or drawing, Irish or Highland dance. Whatever the venue, boys need competition and a way to express their physical, mental, and emotional energies.

GAMES AND ADOLESCENCE

Adolescence is, in a nutshell, the period in which a boy learns to master himself. Suffice it to say that if mastery is the goal in adolescence, then competition plays a vital role in the process. Athletic competition helps him do this throughout his boyhood, but in adolescence it takes on additional burdens, because a boy is starting to take on an identity separate from that of his family, and he is developing an interest in romantic relationships.

In adolescence testosterone levels rise in a way that gives boys a pent up sexual energy. We must teach boys how to deal with it. This is extremely uncomfortable for many parents, but either mother or father (preferably father, since most boys don't want to hear about it from their mothers) must talk to boys about what to expect and to feel. Then they must be encouraged to deal with it in a healthy manner, and that healthy manner can be competitive sports. It can also be directed into the arts or into other forms of competition (like chess tournaments). Where it can't be directed, at least not without great risk to his physical and emotional well-being, is where popular culture wants him to take it. Don't let him do that. I treat too many patients who have absorbed too readily the cheap, nasty messages that come from films, iPods, and televisions.

Sexual energy is no different from intellectual, physical, or mental energy—it must be acknowledged, addressed, harnessed, and mastered. Otherwise, a boy is controlled by his sexual drives rather than being in charge of them. Mastery must occur on all levels of his being.

Achievement in school, athletics, music, or any other competitive venue help a boy to learn self-discipline, self-mastery, concentration, and the proper direction of his energies to achieve desired goals. In short, they can help to build his character. They are not a magic pill—boys need to be encouraged by good coaches, tutors, and parents—but they can definitely help. Little by little, a boy can learn to take charge over one aspect of his character, then another, and then another. Mastery feels wonderful to boys. And it is sad to see so many boys today who have never learned this process, who live without discipline and order, who know only internal and external chaos in their lives. It is sad for them and for us. It is essential that parents teach their sons that living an ordered life, replete with fun as well as discipline, paves the way to a free life, and a successful one. Boys who learn through encouragement of their inherently masculine qualities, who learn to enjoy healthy competition that helps them to respect others and themselves, are boys who have a much better chance of living good lives. But they can't find this all out on their own. We must help them. And we must start when they're young.

CHAPTER SEVEN

A Mother's Son

BENEATH THE ETHEREAL JOY A MOTHER FEELS at the first sight of her son, lies a nugget-sized ache wrapped in fear. Her infant son needs her. She loves him unconditionally. But she also feels the ache of knowing that he will grow into a man and leave, and one day belong to another. The juxtaposition of elation and fear is different for many mothers than the joy and fear they feel when a daughter is born.

She knows from the moment her son belts out his first wail that she exists to love him. She is needed because he needs her. He needs the nourishment, the security, and the love that she provides which will not only keep him alive; but also keep her knowing that she is needed. So she will protect, adore, and nurture this tiny boy until he becomes a man and then, the ache will feel overwhelming. As a man he will leave, and life as a mother will never be the same for her. She will continue to love her son, but the connection will be reworked. Not because she has changed but because one day, he will belong to another.

This knowledge did not exist before his birth. But it presents itself the moment his mother sees him and as her maternal instinct draws her very close to her son. That is the way mother-son relationships are meant to be. From the moment she clings, she prepares herself ever so slowly for the eventual release.

This tension doesn't exist with the birth of a daughter. A daughter can stay connected with her mother forever; mothers and daughters have genetic, hormonal, and psychological bonds that cannot be broken. She can become another's, but her mother can still keep her. They are female together in that bond, and they can stay connected even while life changes the circumstances around them. But the tie a mother feels with her son is more fragile, more tenuous; he is different because he's a man. But for as long as he is a child, he is ours and we feel we must protect him.

There is another difference mothers experience with sons which they don't with daughters. Because he is XY and she is XX, they are disconnected. His maleness is separate from her femaleness and as much as she would want it otherwise, he is distanced. He has a different mind. He will have different physical sensations—different worries and ideas. Will she be able to understand? Intuitively she knows that in order to protect him and bond with him she must graft him onto her like a branch of a grapevine onto a hearty root. At birth, the grafting begins, and a mother's instincts on behalf of her son begin to mound and become bolder and clearer as her son grows.

What about adoptive mothers? Do their instincts erupt in the same manner? Absolutely. Whether through pregnancy or not, the grafting begins equally regardless of biological status. When it comes to nurturing our young, the kindest mother can turn beast on a dime.

A TERRIFYING BEAUTY

In the early evening of a hot summer day I sat at the end of a wooden dock, my feet skimming the tepid water, watching a mother swan. Her coat was so white it shone vaguely blue, particularly as she floated atop the turquoise lake water.

What struck me most, however, was not her spectacular beauty but her calm demeanor. She floated, almost rested, on top of the water. Her head shifted from left to right above her long, graceful neck. Her movements were calculated and secure.

Behind her floated three cygnets, looking like puffy cotton balls with beaks. I recognized them as her offspring, not simply by their coal beaks but by her commanding demeanor. She was silent. They squeaked. And when they spoke to her she neither stopped or acknowledged their presence. She just kept paddling along. Neither mother nor cygnets seemed to pay any attention to each other. Always she kept her paddle feet pulling back the water beneath her breast.

As she passed by, I decided to show her beauty off to my three-year-old niece. Quietly I went to the house, grabbed a handful of bread and my niece, and together we padded back to the end of the dock.

When we returned, the mother swan was still floating by, but her triplets had drifted a ways behind. Feeling sorry for them, my niece threw a handful of mashed bread pieces towards them and they scurried over to get them before they dissolved. By the time the bread hit the water, the mother swan had darted like a shot between them and interrupted their eating. Then, the elegant beauty did something frightening.

She didn't stop when she reached the bread. She raced to the shore and stood up on the sand. Being an inexperienced ornithologist, I suddenly learned that swans not only walk on sand—they can run.

I was stunned by her boldness while my niece simply squealed. Quickly, I pushed my niece behind me. At that moment the mother swan menacingly stretched out her wings in our direction, creating an enormous span of white. I watched her run across the yard, then turn and start, wondering where in the world she was intent on going.

I wondered if she was mad—perhaps she had rabies. No, no; I knew swans couldn't get rabies. Then the swan turned toward me and started racing down the dock. Her feet slapped the boards furiously. "This can't be happening," I thought. " I'm about to be attacked by a bird." I wanted to laugh at the sight of the big white thing running and squawking at me, but I screamed instead.

The swan kept running right at us. I grabbed my little niece and we jumped into the water. Too afraid to turn my back on this mad animal, I jumped backwards, trying to jump high enough and far enough not to land on my little niece who was glued to my back. When we bobbed to the surface, I saw her again. She stopped. For a moment in mid-air, I had reached to the back of my mind for Plan B just in case the swan followed me into the water. Fortunately I never needed Plan B. The gigantic bird stopped and perched on the end of the dock, puffy and gloating.

She paused for a moment to enjoy her victory. Then almost as quickly as she had run at us, she turned and flew off the side of the dock to rejoin her cygnets. Neither my niece nor I suffered any physical injury, but the trauma I harbored in my gut took days to clear. Never before had I been on the receiving end of an animal or human so venomously enraged.

But I knew that was a mother's instinct. What is true for mother swans is true for the mothers of boys. I've never been chased down a dock by one, but mothers are invariably their sons' greatest advocates and defenders.

FEMININE NURTURE OF THE MASCULINE NATURE

Inasmuch as boys are different from girls in their characters, states of development, and emotional and physical needs, in my experience parenting sons is more like parenting daughters than it is different.

Mothers are the love-givers. Whether a son or a daughter is the recipient, giving love well is still very difficult. Showing respect, offering protection, holding ones temper, and being fastidious in perseverance of all aspects of good parenting are equally hard regardless of the sex of the child. Being a mother is tough work.

Mothers offer sons many of the same things that fathers do but mothers offer them differently and—very importantly—sons receive them very differently from a mother than a father. And the reverse is true. That is why both mother and father are needed to parent a son well. Advice that is palatable from a mother's voice may be offensive from a father.

Much of what a mother gives her son is more a reflection of her personality and her character than it is of her son's character. Mothers need to love. And mothers love to be needed. This truth isn't tough to mothers. They live it because they as human beings are egocentric. Mothers intuit that life is better when they are loved, needed, and nurtured, so they expend these important traits to sons in hopes of receiving them back. And a child is the safest place to begin this process.

But there are needs which every boy has that any mother can satisfy. Again this is not to disqualify a father as a provider of these needs. Certainly there are fathers who can meet some of these needs better than mothers I have met. In general, however, maternal instincts act sometimes quite peculiarly on behalf of sons, which can leave some fathers a bit confounded. Let's look at the best of what mothers give to their sons.

A FACE OF LOVE

During the final scene of the movie *Dead Man Walking*, a death row inmate, bound at the wrists and feet, is led into a chamber where he will be put to death. Sister Helen, his companion and confidant, asks if she can accompany him into the room. His guards agree to let her walk with him. At the end of the hallway, before he enters the chamber, Sister Helen asks if she can touch him. His guards say yes. Sister Helen turns to him and says, "When you feel the pain and death closing in around you look up at me. I will be the face of love for you."

Because women are more verbal, they love differently from men. The feeling, the intensity, and the availability may be the same, but the expression of love flows differently from women than from men. Because women talk more, they verbally communicate love more easily. For mothers and sons, the love-giving process starts in infancy. Mothers oogle at their baby boys, make up pet names for them, and tell their sons they love them. Talking to, holding, bathing, and touching their babies help mothers communicate to their sons that they want to be the supreme love-giver. He can depend on her to always buoy him when he is sinking.

A mother may disapprove of her son's behavior, girlfriend, sports, or music, but she will always love him.

A healthy internalization of a mother's love is critical to her son because his experience of her love sets a template for how he will regard love with any woman after her. If he has a positive experience with his mother, he will be more trusting of his sister's, girlfriend's, or female teacher's affections. If, on the other hand, he feels an instability or lack of trustworthiness in his mother's love, these will temper the way he views other women's love—whether it is romantic or platonic.

Mothers love to touch. This is wonderful because infants, young, and older boys need physical touch. A mother's embrace tells her son that he is loved: she sees him, she likes what she sees, and she approves. He is validated by her love. Unfortunately, many mothers abstain from hugging their sons as much as they would like because they feel that part of becoming masculine is needing less touch, and that manliness means fewer hugs. This is certainly not true. A father can afford to be stand-offish when it comes to touch, and may refrain from touching their sons as they grow older—but mothers should not follow suit.

Mothers love to talk to their sons, but they shouldn't always expect much of a response. Women are comfortable discussing their intimate feelings; boys and men are not, and sometimes cannot. Their own feelings are a bottled up mystery even to themselves. But teenage boys in particular still want to know that their mother is *interested* in their feelings, even if they cannot articulate them. And while this can be comforting and necessary, at times it can drive boys crazy. Mothers must be sensitive towards their son's responses. For instance, since women tend to discuss their intimate thoughts and feelings with one another, mothers naturally transfer this behavior to relationships with their sons. If something is wrong, a mother asks what it is. Young boys usually don't know. And if they do, sometimes they will divulge what it is; sometimes they won't.

As boys grow into the teen years many don't want to discuss their feelings, at least with their mothers. But the catch is that most still want to know that their mother is interested in their feelings. This can become something of a bad habit in adolescent boys: a game young men subconsciously play with their mothers. They want their mother to see that they are upset, but they don't want to divulge what is going on. They do this because knowing that their mother really does care is a consoling.

Another common way mothers love their sons is through food. The stereotypical Jewish or Italian mother loves her son well by feeding him well. There is a peculiar connection between the digestive tract and mothering. In my medical practice, the most stressed-out mothers I have encountered are often the mothers whose sons have growth issues. If a child fails to eat well and fails to grow, a mother subconsciously feels that she has failed. The reverse is true as well: mothers whose teens grow up strong and tall feel better about their parenting because they can see the strength of their son before their very eyes.

Finally, mothers love through sacrifice. They act. They will surrender whatever is necessary to keep their son alive. Whether it is intuitive or not, that is what love does. And mothers need to be needed. They need to express their love because if they can give it and have it received, then their very existence is worthwhile.

Many years ago I worked in a large children's hospital where we treated children with various forms of life-threatening illnesses. From brain tumors, to muscular dystrophy, to cystic fibrosis, the rooms were consistently full with of children in pain and mothers in anguish.

I will never forget a particular eleven-year-old boy I cared for who had cystic fibrosis. His lungs would fill with mucous so thick that he had difficulty breathing. We gave him medicines and therapies to try to remove this thick mucous before it turned into concrete. Very often the mucous would become infected with various bacteria, which would lead to pneumonia. If that happened, we would pump IV antibiotics into him.

Over time the bacteria would outsmart the antibiotics, so we would give him stronger ones. Sometimes these antibiotics worked and sometimes they didn't. Many times this young boy would be in the hospital for a couple of weeks at a time. He would return home for a few weeks and then come back in for more medication. His mother sat in his room for endless hours. She read to him. She listened. Sometimes in his frustration, I heard him scream at her. He needed someone—the safest one he could find—to blame for his pain. She didn't cry; he cried. She didn't return his rantings; she sat quietly.

One day she asked me if she and her husband could meet with me in private. She wouldn't tell me what she wanted to meet about, only that is was important. We agreed and set a time to meet. My mind reeled with curiosity about what she wanted to discuss. Did she want him to die? Was she so tired of seeing him in pain that she wanted us to give him an overdose of pain medication? I was ashamed to have such thoughts but they were there.

When we convened, the three of us sat around an oval table. "I know that we're all busy," she started, "and I don't want to take too much time or draw this out. So let me be direct and frank. You have seen my son suffer for a number of years now. You understand his dire circumstances. And you understand that his particular prognosis is poor." I waited, wondering if something horrible was coming next. I was prepared to say: "No, absolutely not—under no circumstances will we give him medicine which that will shorten his life."

Her words interrupted my shameful thoughts. "My husband and I have thought things over. We have discussed our situation in depth and we have come to an agreement. We would like you to comply with our wishes." She did not leave room for disagreement.

"I would like to donate my lungs to my son." I stared at her face. She looked me right in the eye and I could feel myself freeze in my chair. I was dumbfounded. I couldn't agree to her request. First she screamed. Then she cried. Then she pleaded. There is no question in my mind but that she was sincere. And there was even less ambiguity about her love for her son. At first I believed her to be crazy but I realized that day that I had stared at the face of a mother's love.

THE EYES OF A HAWK

Before mothers can protect, or even become over-protective, they must employ each of their sensibilities in order to engage the protective action. Before they know how to keep their sons safe, each must identify the enemy. Something somewhere threatens his boyhood every day and because mothers are instinctively protective, they watch and listen for threats to their sons. When mothers respond to these threats—which today are often electronic—they attack.

In our sophisticated, electronics-saturated, post-modern culture, the threats to a boy's health are insidious and terribly elusive. So good mothers keep their eyes wide open and their ears alert. Then their sons attack them for doing so. Usually this comes in the (manipulative) form of "you just don't trust me." But don't be put off. Just as they don't want to talk about their feelings but still want you to be interested in them, boys can't say that they like restrictions; but they do, because that means their parents care. And deep down, it feels good to be watched. Again, like communicating their feelings, even though being watched feels good boys still reject it. This is another push and pull dynamic in a son's relationship with his mother: do it, but don't let me know you're doing it.

Sadly, however, often when mothers hear their sons admonish them about a "trust" issue, they abdicate their better senses. Well, they reason, I guess you're right. You're a good kid. I should trust you. And their eyes turn away and their ears go deaf to make the young boy feel more grown-up. *Big mistake.*

Smart mothers know that the issue is not trust—mothers don't watch because they don't trust sons. They watch because life is tough, unfair, and cruel. Mothers have lived longer and endured more blows; they understand more about the dangers to young boys. Boys can't see what is behind them, much less what will harm them, so mothers must vigilantly guard them.

Maddie came to see me alone because she was concerned about Sam's moods. Ever since he turned thirteen, she said, he had become more sarcastic and volatile. Prior to thirteen he had been an easy-going, quiet boy who rarely talked back to her and pretty much did what she asked. He was particularly close to his father, a pilot with a major airline carrier. His flight schedule meant he was away from home one week, and at home the next. Her husband was quiet, she told me, just like Sam, and perhaps that was the reason the two were so close.

Maddie was particularly bright, articulate, and caring. She worked part-time as a unit clerk in a hospital and always arranged her schedule to be home when Sam was. They had always communicated easily and this made Sam's sarcasm and negativity that much harder for her to understand. He was an only child and she was quick to point out that with her husband's income and her salary, Sam enjoyed many comforts that his friends didn't.

I queried her about his friends. He had not changed peer groups, but a new boy had recently joined his eighth grade class. Sam had befriended him, and she was proud that he had reached out to the new kid.

I asked what Sam did after school. The usual, she said: track practice, homework, some downtime, then bed. Pretty uneventful.

From all accounts Maddie sketched a healthy, stable home, which she had worked hard to achieve. There was minimal familial friction, except for Sam's new attitude. She and her husband were role models of polite behavior, and had taught Sam to be polite. They couldn't imagine what had gotten into him.

Truthfully, I was mentally preparing a diatribe on the normal attitude fluctuations of adolescence, when something caused me to dig a little deeper before I launched into the lecture.

"So what does Sam do with his downtime?" I asked, half thinking of my talk, half awaiting her response. "Oh, I don't know." she answered. I waited for her to say something more. She didn't. Then I realized why: she really didn't know what Sam did with his downtime. "Does he like to play video games, chat with friends online, listen to music?" I pressed. "Probably." She raised and lowered her shoulders as she spoke. "I let him be. You know, I respect his privacy. He has a TV in his room, a laptop, an iPod, and his cell phone. Although I know he doesn't talk on that too much."

I could tell that Maddie's speech became more tenuous yet pressured as she continued. Something clearly bothered her about Sam's free time, so I pressed her on it. Yet, she couldn't pinpoint her discomfort. "What do you think he does in his room after school?" I kept on. "Like I said, I really don't know. Sometimes he and a buddy—not a girl of course—will go to his room. I guess they play games." She looked up at me with a mixture of sadness and fear. "Have you asked Sam what he does?" I said. "No, no, we respect him and certainly trust him. He is a good kid. Since he has never given us a reason not to trust him, we do," Maddie rationalized.

Interestingly, when I asked about the possibility that Sam might be looking at pornography Web sites (he wasn't), or sneaking beer into his room (he wasn't doing that either), or engaging in any activity she thought was wrong, Maddie became agitated with me. How dare I question the integrity of her thirteen-year-old son?

Realizing that I wasn't getting anywhere, I asked if I could talk to Sam, and she reluctantly agreed. I purposely spoke with him alone first then asked if Maddie could join us. Sam began describing his attitude shift. He admitted that he felt angrier, moodier, and overall more agitated than he had ever felt. When I asked about what he did in his room during the afternoon, he simply said: "Nothing. Just guy stuff."

"Do you have a MySpace page?" I asked. "Sure, everybody does," he said defensively. "Who writes to you?" I asked. "Lots of people, I guess. Guys; a few girls." He spoke with increasing discomfort, refusing to make eye contact with me. He shifted in his seat. "How about you show your mother your page?" I asked, waiting for a dual yelp. "No way. No way. That's guy stuff!" he answered. "Really, Dr. Meeker," said Maddie, "I disagree. That's private. And Mark and I don't agree with invading his privacy."

Bingo. We all three realized at that moment that something was awry with Sam's MySpace page. Sam wanted to keep it secret. I knew that he was hiding something that he was torn about and Maddie refused to budge. She didn't want to know what her son was doing because she didn't want to be upset if she didn't have to be. She didn't want to see because then she would realize that perhaps she wouldn't know what to do. She would be upset—she might scream at Sam, take away his laptop, cell phone, iPod, or all three.

But she couldn't; she shouldn't, her mind reasoned. It'll drive a good kid away and mess him up for life. The safest action to take, she concluded, was to remain distant, unknowing, and inactive. When she thought over the bad attitude and sarcasm of the previous months, she rationalized that they were probably just an adolescent phase. Yet in her heart she knew better, which was why she had come to me in the first place.

The truth is that while her mind rationalized, her instincts brought her through my office door. She knew her son; she knew that something was wrong—she was simply afraid to face it. Because if she faced it, then she had a decision to make: what to do about it. This was what frightened her even more. If she made him get rid of his MySpace page, or even his computer, she was terrified that he would rebel—even run away. She was afraid if she handled the problem the wrong way, she would be a miserable mother and turn her son into a rotten kid.

In my experience, Maddie's feelings typify the majority of parents I encounter around the country. We are afraid to really see what our boys are up to, not because they're bad kids, but because we're afraid of disciplining them. Discipine takes energy and it's unnerving. We want them home, even if they're engaging in unhealthy activities because we're frightened that if we stop activities which we know are unhealthy for them, we'll lose our sons. Let me assure you of one thing: half-way homes and jails aren't full of boys who have been disciplined, they are full of boys whose parents have left them alone.

Fathers approach these issues differently. Many have difficulty believing in the convoluted thought processes mothers can engage in when making parenting decisions about their sons. When a father recognizes a problem, he usually tries to find a solution, and then decides if and when to implement that solution.

But that's not the way mothers think. Problems with sons aren't simply there in isolation. For mothers, all sorts of personal feelings enter into the equation. If the problem is severe, she may call into question her responsibility for creating it, perpetuating it, and then solving it. Because she feels responsible for her son, she fears that his problems reflect her character flaws. Mothers are often a little insecure with sons because they know they cannot fully understand a boy's mind and experiences.

Most mothers travel many mental miles when confronting their son's problems. First, because she is female she is disadvantaged in understanding his male mind and experiences. This makes her insecure and ill at east. Second, some mothers (and some fathers too) consistently personalize their sons' problems. Women are professional blame bearers.

Maddie wanted to be a fabulous mother to Sam. She adored him. His grades were excellent and his character was good. This made her feel successful as a mother. When she realized that he was probably engaging in activities that were harmful, she rejected confronting him for fear that he would not respond well enough and she would therefore fail. So she had two problems on her hands: his activity and her fear of failure as a mother.

The great irony is that she handled the situation beautifully. When Sam showed her his MySpace page in the examination room she went ballistic. She saw lewd and graphic sexual language that he had exchanged with other girls whom he claimed not to know. She rationally yet angrily informed Sam that he had violated these girls and that they had violated him sexually.

She told him that as part of their family, she expected him to speak respectfully to others at all times. Furthermore, she told him, he owed those girls apologies; and those who had spoken so vilely to him owed him an apology as well.

Maddie, in atypical fashion, pounded her gold-braceleted wrists on the exam room table. Sam broke down in tears. He sobbed. I'm sure he felt humiliated, but I'm also certain he felt relief that his secret was out.

Many parents make the terrible mistake of trivializing boys' mischief. But there's mischief and then there's mischief. Boys should be boys when it comes to playing with bullfrogs, and tree forts, and the kindergartner who sprays shaving cream on the sofa. But when teen mischief has a particularly sexual or a violent nature, parents are wrong to brush it off. Mischief that reveals an innocent heart is innocent. Mischief that is sexual or violent violates the innocence that even teenage boys should have. Our culture wants to deny that innocence, to degrade and corrupt it, and to market and sell to the low tastes that result. But we as parents need to protect our sons' innocence if we care about their mental and physical health, not to mention their character. Watch your son like a hawk. Through an adult's eyes, a written conversation which is vile in its sexual content can seem silly and just written for shock value—and many dismiss it as simply something boys do.

Maddie's fearful desire not to fail was ultimately overcome by her maternal instinct to protect her son. If only more mothers would act wisely on their instincts rather than behave as fools and march into their son's problems, how many more boys could experience the relief that Sam did?

KEEPER OF DIGNITY

Mothers are acutely aware of the need to preserve theirs sons' dignity as they mature into men. Mothers embody pride for sons and their daughters from the moment they are born. They are proud because the child belongs to them, but beyond that defensive ownership a mother feels pride for her son because he is male. She sees herself as the one who must transfer her sense of pride in his masculinity to him so that when he is older he will internalize that pride in his masculinity and protect his dignity for himself.

The beauty of a mother as keeper and teacher of her son's dignity is that it transcends all aspects of his character and his capabilities. In her eyes his very existence warrants dignity. He may have spastic quadriplegia from cerebral palsy, be bound in a wheelchair and unable to mutter any words, but he has dignity and she will teach the world this. He may be a concert cellist, a professional athlete, a broker on Wall Street, or a janitor; in every case she will see, expose, and protect his dignity because he must have it. She is his number one fan, and will demand that others honor him because he is a boy transitioning into a man.

I am implying nothing about a mother's lover for her daughter. Mothers most certainly love their daughters and value them (or they should) equally with their son. My explanation of a mother protecting her son's honor does not imply that she feels any less toward her daughter. My point is simply that her feelings—and therefore her behavior towards—her son is different than it is towards her daughter. Sons are different than daughters. Gender differences matter and they are good.

Sometimes a mother's diligence in demanding respect for her son can go overboard. I had a patient who was quite small for his age through elementary school and junior high school. He was a likeable, rambunctious boy and performed well academically. But his mother was extremely sensitive about his size. Her mannerisms told anyone near her that they best not make fun of her son. She felt that she must teach the world that while he was small, he was masculine. One could sense when they were near her, particularly with her son present, that she was anticipating a slur against his maleness, an affront to the dignity he deserved.

To keep his friends and their parents, teachers, and coaches aware of his masculinity, she followed him everywhere he went to make sure that no one made fun of him—that everyone respected his masculinity. She was room mother or at least co-room mother in every grade in elementary school. When he played sports she watched from the team side of the playing field, rather than the parent side. Every game, she argued with the coaches about equal playing time for her son.

And much to the child's dismay, she made him play football in junior high. He didn't make the weight cut so he played a level down but she didn't care. When the poor boy was invited to birthday parties, she not only brought him, she stayed to "help out" at the party. Interestingly, if girls were there she would leave, but if there were only boys she stayed.

Fortunately for the poor child, when he was sixteen he started to grow. And he grew and grew. By the end of his junior year in high school, he had acquired androgenized muscles, a hint of a beard, and he could buy thirty-two length blue jeans. And guess what happened to her following him around? It stopped. She felt vindicated and proud—in her mind she was finally secure that she had "transferred" her son's dignity to a permanent place on his shoulders.

Of course, her son grew and matured despite this over-mothering. By gluing herself to her son she only reinforced to him that his masculinity was fragile. It was up for grabs and since he wasn't able to stand up for himself, she had to be the replacement. Her presence was a constant reminder to him of his inadequacy. This was something that he had to deal with as he grew up.

Perhaps it is because mothers are not male that they guard maleness so fiercely in their sons. They do not take it for granted. The same way a father intuitively protects his daughter, a mother preserves her son's dignity.

DISPENSER OF GRACE

Grace is love that is undeserved. Because a mother can see through a gnarled physique, a low IQ, a beast-like temper, or a chronic disease right to the soul of her son, she can spot the beauty within him, which allows her to love him. She can forgive him, excuse him, accept him, and love him when no one else will. Because her eyes pierce through the layers of this ugliness and find the lost part of his self, she can extend him grace when no one else can. While fathers can do this with sons as well, in my experience mothers have this ability in far more abundance than fathers do—or at least impart it far more frequently. I believe this to be true because mothers don't expect as much from sons as fathers since they and are not in competition with them.

Every son needs to experience grace. I don't think that any human experience changes a boy's character as dramatically or elevates his sense of self-worth so clearly. To know that he is not good enough, not smart enough, or too mean to be loved is devastating to a boy. But the experience of a mother's embrace and acceptance is life changing for a boy. When a mother extends outstretched arms to a son who has failed in sports, or school, or socially, or been deemed not smart enough, "manly enough," or just plain not good enough, he begins to understand what love is all about. The moment a mother extends her grace, he begins to understand that goodness in being a man isn't all about his performance. It isn't about his successes or his failures. It is about being able to accept love from another and then return that love. He learns this lesson when his mother accepts him in the midst of life's lowest points. And when he learns to accept love when he feels humiliated, he learns to stand a bit taller. He learns to trust in himself as a man.

EMOTIONAL CONNECTOR

The very qualities which cause men to be attracted to women can often become the very qualities which men come to hate later in life. And the reverse is true. Some women are attracted to men because they are hard-working and show great commitment to their work. Later on, those same women complain that their husbands are workaholics and never around.

This is true for men. Studies reveal that most women talk about twice as much as men over the course of the day. Women are expressive, and that expressiveness helps mothers become the emotional connector within a family. Fathers are good at setting rules and finding solutions. Mothers are better at understanding. At first a man is attracted to a women because she is expressive— she talks about the relationship and its positives and negatives. Years later, he leaves home frequently because he is talked out.

The fact that women use more words and are in general more openly expressive serves sons very well. Mothers teach sons about their feelings and thoughts and help boys become comfortable with them. This lends itself to helping boys establish healthy connectedness with their mothers and, importantly, other people. Her words help him become a better man.

She can teach him to become comfortable putting words to his feelings and that he has a choice as to when and how he verbalizes his feelings. A mother can teach her son about girls, because a son respects his mother even when he finds it hard to tolerate the girls at school. She teaches him to tolerate girls at various ages, to excuse their feminine behaviors that he finds ridiculous, and to appreciate that the differences between boys and girls are not good and bad, but two beneficial aspects of human nature. Later, she can help him understand and, therefore more easily accept, how women think and why.

Sometimes mothers pain their sons by explaining and talking too much, and women do need to understand that while they, mothers, are responsible for helping sons to understand others, to love them and connect with them, boys may choose to do this in different ways. Grown men don't always bond through verbal communication. They often bond with others through action, which can be anything from athletics to shared hobbies to work, rather than through sharing feelings and emotions.

Mothers need to remember that her goal is to help her son be comfortable enough with himself to form deep bonds and respect his way of doing it. Mothers earnestly teach lessons by talking more but it is important to realize that as their son matures his thinking does as well. As he ages, his cognitive skills help him think more pragmatically. This allows him to see what she is trying to say and absorb it quickly, if he can identify the lesson she is trying to teach.

Beyond words, her physical affection allows him to feel more comfortable being affectionate with others. Her open communication lets him understand his own thoughts and appreciate those of others. As she makes herself trustworthy, he learns to trust other women. All of these aspects and many more of her femininity open a path for him to connect more soundly with others—both men and women.

Mothers ideally bring all of these qualities to their sons. They love adoringly, protect until death, guard their son's dignity, extend grace when it is needed, and ensure healthy relationships for him in the future.

WHEN LOVE COMES OUT SIDEWAYS

The reality of a mother's love is that it sometimes comes out sideways. Mothers are often tired, manipulated, and they make mistakes. They scream when they mean to apologize. They feel guilty that they have to work rather than stay at home with the children. They worry about all the things that can go wrong.

But there's an easy way to take some of the pressure off—and that is to allow both you and your son more time to relax. Some of the most important moments of being a parent consist of just being there for your kids and sharing the most mundane aspects of life with them.

Mothers who spend too much time with other mothers often compare notes and feel they are doing too little. But motherhood isn't a competition. It is a state of being. Twenty-first-century, post-modern mothers site many reasons they are anxious.

Peer pressure heads the list of influences operating in a mother's life which dramatically alters how she raises her son. Peer pressure usually has a very negative affect on sons because it rarely causes mothers to make better decisions for their son. It acts against their own instincts and is therefore usually detrimental to the son.

Mothers ungulate ceaselessly about their concerns over the peer pressure their son experiences. But peer pressure that parents feel affects a boy more significantly than the peer pressure he feels from his contemporaries. Usually the mother is influenced more heavily by peer pressure simply because most women spend more time with other mothers than fathers do with other fathers.

Consider the number of scheduled activities boys have. Why does Johnny go to piano lessons, soccer, and football practice all at the same time? Because other mothers have their sons enrolled in two to three extra-curricular activities. Mothers want their sons to be similar enough to other boys so that they will be accepted among their peers. This is a healthy desire. But if it leads to enrolling Johnny in piano lessons, soccer, and football practice all at the same time because other mothers have their sons enrolled in two or three extra-curricular activities, then it's not. The problem is, two to three scheduled events stress some sons unduly. We know that sons who have healthy relationships with their parents fare much better life. Your sons don't need more activities that separate them from you, they need more time *with* you. And guess what? A night spent reading at home with your sons is a night that's a lot less stressful for *you and them* than a night spent running between this practice and that recital. Further, it decreases the amount of time a son spends with his mother and father and we know that sons who have healthy relationships with parents fare much better in life. But we sign them up anyway.

The United States is the wealthiest country on the planet—but prescriptions for anti-depressants and anxiolytics have soared over the past five years. Why? Because mothers and fathers are stressed by the demands on them—the demands of work, family, and keeping up with the Joneses. And much of these demands come from trying to get to work on time, to make enough money to pay for the shoes, lessons, and tuition for our sons that other boys have. But you don't need to keep up with the Joneses. You only need to keep a roof over your head and raise mentally and physically healthy children. You'd be better off going for family walks together than working harder to make extra money to pay for more activities for the kids.

Peer pressure perpetuates a mother's stress to be all and do all for her son in order for him to grow up and be happy. But many times—most times in fact—a son cannot be happy in a home where there is so much stress created because his mother feels an obligation to perform well or at least better than many of the friends that she sees around her.

When Caroline came to my office with her six-month-old boys, I knew the visit would be long: her mother was in tow. I entered the examination room to see her twin boys, Caleb and Connor, sitting on a blanket in on the middle of the exam room floor. Caroline looked tired, her shoulders sagged. I noticed that her shoulders had lost their squareness as she leaned over to give a Cheerio to Caleb. Clearly she had dressed up for her appointment, and wore heavy makeup, as if to disguise her fatigue. She had concealer caked on her eyes and pale tangerine lipstick covering her lips. As we chatted, I noticed movement only on the right side of her mouth. The left eyelid and the left side of her mouth were drooping. There was a crack in her voice. She cleared her throat to conceal it. She wanted to show me and her mother that she was doing extraordinarily well. But I recognized the symptoms and realized that Caroline had developed Bell's Palsy.

As I asked pertinent questions about the boys' development, eating habits, and sleep patterns, her answers were encouraging but abbreviated. When I started to place the twins on my exam table, she quickly stood to help. While I examined Caleb, she played with Connor while consoling his brother. When I switched to Connor, she continued to concentrate on the two at once.

Her mother sat patiently on the plastic chair beside hers, but I sensed from the moment I entered the room that she was anxious to speak. Realizing that the visit was coming to a close, Caroline's mother blurted out, "Dr. Meeker, I'm terribly worried about Caroline."

"Mother, stop. Please don't." Caroline interrupted.

"No, no, this is important. I think we need her opinion" her mother persisted. Caroline complied.

"What are your concerns?" I asked, looking at the mother.

"Dr, Meeker, I'm worried about Caroline's health. You can probably see she has developed Bell's Palsy. Her doctor gave her some type of steroid medicine for that and she cries a lot. Her doctor also said that she is depressed so he gave her another medicine for that. She started it a few months ago but it's hard for me to tell if it's working or not because she is exhausted all the time. You see, she hardly sleeps. One of the boys is awake every couple of hours wanting to eat. Since she insists on nursing them, she won't let me help. I can't give them a bottle and she won't feed them back-to-back. She lets them eat whenever they want to." Caroline's mother paused long enough for Caroline to interrupt her.

"Mother, you just don't understand," she said. "Things are different today. Breast milk is best for the boys and they need it—everything I read about nursing says that they should eat on demand. You didn't feed me that way in your day."

Caroline's efforts valiantly attempted to insist that she was right but beneath her words I could hear that she wanted to be convinced otherwise.

"Wait a minute," I said. "Let me get this straight, Caroline. You nurse the boys whenever they want to nurse, you are taking steroids because half of your face can't move, and you are suffering from depression, for which you take medication every day."

"Right." she complied.

"I can see that you feel confused, exhausted, and guilty. That's the way any normal mother in your situation would feel." I waited.

"Yeah," she nodded reluctantly.

"Do you think the boys need a happy mother or do they need breast milk more?" I asked.

She seemed surprised by the question. "Breast milk. It boosts their immune system, it wards off infections; there are antibodies in breast milk that they can't get any other way. And it helps me bond better with them. I've read that babies find breast milk emotionally gratifying. How can I not give that to them?"

Like any enthusiastic, loving mother, Caroline had scoured the Internet for information on nursing and had found volumes. Most of what she had read was correct, but some was false. But more important, she had completely lost her balance.

Her instincts told her that she needed more sleep, the drugs (which would be present in the breast and the milk) weren't good for her babies, and the four of them (she rarely thought of her husband's opinion) would be healthier and happier if she stopped nursing.

So why didn't she? Peer pressure. Most mothers feel extraordinary pressure from friends, doctors, and baby books to nurse as long as possible. Certainly I advocate this but I encourage more maternal intuition and common sense.

After a long discussion I tried to convince her that the boys needed a less sleep-deprived mother more than they did breast milk. I encouraged her to wean the boys, start them on formula in a bottle, let someone else help her (heaven forbid their father gets a little bonding time while feeding them), and get some sleep.

She shook her head. I explained the seriousness of post-partum depression and the role that elevated oxytocin, which is associated with breastfeeding, played in the depression. I discussed the potential impact of her depression on the boys.

She dug her heels in. Without words she told me she would sacrifice anything, including her health (and ironically, the health and happiness of her family), for her boys. And giving up nursing was not an option. Mothers are a competitive lot and I sensed that part of Caroline wanted to be Super Mom. Her friends nursed only one child at a time. She could do two. Her mother pleaded with me to convince Caroline to show some common sense.

Realizing that I wasn't making headway, I finally said, "Well, let me tell you. If they were my sons I wouldn't want them to have steroids or anti-depressants in their systems for this long." She stared at me. Her lips were tight, then they relaxed. Her shoulders straightened and she looked at her mom.

"Well, all right. I will wean them a little bit," she said.

Sometimes mothers of sons get crazy. We just do. In our longing to make our sons psychologically sound, physically strong, and developmentally on track (usually we want them advanced) we toss common sense aside. We believe, usually errantly, that others know a better way to parent than we do. So we follow the lead of our peer group. And, I might add, parents of teenage boys are the worst at committing this travesty.

The fact is, your intuition as a mother is better than comparing yourself to other mothers. A mother needs to take a hard look at why she does what she does. Why does her son do what he does? If she recognizes honestly that her motives stem from peer pressure to keep her son ahead of the others, she must buck that peer pressure. Sons need more stress-free homes—which will dictate how they behaves in school much more significantly than does the behavior of their friends.

And one lesson we should all learn is that while mothers want more for their sons, the truth is that sons need less. Boys need fewer toys and fewer clothes. They need more time with their mothers and fathers, less time in structured events, and more time being bored—yes, bored—so that *they* can use their imagination and creativity and figure out what to do. Young men need less time face-to-screen with electronic life and more time face-to-face with people. Less television, video games, clothes, telephone bills, sports events, and preschool hours mean less stress for mothers and more time for boys to figure out who they are and what they want out of life.

All of these things—electronics, clothes, sports events, *ad nauseum*—make their way into a boy's life because his mother (and his father) yield to life as their neighbors live it, the way they see it around them rather than the way it ought to be.

MATERNAL CONFLICT: ENMESHMENT

When a son enters a mother's life, many feelings from her own childhood are triggered. As she swaddles her new son and pulls him towards her chest, he becomes a catalyst for the eruption of emotions that may have been repressed many years earlier. This isn't his fault. This is the normal and often healthy reaction of a parent.

Often these feelings are warm and pleasant—a reliving of a sense of trust, affection, and comfort. Sometimes they are painful—a sense of abandonment, fear, and perplexity. Many mothers experience myriad emotions which can seem frightening and perplexing.

Bruno Bettelheim asserts that if a mother had an unhappy childhood, she may see her son's happiness and avoid responding to it.[1] His happiness feels uncomfortable, so in order to avoid embracing his happiness she becomes aloof and indifferent to him. This is much the same as a melancholy friend becoming irritated by an exuberant one.

Mothers relive their childhoods through their sons. They re-experience feelings of trust, abandonment, affection, and comfort.

But a son can also trigger deep-seated pain for many women. Mothers who have experienced sexual abuse at the hands of men (particularly a father) have serious challenges in their relationships with their son. It is not uncommon for the birth of a son to trigger repressed memories of abuse in mothers along with the concomitant fear and anxiety.

If she had a good relationship with her own father (and has a good relationship with the father of her child), the odds are that these feelings will be positive. But if her relationship with her father was troubled, or if she is a divorced or single mother, and if she fails to recognize what is happening to her emotionally, a mother will transfer the ugly feelings she has from her experiences on to her son. This can complicate her relationship with her son terribly.

Feelings mothers have towards sons can be convoluted, overlaid with conflictual experiences with other men or perhaps other children. But a mother's goal should always be to keep her feelings towards her son as honest and clean as possible. She should feel affection for him and not confuse her affections for him with her feelings for another person. She should love him as a masculine being and this love should be free from an overlaying of love towards other men. Any disappointment towards her son should stem from something he has done—not from something other males have done to her in the past.

In my experience, four patterns of a mother's love toward her son erupt when she is unable to emotionally separate her past bad experiences with men from her present relationships with her son. Divorced or single, mothers are particularly vulnerable to any one of these patterns. They are: enmeshment, estrangement, over-dependence, and unavailability.

Enmeshment between a mother and son occurs when a mother cannot identify where she ends and her son begins. She feels his feelings and very often he feels hers. She is compelled to fix his life because she feels that she is living his life. His hurts are her hurts. His anxiety is hers. Because she is unable to "peel" her emotional self off of him, she experiences his trouble and will do everything within her power to fix it.

Mothers who feel that their lives are devoid of substance are prone to enmeshment because they must cling to someone to give their own life meaning. Her son and his feelings, needs, and desires become fused with her in order that she can feel satisfied on a deeper level.

The problem is, satisfaction never comes. He cannot give enough or be enough for her. She cannot shape his life or navigate it to her liking. So he becomes a chronic disappointment. As for her son, he can feel his mother's emotional entanglement with him, and it naturally makes him uncomfortable. In the tale of the Great Divorce, the mother of Elisha is forced to leave her son. She has attached herself as a leech in her son's life and when the time for separation comes, she screams in anguish. She cannot let go of him. One can sense a tearing of flesh as he pulls himself away from her. Her fingers are clawing at his back. She screams because she literally feels as though her person is being torn in two. Mothers who feel empty, insecure, or struggle with a longing to fill a deep void in their lives must exercise great caution. The emptiness can be filled and the longing can be satisfied but never through a son.

ESTRANGEMENT

Though estrangement is the flip side of enmeshment, it is often the result of the same causes: divorce, single motherhood, or a history of sexual abuse. In this case, it causes a mother to feel estranged from her son simply because he is male. She might regard normal boyish pranks as malevolence. When her son wants her affection, she might push him aside to keep him from becoming "a sissy." When he becomes a teenager she might reprimand him constantly for behavior that reminds her of her former husband, or his deadbeat dad.

There are subtler ways in which a mother can undermine her son as well. She can pay more attention to other women—friends, her daughter, her mother—and brush his needs off easily.

She may verbalize affection for a daughter and rarely verbalize affection toward her son. She can use sarcasm to joke about the shortcomings of his father and his own shortcomings as a boy or as a young man. When a boy realizes that he is being rejected because he is a male, he pulls away, and his mother, in turn, pulls even farther away.

Mothers who have had bad experiences with men need to come to terms with those experiences and accept that their son is an individual, and not the representative of the men who have hurt her.

Mothers who are divorced, particularly those who have endured a very hostile divorce, must heed tremendous caution. When there is dissention between a mother and a father, very frequently a mother can unwittingly take this out on her son. Far too many sons end up in the crossfire after a parent's divorce. Another word of caution is warranted here when considering divorce. Very frequently sons become overly protective towards their mother after a divorce. An oldest son might feel compelled to become the "man of the house." A boy who does this is obviously well-intentioned, but he remains a boy and shouldn't be required to take any mental and emotional burdens for which he is developmentally unprepared.

Divorce is a tragedy that takes a very heavy toll on boys, as well as mothers and fathers. Boys who had previously behaved very age appropriately can suddenly behave very age inappropriately after a divorce has occurred. The best gift for any child is a stable, loving home with a mother and a father. If you have that gift, preserve it.

OVER-DEPENDENCE: MAMA'S BOY

There is a world of difference between a mother having a healthy emotional connection with her son, and a son becoming so emotionally reliant on his mother that he becomes the prototypical boy who is overly dependent upon his mother—a "mama's boy." Sadly, many women have misinterpreted this as a state of emotional connection with sons and pushed their sons away far too early. There is a very significant difference between over-dependence and healthy connectivity.

Most infant boys cling to their mothers. Of course, as an infant, he will want to be attached to her, often literally. As a toddler he will begin to wander a little, while always running back to her. During his elementary school years, he will mimic this toddler-type of wandering then reconnection but the psychological distance he wanders and the length of time he allows to elapse between returning to the safety of his mother will increase. Growing boys value their growing independence.

Over-dependence occurs when a mother consistently communicates to her son that he needs her. She must clothe him, feed him, drive him places, help him with his homework, and assist him in every way, and no one else can fill her spot. This is particularly harmful to a son because it communicates to him that his father has no significant role in filling his needs. And it's terribly painful for fathers. She must help him with his homework because only she can teach him. The lesson a boy learns is that he cannot succeed on his own. Of course, most of what a needy mother communicates is too subtle for a son to identify; but all he knows is that it feels awful.

Mothers who have experienced a poor relationship with their fathers or who have been through a bad divorce are very susceptible to this behavior. But to be warned about it is to guard against it. Since they feel wounded by men, they experience a significant drop in their self-esteem, and they purpose to make up for this loss by being terribly important in their son's life. When such a mother feels her son (a male) need her, she feels that his neediness of her and her alone validates her ability to be in a non-hostile relationship with a male. Unfortunately, over-dependence blunts a boy's emotional development.

UNAVAILABILITY

When mothers entered the workforce with renewed intensity during the last half of the twentieth century, many came under attack for abandoning their families. Numerous research studies appeared on the effects of daycare on children and the effects of maternal absence on the psychological development of children.

Women who worked (without pay) in the home raising their children and women who worked jobs outside of the home felt pressured from all sides. Women who stayed home to raise their children suffered from feelings of inadequacy to lower self-esteem to anxiety about not bringing money home to the family, while women who worked outside the home experienced guilt and sadness about being away from their children. Mine is a generation of women who determined with a fresh ferocity to shift the worlds of finance, law, medicine, and any other workplace dominated by men to accommodate us. We were tired of limited choices, disrespect, and often just plain bored with the mundane task of keeping our homes in order and our children well cared for.

Mothers can find research and books to support and encourage their lifestyle choice, whatever it is. Where parenting is concerned, there is no positive research or advice. That's why I hold much of it loosely. My belief is that if we mothers are tough enough to be honest with ourselves, we will know what our sons need. We know the moment they are born our sons need to form strong emotional attachments to their mother or their father in order to learn to trust that they will be cared for and that they are worth being cared for.

Many argue, and even some research shows, that as long as any adult consistently provides for a boy's basic needs during his first one to two years of life, he will fair well psychologically. The problem is, for the majority of mothers, we know better. We believe that our son needs a strong bond with us, and we with him.

Boys need to form emotional bonds with their mothers over time in a consistent manner. We do know that boys who fail to form these bonds in the first two years of life suffer attachment issues for many years and are at risk for of never being able to form healthy attachments to others. And boys can't form bonds or learn to trust others if their mother (or consistent mother figure) isn't available or dependable.

We need only to look at the psychological health of many boys in orphanages from the old Soviet Union. Many were adopted by families in the United States. Many of the older boys in particular demonstrated serious attachment disorders and parents of these boys were distraught and frightened because while many of these orphaned boys acted quiet, compliant, and sweet externally, internally they were almost vacant. Many were so emotionally bankrupt that the only feelings they were comfortable feeling were anger and hostility. The circumstances of their infancy years demonstrate why their comfort with only negative feelings makes sense.

When my patient Andrew was born in Ukraine, his mother was very poor and placed him in an orphanage. He was given a crib and fed several times a day, but was removed from the crib and held only one or two times a week, his adoptive mother was told. He walked at age two rather than age one because he never had the opportunity to be out of his crib.

In short, he experienced a profound sense of abandonment. And abandonment, I believe, is the most painful human experience possible. Andrew was deprived of touch, affection, eye contact, and love, and was given the minimum calories needed to survive. He experienced a profound emptiness because no one was available to him: physically, psychologically, or mentally.

And I believe that even in those first months of life a child understands his own value on some level. If his needs are met by another, he feels valued. If they are not, in a very fundamental way he feels worthless.

Andrew had no one available for him in any meaningful way. He became invisible, probably even to himself. Lacking emotionally security, he could not laugh or smile. As he grew, he could not show or feel any affection, because none had been offered to him when he was young. He walled himself off from receiving any positive affection from another (even though it was probably never offered) because feeling any affection or warmth would remind him of all the affection he failed to receive.

Andrew felt safe feeling angry and hostile because these feelings do not presuppose a sense of security or value. But they do offer a sense of control, of "getting even;" anger is a safe way of releasing sadness, loneliness, or grief.

Because Andrew lacked a mother to give him physical and emotional contact for the first six years of his life, he locked himself into an emotional glass cage. He was safe there. And because he had been there from such an early age and at such a crucial point in his development of trust, his adoptive mother wondered if he could ever be removed. Even the best child psychiatrist in our area wondered the same thing. Andrew became physically violent by the third grade. He hit another boy so hard he broke his leg. By the time Andrew was in sixth grade, his parents were gravely concerned that he might harm his siblings—or even them—while they slept at night.

Andrew's upbringing demonstrates the extreme damage done to a boy when a parent is unavailable. But all around us—in our schools, sports teams, and daycare centers—there are boys who suffer attachment issues and healthy emotional development issues because they have mothers who are physically or emotionally unavailable.

Mothers who are drunk are emotionally unavailable to their sons. Mothers who compulsively work or play are unavailable. Mothers who suffer from depression, obsessive compulsive disorder, attention deficit disorder, and excessive stress are physically and emotionally unavailable at times to their sons. In short, many of us are unavailable to our sons at various points during their lives.

Every mother must examine her life, take inventory of her energy for work and motherhood, and then ask how she can be present more for her son. This is really hard stuff because all mothers struggle at different times with different issues. But raising great sons demands that we take inventory of our energies because boys need their mother's time, attention, and affections.

There is a good reason why many adult men fail to trust women. They do so because many have never experienced healthy bonding with their mothers. And if a boy grows up with an alcoholic, workaholic, or absent mother, he quickly learns to withdraw from women. But the hurt doesn't stop with the withdrawal. He pulls away to guard himself from further insult. He subconsciously concludes that she is not available for him because he is not worth her time or affection. And if he is valued this little by his mother, he must be valued less by others who aren't supposed to love him. Ultimately his affection and respect for himself suffer and he feels quite alone.

The investment of physical and emotional energy which a mother gives a son is very serious stuff. When a mother chooses to be away from her son, regardless of the reason, the impact on her son is greater than she realizes. Sometimes mothers can't help being separated. My purpose in reminding mothers of this is not to incite guilt—I myself am a working mother—but simply to state a fact: to be blessed by sons is to be called to a great responsibility. Every choice we make as mothers has farther reaching effects on our son than we realize.

The choices, loves, and beliefs of a boy's mother craft his character. Mothers are a powerful presence in their sons lives. This knowledge shouldn't frighten us; it should motivate us. Boys need more of their mothers in order to be greater men. And any mother who follows her maternal instincts, examines her own motivations, and does the best she can, will be a good mother. Boys don't need perfection; they just need you there.

Jimmy O'Donnell was a mean kid. In his short ten years he had successfully and single-handedly terrorized every young boy on his street. The girls in his neighborhood dodged him; one look at him and each of them knew that Jimmy O. was nothing but trouble.

Even Jimmy's mother feared him. She never admitted it, but it was clear to Jimmy's teachers, his school principal, and other parents on Jimmy's street. She avoided him. Like an irresponsible dog owner, she shooed him outside to roam the streets.

Seven-year-olds Mike, Bobby, and Evan lived on Jimmy's street. Whenever Jimmy hopped on his scooter, one of two things occurred: either they would chicken out and run away, or, if they were feeling particularly tough and united that day, the threesome would stand in a yard and withstand Jimmy's taunting.

One day, Jimmy made an enormous mistake. He hopped on his scooter and came to terrorize them. "Mike, Bobby!" he shouted at the two of them from his scooter. "Hey, get over here, you mother-loving, booger-eating turds!" The two boys froze. They were not a threesome. Today they were a twosome and each looked at the other anxiously, knowing that they needed to decide very quickly what to do. Should they run? Should they look up and risk making eye contact with Jimmy? If they did, their day was doomed. Or so they thought.

"Whatcha want Jimmy?" Mike blurted. Bobby was stunned. Blood drained from his olive face and suddenly he felt nauseated. "What's the deal, Mike? Are you crazy or something?

"Let's get out of here!" Bobby blurted.

Mike shoved his fists deep into his jean pockets and started at Jimmy. "No," he said. "You don't scare me Jimmy O'Donnell."

Jimmy leapt from his scooter and tossed it on Mike's freshly mown lawn. Jimmy had a fresh velvety buzz cut and Mike saw snippets of his pink scalp beneath the trimmed stubble. Rumor had it that Jimmy shaved. Some said that he could actually grow a beard at age ten—and this made his steps more daunting as he approached Mike.

"What do ya say, punk? Did I hear you say something to me?"

Mike blurted, "Yeah, Jimmy. I did." Mike stretched his neck and pushed his bony shoulders back. Without a shirt his scrawny frame looked like it could snap like a chicken bone. Bobby stood beside him with a short-sleeved madras shirt buttoned to the neck. He was still frozen.

"I'm sick of your bullying everybody. Me and Bobby here, we want you to get lost. And now." With that command, Jimmy darted toward Bobby, chasing him like a rooster chasing a chick. Bobby's skinny arms flailed as he ran and screamed, Jimmy pursuing him easily.

"Knock it off Jimmy," Mike demanded. "Why don't ya go chase someone your own age? Suddenly Jimmy turned towards Mike, spit flying from the sides of his mouth, beads of sweat erupting from his scalp and resting atop his buzz. "I'm gonna make you eat that. Come over here, you weenie!" Jimmy shouted at Mike.

Mike ran out of his yard and into the McNally's next door. Jimmy followed. Without a thought, Mike threw himself up into a branch of Mr. McNally's maple tree and scurried toward the sky. His heart pounded in his palms and now he felt sweat running down his bare back. When he reached the branches that could no longer hold his forty-five-pound frame, Mike stopped. He was ashamed that his heart was racing so fast and that he was panting.

Suddenly Bobby jumped into the tree and climbed up to Mike. They sat there like frightened cats, while Jimmy snarled below. Mike looked down and there stood Jimmy, standing guard at the foot of the tree.

Little did they know that Mike's mother looked out through her kitchen window at just this moment. She searched her yard for the boys. When she couldn't see them, she opened her back door to get a better look. Then she saw Jimmy, standing there in front of the McNally's big maple tree with his arms crossed and a smirk on his face.

She watched for a moment to see what the two would do. She saw Jimmy look up and yell something at the boys then turn and laugh. Enough was enough, she thought.

She slammed her back door and marched over to the tree. Her glare fixed on Jimmy O'Donnell's face. Mary wasn't a large woman, but one thing was certain. She was bigger and stronger than Jimmy and she was a mad mother.

Jimmy never saw her coming. He was too engrossed in his glee. When she reached him, Mary grabbed him by the shoulders and spun him around. "Just who do you think you are, Jimmy O'Donnell? You think you can come and bully younger kids whenever you want? Well, those days are over. You won't scare my son or his friends anymore."

With that resolved, Mary grabbed his elbows and locked his arms in an "X" behind his back. "Come on down here, you two," she yelled up to Mike and Bobby. "I've got a job for you." The two stunned boys scampered down the tree and saw Jimmy desperately trying to wiggle from Mary's angry grip. When they landed on the ground, Mary marched all three away from the tree and into her backyard.

"Boys," she started, "Jimmy won't be bothering you anymore, because if he does he has to deal with me. I'm going to hold him here for a minute. I want each of you to take a swing at him."

Mike's mouth fell open. Hit Jimmy O'Donnell? Was she out of her mind?

"Come on boys, step up here. Take a swing. Mike, you first," she insisted. With that, Mike balled his small fingers into a fist and swung his birdlike arm smack into the center of Jimmy's belly. "One more, a little harder, Mike, then it's Bobby's turn." Again, he readied his aim and smacked Jimmy in the belly.

Bobby followed and took two swings, just the same. Jimmy didn't cry. The punches were so weak and his muscle so strong, but still Mike thought he saw tears tucked in the corner of Jimmy's eyes.

After Bobby swung, Mary released Jimmy. He ran from the three of them back to his scooter. As he ran away, Mary thought she heard him utter, "Just wait, Mrs. Winter. My dad's gonna come and beat you up."

From that day forward Jimmy left Mike and Bobby, along with many of the other neighborhood boys, alone.

This incident occurred many years ago and if it happened today, Mrs. Winter would probably have been charged with assault and battery. She wasn't a violent woman and she knew that two scrawny boys couldn't hurt any part of Jimmy save his ego. Forty years ago mothers seemed to understand more about young boys. There is a pecking order at work in male groups regardless of a boy's age. And in the periphery of each group waits another boy watching for opportunities to push his way in and pounce on whomever he can. He doesn't want to join the order, he wants to crush it and crown himself king.

Mary saw this and she responded. With no intention to negotiate she identified a problem and allowed her maternal instincts to drive her actions. Bullies must be confronted and she realized that she was the one to dethrone Jimmy.

I'm certainly not advocating that mothers follow their young boys and make their sons punch the lights out of bullies. But we mothers have become confused by listening to too many experts and over-reading and over-thinking everything about young boys' behavior. Just follow your instincts, use common sense, and remember that not only should boys be boys, but mothers should be mothers. Papers have been written in journals on bullies. Teachers have lectured and parents have argued with each other over the behavior of their boys. But bullies have remained on their thrones on playgrounds across America, because we refuse to confront very real truths about boyhood behavior and then do something about it. We will examine the behavior of bullies and the pecking order of boys in a later chapter. So for a moment, let's rewind and look at a mother's response when her son is bruised—whether physically or emotionally. A ferocity is triggered inside a mother. Is this anger more intense when a son rather than a daughter is hurt? Yes and no.

Mothers view sons differently than they do their daughters. They have an instinctual desire to preserve their son's masculinity and this means preserving the perception that her son is physically and mentally strong. She will never allow him to be at the bottom of the pecking order.

CHAPTER EIGHT

The Difference a Dad Makes

IT TAKES A MAN TO RAISE A MAN. And just as mothers should listen to their intuition, fathers should listen to their sons. If they did, the conversation might go something like this.

"Hey, Jack, I'll see you later. I'm going to a seminar now on how to be a better father to you!"

"Oh, that's easy, dad. Just pound more nails with me."

After the class, Jack's father returned and announced, "The teacher told me I need to spend more time with you."

"That's what I said, dad, but you left anyway."

If a boy is going to grow into a healthy man, he needs to have a dad who shows him how. Does this mean that a single mother cannot raise a man? No, but one thing is for sure. If a single mother's son grows up to be a strong adult, chances are excellent that he has rubbed shoulders with a good man along the way.

Let's take a look at the state of boys in the country with regard to their exposure to their fathers.

- Sixty-seven percent of children under the age of eighteen live with both parents and 27 percent live with one parent only (usually mom)[1]
- Sixty-seven percent of teens live with their biological father; 91 percent of teens live with their biological mother[2]
- Sixty-three percent of black children do not have their biological father at home; the same is true of 35 percent of Hispanic children and 28 percent of white children[3]
- Eighty percent of African American children can expect to spend at least a significant part of their childhood years living apart from their fathers[4]

Many of us have seen these numbers. We know that our boys spend far too much of their lives outside of the influence of their fathers. We know that out-of-wedlock births are a problem. We know that divorce has wreaked havoc in the lives of young boys, as it has in the lives of fathers. But we have nevertheless failed to face up to the problem. There is no paucity of research regarding the impact of fatherlessness on boys.

- A boy living in a single-parent home is at double the risk of suffering physical, emotional, or educational neglect[5]
- Seventy-three percent of adults and 68 percent of teens said young people "are more likely to be violent and commit crimes when their fathers are absent from home"[6]
- In single mother households, older boys are more likely to commit criminal acts than their peers who live with two parents[7]
- Children growing up with a single parent (usually a mother) are at increased risk for: behavior problems, educational problems, extreme hyperactivity and withdrawal, poor deferred gratification skills, school misbehavior, dropping out of school, smoking, drinking, early and frequent sexual activity, drugs, suicide, vandalism, violence, and criminal acts[8]

There is plenty more such data, but I'll spare you. When we read the data on the state of our boys across the country, we feel sick. We stew over and fear for the future of these boys. Our hearts sink not only for their lonely lives; we worry for our country; we worry about what life will be like for the generations after us, with so many boys growing up in such circumstances.

As fatherless homes have risen dramatically, life has changed dramatically for our boys and for our society. Let's start by reversing the data we just looked at. A boy living in a home with his mother and father is less likely to experience physical, emotional, or educational neglect. He is less likely to commit violent crimes. He is less likely to commit violence at school. A boy growing up with a father and a mother is at decreased risk for behavior problems, educational problems, hyperactivity, and withdrawal. He is better able to develop deferred gratification skills, less likely to drop out of school, less likely to smoke, drink, have early or frequent sex, use drugs, commit suicide, or commit vandalism or violence or any other type of criminal act.

It's not just nostalgia that makes us think childhood was better in our day. In many ways, it was.

We can blame many things for this terrible situation: the sexual revolution, feminism, the idea of a "gender-neutral" society, a toxic media culture, and so on. What I can say as a pediatrician is that the science is clear that boys thrive in stable, two-parent families. Both mother and father are irreplaceable, but for different reasons.

WHAT A FATHER GIVES A SON

In a son's eyes, his father is the source of all correct answers. He knows what's going to happen next. He is smarter, stronger, and tougher than the rest. A boy's world is shaped by how his father responds to those around him. Fathers are the authorities. They set rules, because they know the rules.

Dads are also protectors. A father is a son's hope. The future will be better, safer, more fun, because dad can make bad things disappear. Monsters flee from beneath beds, harsh words from a soccer coach sting a lot less when dad can tell a son about his own days as a failed soccer player, and dad can tell him convincingly that girlfriends who cheated on him weren't right for him anyway.

In a much broader sense, a son watches his father and subconsciously kneads each of the qualities in his father into his own character. He does this so that he too will become a man. The dynamic is so powerful that it works negatively as well. Boys who see their fathers come home drunk every night have a higher chance of doing the same when they are grown, than boys whose fathers aren't. Masculinity begets masculinity, be it good or bad.

The highest compliment a father can be paid is having a son mimic his character and take it as his own. This is comparable to a father giving a son his name. In the act, the man lives on into the future. Part of him is present long after he is gone.

The beauty of the father-son relationship is that both parties unknowingly aspire to achieve the same goal. Fathers want the best of themselves integrated into another person so that they can become "eternal" and sons want their personalities to fuse with their fathers. Both of these desires stem from a healthy masculine pride inherent in every man.

What does every son need from a father? What can his father alone give him? He needs three things. First, a boy needs his father's blessing. Second, a son needs love from his father. And third, he needs his father to teach him self-control.

THE BLESSING

From the first years of his life as a little boy until the days before his death, every man is haunted by the question: *Am I good enough?*

The yearning is broad and persistent. He doesn't want to know if he is good enough at anything in particular—a sport, an art, or any utilitarian act. He doesn't even long to understand his capabilities. The question is far deeper.

The question for every boy is: am I good enough for my dad? A son's desire to "be good enough" in his dad's eyes is complex, because it has no simple end point. The question is not simply whether he is good enough for this dad to "like" him, or "love" him, or "approve" of him. It might include all these things, but it goes deeper, and boys themselves (and men too) cannot explain it. It certainly goes beyond a father's approval of some particular characteristic or behavior of his son. What is wanted is a fatherly affirmation of a boy in his entirety, as a whole person.

This fatherly blessing is mysterious and unquantifiable, but it is a rite of passage every boy desires. It is so personal that only a son will know when it occurs. It can come in an instant, with a father's smile or nod, or it can be full of ceremony. But when a boy receives his father's blessing, he has a sense of having been affirmed, and he feels he can live boldly.

In their book *The Blessing,* family counselors Dr. Gary Smalley and Dr. John Trent wrote about the importance of a father conferring his blessing on his son.[9] Looking at the tradition in orthodox Jewish homes where sons receive blessings bestowed upon them by their parents, the authors give readers insight into why this tradition is so important to children. Through their many years of counseling, they have come to the conclusion that boys who fail to receive such a blessing from their fathers often have greater difficulty establishing strong attachments to others, such as a spouse, in the future. Men, they explain, who never experience a deep sense of acceptance, validation, and love from their fathers feel incomplete, and their ability to become intimate with others suffers.

And the reverse is true as well. A man who feels that he has been affirmed in his personhood (who had his father's blessing), has confidence that can withstand the loss of a job or other difficult times. He can love his family and friends easily and with vigor. He can adapt to changes in his life with ease.

Boys who have felt their father's blessing know it; and boys who haven't feel the lack. This is how men who have their father's blessing describe it. They say that "I know that in my dad's eyes who I am is worth loving." Or others say, "In that one moment, I knew and I don't know how I knew, I just did." Or, "While my dad didn't approve of everything I was doing, he let me know he liked me for who I was and he had a special pride he extended just to me. The moment I realized it, I felt like I was flying."

So the natural question for a father is, how do you make sure that your son has your blessing?

A man who has a son must courageously search his real thoughts and feelings about his son. Is his son a disappointment to him? If so, why is he a disappointment? Does he feel only pride and affection? Is he angry with his son continuously?

This is one of the hardest exercises a father can undertake, but it is simultaneously one of the most freeing exercises of his life. Fathers must not be afraid to confront their real feelings about their sons. Why? Because while a father may not be able to articulate his deep feelings about his son, his son can.

Boys are so needy of knowing how their father feels about them that they read into their father's every behavior. They watch their father's moods, body language, and tone of voice. And every day, many times a day, they ask themselves: How does my dad feel about me? What does my dad think about me?

The great wonder of sons is that they can't be buffaloed. If a dad lies, a son knows it. So a father needs to honestly examine what he thinks about his son, and find a way to reconcile himself to giving his son a sincere blessing. This process can be hard or it can be easy, but it is necessary.

I will never forget a conversation I had with Ben when he was in eighth grade. His mother brought him in at the beginning of the school year for his annual physical. The moment I walked into the room I felt a tense silence. Neither mother nor son was reading a magazine nor talking. They sat side by side with their elbows tucked away from one another so as not to touch.

Ben's mother greeted me and said: "I'm not going to stay in the room long, you know. Ben is thirteen and all. I just wanted to ask you if you could talk some sense into him. He and I argue all the time. Since his brother left for college it's just the two of us and, well, it's not a whole lot of fun. He never wants to be home. He won't do his chores and whenever I try to ask him why, he either yells at me or goes to his room and slams the door. Honestly, we haven't had a normal conversation in months."

While she talked I regularly swept my eyes from her face to Ben's and then back again. She was teary and frightened. Ben never looked up at me or at her. He eyes focused on his shoes. I could sense that he too was sad and upset. I was glad to see his cheeks flush and his eyes well with tears. I knew that he wasn't hardened with anger. He wanted to change things at home too.

"Where's dad in all of this?"

"Well you know, Dr. Meeker, we got divorced last year. Ben's with me most of the time. His dad travels. But when he's home he wants Ben with him at his house. He lives just five miles from us. I don't think that's fair to Ben. Weekends away with his dad are enough. He needs a good night's sleep during the school week and his dad gets him all jazzed up."

When I had Ben alone, I asked him to tell me about his dad. He brightened up immediately.

"I really miss him, you know. Our house just feels awful without him there. Mom says he travels more but he doesn't. He has always done that. He has to; that's his work. I just want to be with him whenever he's home." Ben began to cry quietly.

"Tell me about a special time you had with your dad recently."

"We just have fun, I don't know. We do guy stuff, that's all."

"Do you and your dad go to football games or baseball games?"

"No."

"Did you take any trips this summer?"

"Yeah."

"Tell me about one."

"Well, me and my dad every summer we go camping together. We went to the Upper Peninsula and that was really fun."

I waited him out and he finally continued.

"Well, I guess our trip was kind of special. Dad let me be in charge of a lot and that was pretty cool."

"What kind of stuff?"

"See, every summer we camp and fish. We love to fish. Dad packs the tent and our gear and I pack the food. He does the cooking though."

"Anyway, when we got there he said that he wanted me to pitch the tent by myself while he went and got wood. I was kind of scared. I guess. But I did it. But not very well." His cheeks and nose began turning red and I could see tears coming.

"That sounds really fun."

"It was. The first night it rained really hard. The fly blew off our tent and rain started coming in on us. I ran outside and saw that I didn't pitch the tent right and that's why we were getting wet. I guess my dad should have been mad but he wasn't. The rain kept coming. All my dad said was to move to the back where it was dry. We went fishing the next day. We got some trout and he asked me if I wanted to cook them. I didn't know why he was asking me to do all this stuff. Maybe he was sick but I didn't think so. So I tried to cook them, but I wrecked them. They fell into the fire."

"Did your dad get mad?"

"No," he said, sobbing at the memory. "No, he just smiled at me real funny. He wasn't laughing. He was just really happy, I guess. He told me he wasn't in the mood for fish and we ate marshmallows and saltines for dinner. I kept making stupid mistakes the rest of the week. The tent almost blew away by the end of the trip."

Ben's body relaxed and his tears slowed.

"I just really miss my dad. He gets me. My mom just constantly tells me what to do and she drives me crazy. I just can't stand her sometimes. I want to be with my dad."

I had never met Ben's father, but after hearing about their trip that summer I respected him greatly. His son was thirteen, and Ben's father wanted Ben to know that he could do things; maybe not well, but he could learn. It was a way of telling Ben that he was growing up, and that his dad approved. He was giving Ben his blessing. Ben got it. It was obvious that the camping trip with his dad had made him good about himself. But it also made it terribly painful for Ben to be away from his dad.

I spoke to Ben's mother in private and told her Ben needed to spend more time with his dad. I reminded her of the importance of fathers to sons, and that she needed to put Ben's needs before her own.

About a year later I met Ben's father. He was small and painfully shy. I was surprised. I suppose that I expected him to have a greater presence. He was so big in Ben's eyes, and I had come to respect him. I told him that Ben had described their summer camping trip, and that I admired him for what he had given Ben that week. He smiled.

"I really love the boy, Dr. Meeker. He's my only son. My dad left my mom when I was eight. Ever since I felt like I was undone. Nothing was right. I spent years trying to get a better job or do something special that I guess I thought would make my dad proud. Just notice me. It darn near killed me trying to make the guy happy and the sad part is, it never worked. I didn't want my son to live with that. He's a good boy, Dr. Meeker, a real good boy. No matter what he does, I want him to know he's just fine by me."

The blessing takes on many shapes and can be given once or repeatedly. Some sons get it at ten, some at twenty-five. But it must come and it must come from a boy's father—from man to boy. A mother can't give a blessing in her son's eyes because she has to love him. But a father's respect has to be earned. I will state here that if a father is unavailable, a boy can draw close to a stepfather, uncle, or an adult male mentor. His father is ideal, but if circumstances make that impossible, any adult male can serve as a surrogate.

Dr. Smalley and Dr. Trent say that there are five elements of a healthy blessing. These are: meaningful touch, a spoken message, attaching "high value" to the one being blessed, picturing a special future for the one being blessed, and finally showing an active commitment to fulfill the blessing.[10]

Concerning the first element of touch, many fathers might balk at the idea of hugging their son (particularly if he is a teen). In fact, most other countries around the world touch more frequently than Americans do. Customs aside, I can say that people respond to touch, because it is an act of affirmation. Fathers should not be afraid to hug their sons, or if that is too much, at least to give them a manly pat them on the back. When it comes to a spoken blessing, ironic as it might sound, many fathers find it easier to talk to their daughters than to their sons, at least when it comes to talking about feelings. Perhaps this is because girls talk more frequently and because it doesn't seem embarrassing talking to a girl about emotions. But what is important is to understand is that boys need a father to make his blessing verbal. A father needs to tell a son how much he values him and approves him.

Fathers often assume their sons know they love them. Don't be so sure. A father might know in his heart that he cherishes his son, but children are egocentric. They need that affirmation made plain, and they are quick to blame themselves if they don't feel it. Many boys actually harbor strong feelings of contempt toward themselves, about their athletic, academic, or practical abilities, and many parents can't see this because boys don't verbalize their feelings freely. Moreover, many fathers try to 'toughen up" their sons, especially as they grow older, by using sarcasm, criticism, and mildly demeaning language. But while a father might think his comments are mild, he judges them as an adult, not as a child—much less as a son who wants to please his father. A father's words carry significantly more weight than the words of others. That's why it is so important for a father to tell his son how highly he values him.

Sons look to their fathers in order to find hope. Every boy wants to know that his life has meaning and purpose, that his future will bear witness to his meaning. A boy's father gives him a sense of what a successful future might be like, because he is the most meaningful adult in a boy's life. And a boy needs to know that his father thinks he too can have a successful future, that there's a reason for him to study hard for that scholarship, to apply for that internship, to take that part-time job that will teach him valuable business skills. A boy needs to know that as he works hard for that future, his dad is committed to helping him. A boy knows that if a father is willing to make that commitment, he must be worth it. He and his father have a connection to the future.

This is no insignificant life event for a man. If he never gets the blessing from his father, he'll have a gnawing ache, a sense of failure, a void where something positive should be for the rest of his life.

And that means tripping up the blessing is a problem too; it can become a painful experience for a boy when good intentions are executed poorly.

Several years ago, Timmy came in to see me for an office visit. He was sixteen, struggling in school, and his parents were concerned about his "bad attitude."

I had watched Timmy grow, so I knew his history. Timmy told me he no longer enjoyed doing anything. I asked him to think back to when he did love doing something. His eyes lit up.

"Easy," he said. "When I was a kid I used to play outside all the time. My dad and me had this game we played, whenever we were bored. If we were at my cousins' and everyone was talking or watching TV, my dad would look over at me. He'd give me this look 'let's get out of here.' It became kind of our secret. We'd go outside together into the front yard. We'd look for branches or a stick to hit stones with. Then we'd stand in the yard and hit stones into the street. We'd try to send them across the yard and try to hit the neighbor's mailbox or a tree in their yard."

Timmy suddenly became quiet.

"So," I asked, "Do you still play it?"

"No. After a few years, my dad told me that he wanted me to play Little League. He said it was because I was such a good hitter. I really didn't care if I did or I didn't. But when he signed me up he became my coach. He told me how to hold the bat so the ball would go farther. Pretty soon it wasn't fun anymore. I was kind of like a specimen and he didn't play with me anymore. He just told me how to do things better and critiqued me and the rest of the team."

"Do you still play baseball?"

"No. I stopped a couple of years ago. I know my dad was disappointed but I just didn't like it anymore."

Timmy's experience is a common one for boys, particularly as they mature into the teen years.

When his father played with him, they shared a special bond. They had a fun activity they enjoyed doing together. But when hitting stones turned into a more serious game, what once was a source of pleasure and closeness with his dad became an irritant. He became watched and critiqued. His father's intentions were excellent. He wanted to bolster his son's self-esteem by making him "better" at baseball. He thought that Timmy had potential as a ballplayer, and that if he could help develop that potential, Timmy would feel better about himself. But from Timmy's perspective, experiencing his father's pleasure in his company was the important thing. He loved that his father simply wanted to be with him. If Timmy and his dad had continued to slip away from others and pass the time swinging sticks, you can bet that at sixteen, Timmy would have felt his father's blessing. And the blessing would have communicated: I delight in your company, you are fully acceptable to me. The moment that dynamic shifted to Little League and coaching and critiquing, the fun went out of it for Timmy, and so did his sense of self-worth, his sense that his father approved of him just for himself.

Fathers must be very careful. The blessing can't come through coaching, criticism, or competition. It is much simpler and deeper. It comes only through the honest expression from a father to his son that he is pleasing just as he is.

LOVE FROM A FATHER

Father's aren't just authority figures who give their blessings, they need to be loving parents. We know from scores and scores of studies that a loving father is crucial to a child's happiness, well being, and success, and that children who lack a loving father are at a much greater risk for drug abuse, depression, and many other problems. Sons need fathers to express their love in three ways: by giving time, by showing affection, and by refusing to ever give up on a son.

TIME

The great news is that overall fathers are trying harder at loving their sons. Fathers, on average, spend about four hours a day with their children. That's more than an hour longer than fathers spent with their children forty years ago.[11]

Nothing boosts a boy's self-esteem more than his dad showing that he wants to be with him. Sons need to be reassured that they are valuable to their fathers and worthy of their attention. A boy who sees his father giving up time at work, time with his hobbies, or time with recreation in order to be with him, knows that he matters. When dads don't seem to value their sons, their sons don't feel that they can value themselves either.

In many respects, boys equate time spent with their fathers with love from their fathers, and that love brings boys all sorts of benefits. Boys whose fathers are more involved in their upbringing tend to be more empathetic. When dad shows empathy and love, so does his son. We know that when a father spends more time with his son, his grades go up. Boys with strong, loving, involved fathers are less likely to be bullied at school. And as boys grow older, those whose fathers remained highly involved had better self-esteem, obtained a higher level of education, and got better jobs later in life.

The National Fatherhood Initiative published an extensive review of literature researching the effects of fathers on their children in their book *Father Facts*. They found that boys with fathers who spend time engaging them: act out less, have lower levels of delinquency as they grow older, are psychologically healthier, and are at less risk for substance abuse and early sexual behavior.[12]

In short, the more time a father spends with a child (assuming the relationship is not abusive) the more a boy feels loved and the greater his chances for overall psychological, academic, and social success in life.

AFFECTION

Most fathers and sons are more comfortable with physical affection when a child is young but when a son grows into puberty and adolescence, fathers tend to show affection in other ways.

Mothers often want fathers to talk to sons, to find out what they think, what they want. Fathers, however, know that what really helps males to bond is doing things together—whether it's work, exercise, or hobbies. As a matter of fact, play can be a great source of nurturing and teaching by a father to his son. Dr. William Pollack writes in *Real Boys* that playing with a father helps a son develop important emotional mastery skills.[13] As they recreate, many emotions emerge: excitement, competition, anger, disappointment, happiness, and achievement. By playing with his father, a son learns how to handle these emotions.

Play also brings a son closer to his father. Physical play affords an opportunity for father and son to interact with one another in a physically affectionate way without feeling awkward. Wrestling is comfortable for them, because while it is competitive and athletic, when it's between a father and a son it is also an expression of affection.

LOVE: STICKING IT OUT

Parents often ask what the biggest mistakes are in raising sons. There is no question in my mind that the biggest and most damaging mistake a father can make is giving up on his children. By the time a boy turns fifteen or sixteen, most fathers have experienced a multitude of hardships that have worn them down: everything from marriage trouble, to work strains, to health issues. All of these drain energy from fathers. Many men just try to make it through the day, and then through the week. They don't feel they have the energy for much else. Too often they turn their sons over to electronic gadgets—and then both men lose. Time together requires more mental, physical, and emotional energy, but it also makes for a richer life for child and parent. It's worth the effort. Sons are always worth the effort, even when they hit the early teen years, and you're likely to be on the receiving end of grunted, one-word answers and facial expressions that communicate that you're an idiot. Boys have temper tantrums during the teen years and fathers take those tantrums far too personally. If the son and father have similar personalities, the tension between them can be strong as a boy matures. They can become competitive with one another and tempers can fly. And unfortunately, many fathers withdraw support and love from their son when tensions mount.

With the proliferation of books on parenting, marriage, and relationships that have inundated us over the last forty years, expectations for relationships have been raised to an unreasonably high level. Husbands want happiness in their marriages and look to wives to fulfill their needs. Women want compassionate husbands who work hard at their jobs but are also highly involved with their children. And fathers expect their relationships with their sons to be pleasant, deep, and unique from other father-son relationships.

While it's wonderful to have high aspirations, all healthy relationships need to be able to handle disappointments, because disappointments are inevitable, though that simple truth is often denied. We tell ourselves that with so much research, thought, and focus on human relationships, there must be solutions to every problem in a relationship. We believe that love should be magical and that it should work better and feel better. If it doesn't we seek to find the guilty party, and if we can't correct the mistake, we withdraw our own emotions and give up. But that's not the way real life works. Relationships require commitment and hard work. They require getting through the hard times. And with fathers and sons, they require dads to realize that their sons need dads who stick with them—even when the son pushes his dad away (which he might to do just to see if dad will push back).

The good news is that dads have the strength to tough it out during the painful times; they're big enough to set blame aside;

they can be stubborn enough to see things through; and they can be loyal enough to stick by their sons no matter what. Nothing launches a boy into manhood as powerfully as learning these lessons in character from his father.

SELF CONTROL

As a boy matures and feels his body strengthen and his energy and new emotions arise, he begins to have a newfound sense of power.

Again, play is a wonderful means with which a boy can confront his own power. When a boy plays with his father, he can feel free to push his physical strength to its limit because he knows that he can't hurt his father. William Pollack writes: "fathers provide a flexible surface for their sons to bounce off of. A play space with elastic but firm limits, a secure sense of love expressed not just in words but through actions."[14]

What is it about a father that supplies such a sense of security and protection to a son? It is his strength: sometimes his physical strength, sometimes his emotional strength.

As Shawn Johnston, forensic psychologist says, "The research is absolutely clear...the one human being most capable of curbing the anti-social aggression of a boy is his biological father."[15]

Jesse's father changed his life one afternoon. While he was arguing with his mother, seventeen-year-old Jesse became increasingly hostile. His mother demanded Jesse stop yelling. She could see that his anger was escalating out of control. His mother told me that Jesse always had a volatile temper, but it was worse now because he was tired from little sleep the night before and was stressed over a recent break-up with his girlfriend. Lynn, being a strong and assertive woman, calmly insisted that Jesse leave the room and that the two of them would finish the "conversation" when he was calmer. As she recounted the story to me several weeks later, she couldn't even remember what they were arguing about because the incident was so trivial. Nonetheless, when she told Jesse to clam down he lashed out at her. "You are a bitch!" he screamed to her face.

No sooner had the words escaped from his mouth than his father appeared. He flew off of the couch in the nearby living room and planted his face against his son. He was considerably shorter than Jesse. Stan grabbed the seventeen-year-old by his shoulders and pushed him hard, up against the refrigerator. "Don't you ever call my wife that name again!" he commanded.

Jesse fell silent. He was stunned. His yelling stopped and the moment his father released him, he scampered off to his bedroom like a puppy, a six-foot, three-inch puppy. Never again did Jesse even raise his voice to his mother.

A boy can learn self-control in a matter of moments from a man he respects and who exhibits self control. Jesse's dad didn't scream or hit. He didn't repeat himself, belabor his point, or lose control. He flexed his muscles and taught his son to gain control because Jesse couldn't do so on his own. Testosterone must bump up against testosterone in order for boys to learn how to gain control over themselves and their passions. Learning to master their emotions gives boys a sense of security—and dads are the ones best placed to teach them that. A boy watches his father to see what he does with his strength. He watches to see how his father controls his temper when he is angry, how he talks with people when he is irritated by them. He watches how his father spends his money and spends his time. He watches to see how committed he is toward his loved ones. Does he discipline himself to go to work when he is sick? Does he continue to be patient with the boy's mother when they're arguing? When a boy sees how self-control benefits his father, and everyone in the family, he learns an important lesson.

In my experience, boys who grow up without fathers are scared to death. They are afraid of themselves and their masculinity. The intensity of their feelings frightens them, and can drive them in unhealthy directions. They are afraid of feeling too much or feeling too little. They are frightened by their physical strength because they know it can get them into trouble. In short, they are frightened because they lack a father to channel their masculinity, to teach them proper limits, and to model for them self-control. When teenage boys feel afraid, when they lack a father to bump up against, they can unleash untold damage upon themselves and the people around them.

Fortunately, the reverse is also true. A son who grows up with a father learns not to fear himself. He learns to be grounded in his father's love. He is girded by his father's acceptance and approval. He has learned to be a leader because his father has led him. He has learned to become a provider because his dad has filled him up with the ingredients of good character. And he has learned to become a protector, because his father showed him how strength should be used and how self-control should be practiced. He has become a man, because he was raised by a man.

CHAPTER NINE

The Forgotten Step
from Boyhood to Manhood

HAVE YOU EVER MET A FIFTY-FIVE-YEAR-OLD man who forgot to grow up? Of course you have. We all have. He is the one who won't stop talking about his good old college days when he could drink the next guy under the table and stay standing. Or the neighbor who can't let go of his college sweetheart and constantly laments about his wife's shortcomings. He screams at his Pop Warner football team (the one your eleven-year-old son is on) like they are getting ready for the Super Bowl. Or he flirts with his nineteen-year-old daughter's friends.

You know him, because perhaps part of you feels like him. The truth is most boys aren't schooled well when it comes to growing up. Who taught you? And who will teach our boys?

Most men who reflect on their transition into manhood conjure an image of another man—their father, a teacher, a grandfather, or a coach—who shaped a picture of what manhood looked like. Some of these older men challenged them, pushed them, or simply walked in front of them and told them to listen up. But one thing is certain—boys who leave childhood must have pictures in their minds of what lies ahead, they must know that it is safe to leave boyhood, and they must have the confidence of knowing they have what it takes to mature into a man.

THE TRANSITION

Boys are impulsive. They become mad and they yell. When they are frightened they lash out and they run. When they are sad or their feelings are hurt, they run to a corner and sulk.

Grown men don't (or shouldn't) do these things. A man is fully mature when he is able to acknowledge a multitude of intense emotions and then make a deliberate decision about how to react to them (if he needs to react to them at all). Sometimes a man will desperately want to yell back, but he doesn't. He has learned self-control, to separate his feelings from his actions.

Boys don't learn this skill naturally, it has to be taught to them. It feels unnatural to him to refrain from arguing when he thinks he's right and someone else is wrong, or to refrain from pursuing a girlfriend he knows will be a bad influence. In the teen years, the hormonal and social changes a boy undergoes makes these separations of emotions and actions harder. This is precisely why every boy needs someone older who has successfully transitioned into adulthood to help him through.

Sadly, many boys never receive this training. They either lack exposure to mature parents or mentors, or they have misguided ones. Even intelligent, loving parents sometimes inadvertently fail to teach a boy how to separate his feelings from his behaviors. They do this by indulging their son and making pleasure his primary goal. But this effort to make their son happy only keeps him from maturing into a man.

This happens frequently during the teen years. We focus on a boy's wants: for a car, a new pair of skis, a spring break trip, a party with his friends, to quit school, or get a job. The list goes on and we indulge him with the belief that doing so will help him become happier. Intellectually we know better, but we do it anyway, and we shouldn't. I know I said this earlier, but I will say it again. When it comes to material things, boys don't need more, they need less. When it comes to indulging their desire for pleasure, they don't need more of that, they need less of it. What they need more of are parents willing to step up, spend time with them, and show them the virtues of maturity and self-control.

MOVING FROM YOU'RE RESPONSIBLE TO I'M RESPONSIBLE

The egocentrism of children cuts two ways. It is what makes boys blame themselves when parents divorce, but it is also what makes them blame others when things go wrong. How many of us have heard the refrain "It's all your fault!" or a fourth grader blame his teacher for causing his "D" because she made the test too hard, or a young soccer player complain that the refs don't know what they're doing when they continually give him a yellow card.

The hallmark of immaturity in a boy is his inability to blame himself when he is truly to blame. Don't be discouraged if your son does this. It isn't necessarily a character flaw. It is more likely a developmental issue, albeit one he needs to grow beyond. He is self-absorbed during his pre-pubertal and pubertal years because that is the way he is wired to be. It's normal for a boy or a teenager, but it is not appropriate for a man—and your son should be growing into a man.

Many parents fall into a trap with boys. We believe them. If only he had a different coach, then he could spend more time on the field. If only his teachers knew what they were doing, his grades would reflect his true talents. We buy into our son's vision that others are to blame for his miseries, his mistakes, and his hurt feelings. We feel a duty to fix these problems so that we can free our sons to excel.

So we fire coaches. We enroll our boys in different schools. And when they really mess up, we even blame the principles or the other authority figures who act as disciplinarians. Defending bad boyhood behavior has become typical of post-modern parents. But it is a terrible trap that keeps boys from maturing into good men.

I was once contacted by a high school wrestling coach in order to help settle a dispute. Apparently seven senior boys on a wrestling team went out and got drunk one night. Another student who wasn't on the team alerted the principal who told the coach. Quite appropriately the wrestling coach benched the boys for a month because they violated the team's verbal contract, which was that no team member was to smoke or drink during the season. If they did so, they would be removed from the team.

The high school was small and the boys stood as an example to the younger students. But the distraught coach was going easy on the boys, only benching them for a month rather than kicking them off the team, because, he said, they had a shot at going to state finals. Besides, he said, in general they were pretty good kids. He liked them.

The disciplined boys went home and told their parents what happened. They were irate at the coach. He was hurting their careers, depriving them of pursuing a once in a lifetime (albeit high school lifetime) opportunity of competing at a state level. Several parents went to the high school principal and not only demanded that the students be allowed to wrestle, they demanded that the coach be fired. What did the boys have to say about it? Until their parents got involved, they had acknowledged that their punishment was reasonable. After their parents erupted, they rallied behind them. It was a case of parents making their sons' behavior *worse*.

This scenario is a fairly common one across our country, and it severely blunts the emotional development of boys. Adolescent boys instinctively blame others for their bad behaviors because they lack cognitive and emotional maturity. They naturally resist owning responsibility because many lack the capacity (or fear that they lack the capacity) to correct a bad mistake. Additionally, because they lack full brain maturity, making the leap from "you are responsible" to "I am responsible" sometimes requires cognitive skills that they don't have. Many boys, however, do have them. They simply don't want to utilize them.

The male brain undergoes tremendous growth during the teen years, and responds very well to training—the training that parents should provide. To speak in metaphorical terms, parents have the ability, or the responsibility, to help a teen hard-wire his brain for maturity. If a teen is not challenged to do so, his brain might never be adequately rewired into that of a functioning adult, and immature patterns of thought can stay in place. This is why parents who rush to defend a boy's bad behavior harm him so much. They not only send the message that his desires trump the rules, they tell him that he doesn't need to take responsibility for his behavior. These are boys who, emotionally and psychologically, are in danger of never leaving adolescence. If they don't, they will lead lives of constant frustration and discontent, always blaming others, and never realizing the control they genuinely have over their own lives.

Let your son understand that taking responsibility for his bad behavior works better for him than pointing the finger at others. Life is happier when he is in charge—of what he does wrong and of what he does well. Not only will his brain learn to think differently, he will live with immensely greater freedom. How cruel to commit a boy to a life where he believes that if only others would act better on his behalf, then he could be happy or successful. Unless he is prodded and pressured out of this boyish thinking, he will never enjoy life with the mind of a real man.

Men take responsibility for their own happiness. They realize their own limitations as well as the limits of others. By owning their choices, they become less dependent on their spouses, children, co-workers, or bosses. They have a keen sense of responsibility for their own happiness. They learn to reverse boyhood questions. They don't ask how *others* can make life better for them; they ask how *they* can make life better for themselves and those around them.

Every boy deserves the freedom to enjoy manhood. He needs your help in getting there. During his teen years, help him ask questions of himself rather than of others. Don't perpetuate his propensity towards self-absorption and irresponsibility by twisting the predicaments he creates. When you do this, you sentence him to a life of adolescent thinking.

DOING WHAT'S RIGHT

Men live with an ordered set of principles. One man's principles may differ from another's but as a man leaves adolescence, his belief system begins to crystallize. Vagueness evaporates during his early adult years and he finds that he is pressed to make decisions about his present and future life according to something other than what he simply wants. Or, he chooses to decide to live according to his wants over his beliefs. The point is, internally he begins to consciously choose a pattern of life and a formula for living.

Boys can't do this quite as readily. Their belief systems and their moral reasoning are tentative, fluctuating, and still quite easily influenced. Boys absorb influences from parents, teachers, and coaches, in everything from mannerisms to political beliefs.

Parents help them filter differing influences, but all parents brace themselves for a period of adolescent rebellion.

Many teen boys who grow up in a home where they were required to go to church or synagogue suddenly announce that they will no longer go, because they want to make their own decisions about what to believe. They will solemnly declare that they no longer need spiritual guidance from a priest, a rabbi, a pastor, or even parents. A boy will declare that his mind is his own.

The irony (though he doesn't realize it) is that there is perhaps no more prominent time in his life when his mind is less his own than during the teen years. Decisions were easy when he was eight. At seventeen he doesn't know what to think anymore. He doesn't know who is right or who is wrong, what to believe and what not to believe.

Outwardly a teen boy will act confident and assured. Inwardly he might be a wreck. He might feel insecure, confused, and angry with himself because he can't figure out what he wants to believe. He will convincingly assure you and his peers otherwise.

Enormous decisions are up for grabs in his adolescent mind. They are no longer trivial to him. What kind of a person does he want to be? Can he resemble his father or will that make him look like he can't be his own person? He is afraid of being too much like his father and too little like him.

He is no longer content to hear about the importance of being honest. He wants to see if it really works. He knows that some believe God exists and others think believers are fools. He wants to find out for himself if God is real. Does it serve him well to act differently than his friends? What does he think about alcohol, drugs, sex? His parents say no, but some of his friends are doing it.

Adolescent boys wrestle to establish a belief system specifically because everything in life intensifies. His feelings grow stronger and they conflict with what he wants to do. But now, in the conflict, he realizes that he needs to decide what to do—and others shouldn't do it for him. Men want to lead, and as a teenager, a boy is trying to figure out where to lead himself.

As a boy, his moral reasoning is black and white, and at that point, parental authority poses no threat to his identity. But as a teen, he thinks his masculinity is in question if his morals and beliefs are not his own.

The best aid any parent can give a boy is to capitalize on his receptivity when he is a child. Teach him your beliefs and tell him why you believe what you do. Give him a solid moral foundation and then help him practice it. This way, when he is an adolescent he will have a clear structure with which to work. He needs something to work with and if he has nothing when he enters adolescence, he will find something. And that won't necessarily be a pretty picture.

When he is a teen, don't be threatened by his questions. They aren't about you, they are about him. He is figuring things out. He is reordering his moral framework and testing his (or your) belief system. Let him. If what you taught him is true and good, it will withstand his testing.

Be a sounding board. Ask him questions about what he thinks, likes, or wants. Then let him talk. Ask what he thinks about a political candidate or the guilty plea of a baseball player sentenced to jail for drug use. Ask him questions that require moral thought. He might feel a need to come up with answers different from yours. Sometimes he will intentionally try to irritate you with his answers. You'll teach him a better lesson by biting your tongue than by responding to his provocation, because what he really wants to know is whether you respect him and think his opinions are worth considering. Once he realizes you do, his beliefs will likely eventually, if not immediately, closely reflect yours.

It can be gratifying if his beliefs represent yours, but more important is that he has a belief system to help him clarify his sense of morality. Boys, teens, and men need a moral framework in which to operate, one that allows them to move from putting their own interests first (as children do) to putting the interests of others first (as mature adults do). In other words, in his teen years—when parents worry so much about kids getting into trouble—he needs to know how to do what's right, how to find out that virtue is its own reward. When he makes that leap, it can be intensely satisfying, and that transition is one of the most crucial to a boy's ultimate happiness.

The most important decision a man makes in his life (aside from ultimate questions about God) isn't choosing his college, his career, or what city he's going to live in. It's choosing his mate. If a man's marriage is good, life is good. He can lose his job, a child, a home, but if he has a solid relationship with a spouse, he draws strength from it to endure the hardships. If, on the other hand, the relationship is tumultuous and painful, life feels bad. His job leaves him feeling less satisfied, his interests in hobbies wane, and he is more likely to give up hope in all other areas of his life.

One of the greatest gifts we can give our boys is preparation for marriage, if marriage is going to be part of their lives. Even if a man chooses not to marry he still benefits tremendously from the training in healthy adult relationships.

All boys, including teen boys, look for role models. And what do they see? Boys are just as influenced by celebrity lifestyles as girls are, they just choose different celebrities. But the influence is still the same. What pop culture teaches kids is that relationships are intense and transient. That's not a good prescription for a healthy life. But this is what millions of our young men have come to expect as the norm. Tom Cruise leaves Nicole Kidman and their children in a wake of tears in order to move onto, and be celebrated for finding, a new hot babe. Wives, not to mention children, are disposable to the Hollywood elite and boys take it all in. They've been taking it in from Hollywood and other cultural sources for forty years. You yourself might be a victim of a father or a husband who bought into the Hollywood ideal, or who had his so-called "mid-life crisis" (of recurrent adolescence).

Boys act on their feelings, but real men don't. Hollywood elite are not the "men" most of us want our sons to aspire to be. They behave like boys who never grew up. They were never schooled in growing up. Their passions and desires, no matter how transient, run their lives. The tragedy is that any man who lives life like this never wins. He never finds peace or joy, and he takes many in his life down along with him.

Our sons see the norm of relationships redefined and we must correct this. Otherwise they will fail to grow up, their behavior will take their life into a downward spiral, and they will find themselves alone and miserable. And the best way to teach a boy the right way to live is to give him an opportunity to watch a good man at work.

When Henry was ten, his grandfather was placed in a nursing home. He hated going to visit him, he said, because it made him sad and the stale smells of an old folks home gave him a headache.

Henry was an only child from a broken home, and as a result he had grown especially close to his grandfather. He wasn't ready to stop seeing him altogether. Sometimes he went, because he thought that maybe one day his grandfather would get better—just for a little while. Maybe they could play poker again the way they used to. That hope made it worth enduring the smells.

On one of Henry's visits, he met another old man named Bill whose wife was in the nursing home. She looked like she was 112, and Bill looked like he was seventy. Henry and Bill liked one another immediately. Bill was like his grandfather used to be: a kind, quiet man who liked to tell jokes.

Henry's mother said that after he befriended Bill, he hesitated less about going to the nursing home for their weekly visits. Bill didn't live there but Henry knew that whenever he visited, Bill would be walking the halls with his wife, feeding her dinner, or reading to her in her room.

Henry was fascinated with Bill. He didn't have a life, Henry remarked to his mother. All he ever did was take care of his wife. Sometimes Henry became visibly upset because Bill's wife would yell at Bill or even hit him. Then she would just cry and cry.

Her behavior upset Henry. He became protective of Bill and decided that he would help him. He asked his mother if they could invite Bill over for dinner. He felt sorry for the man.

One day, Henry's mother overheard him talking with Bill. She was sitting next to her own father, helping him eat lunch, and Henry sat with Bill as he fed his wife. She had a bib on. She was sad that day. She didn't want to eat. Bill coaxed and pleaded with her. Henry became upset.

"Bill," he said. "How can you keep doing this? I mean, you're not even really helping her." Henry paused, realizing that he had overstepped his bounds. But he was upset, and he hated to see Bill waste his time.

Bill looked at him, then turned back toward his wife. He seemed to smile.

"Sorry, Bill. I'm sorry. It's just that week after week this is all you do. It's so boring. How can you stand it?"

"Listen to me, son. Listen to me. Bev and I have been together fifty-eight years. That's more time than you can ever begin to imagine. This is a tough time for sure, but there have been others. But in between—for years here and there—the good broke through. Real good broke through." He turned back to his wife and wiped egg salad from her cheek.

"Don't you ever forget something, young Henry: staying together—that's when the good stuff comes. Right now, this is love, boy; this is love."

Henry never forgot Bill. Most important, he left the nursing home that day a changed boy. His mother said that he was never the same. He laughed a little more and fought a little less with her. He had hope. Hope that his life could be different than his father's and mine, she said. Bill gave Henry a picture of life filled with frustrations, grief, and love—something deeply admirable. And he saw a man make tough choices, to do what was right in spite of his interests. And Henry saw that when a man did that, everyone involved won.

MEN KEEP MOVING FORWARD

Perhaps the greatest hallmark of the successful transition from boyhood to manhood is perseverance. Boys lose steam and want to quit. Men lose steam, pause to find it again, and then continue on.

One of the greatest masculine character qualities is tenacity: the setting of the will in a direction that a man knows is the necessary one. Boys can't do this for many reasons.

First, they lack the mental and emotional resources to stay focused on a goal over an extended period of time. Boys get bored, they change their minds, they're too busy discovering the world to focus on one goal.

Second, a boy has no grasp of delayed gratification. He can't really envision that saving $10 a week in his savings account will earn him more than $5,000 in a period of ten years. His inability to recognize future consequences prevents him from having any incentive to persevere. In a thirteen-year-old boy's mind, today, and perhaps tomorrow, is all that matters. He doesn't try to think this way; it is simply how his brain functions (which is why parents need to make sure he makes that $10 contribution every week).

Living with tenacity requires motivation. Boys have motivation only if they can see immediate benefits and if those benefits are directed towards them. Building a bent toward perseverance requires that a parent make fairly immediate benefits when their sons behave well. The immediacy of the benefits can be stretched out as the boy matures. A ten-year-old can save money for one month to buy a baseball bat and stay motivated throughout the month. A sixteen-year-old can save money for three or four months and stay motivated to buy the skies he'd been eyeing.

Tenacity also requires deep conviction. Boys like certain things and believe certain things, but they are easily influenced and their beliefs and likes are malleable.

Another hallmark of a mature man is that he knows what he believes and why. Thus he can act on his beliefs even when others disagree. He remains steadfast in carrying them out because they are unshakeable.

Rudyard Kipling summarizes this in his brilliant poem entitled *If*:

> If you can keep your head when all about you
> Are losing theirs and blaming it on you,
> If you can trust yourself when all men doubt you
> But make allowance for their doubting too.
> If you can wait and not be tired by waiting,
> Or being lied about, don't deal in lies,
> Or being hated, don't give way to hating....[1]

Then, says Kipling, a boy will be a man.

A boy's peers can't teach him tenacity because they are in the same boat he is. But you can. Whether you are a man or a woman, teach him to find what is right, to follow what is right, and then to hold onto it. Give him small tasks to follow through on. If he starts six weeks of tuba lessons and hates the tuba after the second week, make him finish. If he asks a girl to a prom, then changes his mind—tough, he must take her anyway. If he commits to a job fifteen hours a week after school and gets mad at his boss, you can make sure he keeps going back to work.

Conscientious, enthusiastic parents too often rob their sons of moving into manhood by letting them quit their commitments. If your son starts something and impulsively decides he hates it, make him wait at least two to four weeks before he decides to quit. And then, the process should be a sobering one. Quitting something should never be done lightly or finished too easily.

> ...If you can force your heart and nerve and show
> To serve your turn long after they are gone,
> And so hold on when there is nothing in you
> Accept the Will which says to them: Hold On![2]

Matthew Benton learned to hold on long before any of his friends did. When he was nine, his father died after a long battle with a rare form of lung disease. His mother was devastated. She had adored her husband. After he died, she never talked about it, because, Matthew said, she didn't want to believe it had actually happened.

One morning, before his father died, Matthew got himself ready to go to school and ate breakfast. He peered into his parents' bedroom to say goodbye to his dad. His father was getting dressed for yet another test at the hospital.

"See you, pal," he said to Matthew. "Same place, same time."

Matthew loved hearing the familiar banter. He and his father had several inside phrases they exchanged. They used "same place, same time" in anticipation of the next time they did something special together. When his father used phrases such as these, the whole world went away. For just a moment, Matthew and his father lived in a private space where only they belonged.

On that particular morning, Matthew ran out of the house and boarded the school bus. He never saw his father again. Matthew was in the third grade. When he came home from school his father's clothes hung in the closet and his half-eaten bowl of cereal was in the sink. His shoes were in the mud room and his jacket smelled of fire wood but he was nowhere to be found.

For several months after his father's death, Matthew's mother barely spoke. She slept a lot and began smoking cigarettes. She never cooked a meal. Matthew made himself a lot of peanut butter and jelly sandwiches.

His grandmother came over and he overheard her yelling at his mother one evening. Suddenly he began to cry and he felt that he cried for one solid year.

Almost eighteen months later, Matthew's mother married a man whom she barely knew. The man had a daughter three years older than Matthew. Matthew wanted the man and his daughter gone. This was *his* house.

Every time he walked past his parents' bedroom, he refused to look in. After that horrible day he never went in his parents' room again. His dad told him a lie from that room. He didn't return to the same place at any time.

Matthew coped over the next few years by closing out the world he saw and he inwardly created a new one. He listened to music, watched a lot of television alone in his room, and rarely went outside to play with his friends.

His stepfather occasionally asked him to go to a football game or a movie. Usually Matthew refused. When he did, his stepfather accused him of being spoiled and rude. Matthew didn't care.

During his eighth grade year, Matthew joined a Little League team. He loved being away from the house. And he loved everything about baseball—the uniform, the smell of his leather glove, even the way his hands stung when he whacked the ball hard. Mostly, he said, he liked Little League because Brian was there.

Brian was a twenty-five-year-old trainer fresh from a farm league who came to practice to help Matthew's coach. Matthew thought he sounded like his dad. When Brian showed up, Matthew said everything seemed okay for a while. He couldn't explain why.

Brian learned quickly that Matthew enjoyed the attention he showed him. So he gave him more. He picked him up at his house and drove him to some indoor batting cages where they could practice hitting. Almost every week they did something together, usually involving sports.

When Matthew was seventeen, he drove to baseball practice. Brian was there. The moment he saw Matthew, Brian knew that something was wrong with him. He went over to him and smelled something peculiar emanating from his sweater. It was dope. He looked at Matthew's eyes. They were hazy, and Matthew was laughing in a sort of stupid way.

Brian didn't say a word until practice was over. Then he brought Matthew to his car and they sat inside for what seemed to be hours. Brian lost his temper: What was Matthew doing? What was he thinking? Why was he running around with such jerks? Why was he throwing his life away?

Matthew began to sob. As he recalled the hours in Brian's car that day, he realized that he had disappointed Brian—and that hurt. But he needed to hurt. Over the years Brian had filled an enormous emotional void for Matthew, had helped him in innumerable ways, and now Matthew realized he had betrayed him.

Something happened to Matthew in the car that day. He grew up. For years he had hated his mother, his stepfather, and even his house. He blamed them for stealing his dad from him, and he wanted nothing to do with them. Brian hadn't taken away Matthew's dad. But he had stepped into his shoes and been a second dad to him. He deserved better from Matthew, and Matthew knew it. Matthew needed to take responsibility for his actions; he needed to take control of himself and his life.

"I realized that day in the car that I had a choice. I could blame everyone or I could take charge," he said. "Brian made me realize that I could take charge. It was okay."

Brian gave Matthew the freedom of manhood. This is what a male mentor can bring to a boy. Every boy who doesn't have access to a father, needs a man—a coach, a teacher, a stepfather, an uncle—to be with him as he leaps the chasm from boyhood to manhood. It requires energy, fortitude, and sometimes a big push. And a boy takes that push much better from a man than he does from a woman. He trusts a man more, because a man has done what he has to do.

The biggest mistake we make with adolescent boys is forgetting that they all need help moving *out* of adolescence. Millions of boys grow older, but few become men. No boy really wants to stay in the banal world of perpetual adolescence, but he needs someone to lead him out. His deepest longings pressure him toward manhood and he needs to respond. He wants to respond but he simply doesn't know how. So help him. Be there to challenge him. Make him a little uncomfortable by stretching his intellect and demanding maturity. As in any other growth process, it will be painful for you both, but his life depends upon it.

If you are a coach, help a player or two. If you are an uncle, reenter your nephew's life. If you are a single dad, engage your son.

Every boy in America needs a man in order to become one.

CHAPTER TEN

The God Factor

BOYS NEED GOD. ALL BOYS. Whether they are three or twenty-three, the single greatest deficit operating in a boy's life isn't education, lack of opportunity, or even lack of stable parenting. It is the faith in a God who cares.

And boys, particularly young ones, know this. Little boys are open to the idea of an invisible, powerful God much more so than older siblings or parents. I have found this to be true in my young male patients and my experience is echoed by the great psychiatrist Robert Coles. He witnessed time and again his young patients describing to him (without his prompting) the character of God. As a trained psychoanalyst, Pulitzer Prize-winning author and professor at Harvard Medical School, Coles recounts with great tenderness hundreds of conversations he has had with children about God. He illustrates these in his book, *The Spiritual Life of Children.*[1] He doesn't write with any hint of a proselytizing agenda. In fact, he doesn't betray his own religious beliefs, focusing solely on what children say to him. I know that his words are dead on, because I have heard the same words, the same naturally exuberant faith, from my own boy patients halfway across the country.

Boys who talk to me about God do an interesting thing: they describe His moods. "I think that when I'm nicer to my mom, I make God happy." Or "I know that God feels really disappointed when I lie." And when boys describe what God looks like, they discuss His face, never His body. He has a large face—wrinkly, bearded, kind, yet somewhat stern. His face, they say, is what's most important about Him because He really isn't a person, He is a spirit, but they need to know what His face looks like so that they can figure out how He feels about them. These comments have surfaced in my discussions with boys over the decades I have treated them.

I find the focus on His face fascinating and encouraging. Young boys want to know what God is like and they seem to understand His character better by imagining how he smiles or frowns, how he expresses approval or disapproval. Boys are naturally straightforward and a bit utilitarian. If God is real, then they want to know what He is like. If He is a reasonable fellow, then they will move a bit closer. If He is mean, then they will shy away. Most important, boys want to know if God is going to help them in any way. Will He listen? Does He really see what they're doing at school, in their bedrooms, on their phone conversations? When they are having a problem, will He fix it? Does He carry a wand? No, of course not, remarked Matt to me one day, only fairies carry wands. But, Matt assured me, God can zap things better—and very, very fast.

God makes sense to boys. Boys find it easy to imagine that God exists in an invisible state without definitive form, that he possesses both male and female qualities (God is as authoritative as a father and as loving as a mother), and that he can see everything in the universe all at once.

One reason young boys find this so easy is that they connect their inner world of thoughts and feelings to the exterior world. In other words, their external behaviors mirror their inner feelings. Boys feel less inhibited and less socially guarded, and are uninhibited about sharing their natural belief in God. It is not until they reach the later elementary school years when they begin to force their inner selves to go "underground." When classmates become cruel, parents divorce, or failing grades come their way, boys learn to push their interior world to a private place.

This is why as boys grow older, their imaginations are less openly expressed. For example, six-year-old Johnny liked spending hours upon hours playing with an elaborate train set alone in his basement. One day, while he played, his sister overheard him talking to someone. When she asked whom he was playing with in the basement, his face flushed beet red. No one, he said. But his sister knew that he was talking to someone—his imaginary friend.

She chided him mercilessly and low and behold his friend simply went away, or at least he kept their conversations within the silent confines of his brain. Johnny's external behavior separated from his internal world.

When boys mature and hear adults ridicule their faith or those representing a faith, they become more uncomfortable with their own beliefs about God. One of the greatest offenses an adult can commit against a boy is to crush his childlike, honest, and very real belief about God. Many adults squelch a child's faith often under the guise of wanting him to "decide for himself." Ironically, that takes the very decision away from the boy.

WHAT BOYS BELIEVE

Many young boys have told me about their experiences with God. I believe them, because many of these experiences share common themes. They are always positive and uplifting, never frightening or discouraging. None of the boys (to my knowledge) shared their experiences with my other patients, so their experiences are unlikely to have come from one boy planting ideas into the mind of another.

When Georgie was ten, he had a very unusual brain tumor. It wasn't malignant, but its location made it inoperable. As you can imagine, his parents felt devastated. He underwent chemotherapy and radiation treatments. He lost his hair and a lot of weight, but remarkably, I never saw his spirits plunge. After about eighteen months of treatment, the oncologist informed Georgie's family that he didn't believe Georgie was going to be able to pull through. The tumor was continuing to grow small tentacles that were pushing their way into Georgie's surrounding brain tissue. Within the next few months, the oncologist said, Georgie would most likely slip into a coma.

Georgie's mother became withdrawn, and cried continually. Georgie's father did the best he could, going to work so that their medical insurance wouldn't lapse. Georgie spent a lot of time alone during those last months because of his father's work and his mother's grief. I will never forget, however, an experience he described to his friends and his family. One afternoon, he was sitting alone in the living room and his mother was napping. The house was quiet and he was working on a puzzle. Suddenly, he said, he felt God speak to him. He didn't see anyone, he didn't hear an audible voice, but, he said, there was no doubt that he heard something inside of him. He knew that it was either God or an angel. Georgie said that God told him not to worry. He wasn't to worry about dying, his parents, or heaven. That was the message, nothing else.

But the message was enough. From that afternoon on, Georgie wasn't the same person. He was happy, calm, and he slept well at night. And he persisted in reassuring his parents, every day, that he and they were going to be all right. Never before, his parents said, had they ever seen anyone so sure about something in their lives.

Georgie died several years ago and his parents continue to
hold onto his experience. Truth persists and I believe that the
reality of his experience is evidenced by its persistence. If he had
had a dream, an idle thought, or simply boyhood belief, it would
not have changed lives the way his remarkable conviction did. I
believe Georgie's experience was real, not only because of its
power and sincerity, but because many patients have described
similar encounters to me: God spoke and He gave them hope and
profound reassurance. Perhaps He speaks more often to kids
because they have open ears.

Take a look at what medical studies reveal about the current
state of faith amongst the boys in our country. (Bear in mind that
this information is from *The Journal of Adolescent Health*, and
the mean age of kids studied was sixteen.)

- 89 percent reported a belief in God
- 77 percent stated that religion was important in their lives
- 80 percent report that God loves and cares for them
- 63 percent feel they have a personally meaningful relationship with Him

So while faith might decline in some teenagers, compared to
their early elementary school years, a belief in God is still overwhelmingly a truth for adolescent boys.[2]

GOD IS GOOD FOR BOYS

Reviewing the medical studies regarding the effects of a boy's faith
on his feelings, thoughts, and behaviors is an extraordinary experience. The findings are remarkably consistent and the impact of
a boy's faith in God on his complete well-being is dramatic.

Many parents read books, seek professional advice, and add
controls to electronic media in their home in order to keep their

boys on the right track. Parents earnestly want to do whatever they can to keep their sons away from drugs, drinking, and pornography. They want to keep depression from being a part of their son's life. They want their sons to be academically, or artistically, or athletically successful. Ultimately, parents want their sons to be happy.

Medical studies show that the best way to accomplish this is to give your child a belief in God.

Let's flesh out the specific ways that God helps boys.

First, religious fathers have better relationships with their sons, which makes for healthier, happier sons. In *The Journal of Marriage and Family*, Valerie King states that religiously active fathers tend not only to invest more in their relationships with their children, but to have greater expectations for healthy relationships with their children in the future.[3]

Research also shows that mothers with a solid faith have healthier relationships with their sons. Moreover, when a son and his mother regularly attend religious services together, mothers report significantly better relationships with their sons.[4]

Boys who are religious are less likely to be sexually active too soon and less likely to become promiscuous during their teen years and later on in life. Boys who have a religious faith are significantly less likely to smoke, drink alcohol, become truant, use marijuana, and experience depression; and they are more likely to have higher self-esteem as well. Boys are less likely to be involved in criminal activity if their parents are religious. And religion helps children from poorer backgrounds overcome the physical, psychological, and behavioral disadvantages often associated with childhood poverty.[5]

Researchers from Princeton University and the University of Pennsylvania reviewed the best literature available on the impact of religion in children's lives. They also completed their own research and found that the evidence regarding the positive physical and emotional health benefits of religion on children's lives was so great that "based upon these findings it is appropriate to suggest that prevention programs which collaborate with, are anchored in, or are offered by local religious congregations should be given attention and support by the wider community when it comes to supporting healthy youth development."[6]

Many of us keep our religion separate from our professional work. The problem is, as parents, but also as doctors, teachers, and coaches, when it comes to nurturing boys into mentally, physically, and psychologically strong men, we cannot ignore the faith factor. We simply can't. The scientific data says so. Regardless of our personal philosophies or faith, the bottom line is that God is so good for boys that we cannot ignore this reality.

BOYS AND FAITH—WHAT DOES IT MEAN?

Most studies describe faith in God as religiosity. But what is religiosity? We know, through *The Journal of Adolescence*, that 89 percent of teens say they pray weekly, and more than half attend church weekly.[7] Thirty-two percent of teens, according to the Barna Research Group, attend church youth group meetings outside of normal Sunday worship.[8]

While this gives a fairly traditional picture of the religious life of American boys, it is also true that that spiritual life has changed dramatically over the last forty years.

Today, many religious believers—particularly teens—no longer think of religion primarily as a means of knowing and worshipping a deity, but use it as a means of self-discovery. This is a generalization, of course, and many young and mature boys in America lead traditional religious lives. They memorize prayers, study sacred scriptures, attend religious services, and seek to understand a God who created them for a deeper purpose.

But the social changes that have affected everything else in the lives of boys over the last forty years have affected their religious lives too. Many baby boomer parents are less traditionally religious than their own parents were; and some religious institutions have reflected this change. Some of this we've discussed in previous chapters in a different way, when we saw how social changes of the last forty years—the jump in divorce rates, the steep rise in single parent households, the dramatic surge in premarital sexual activity (and the explosion of sexually transmitted diseases)—that have had a negative impact on boys. Many of these behaviors or actions were things that traditional religion opposed, but does so less effectively today.

For boys this has been doubly damaging. The fallout from such social changes—fatherless homes, rampant sexually transmitted diseases in ever younger patients, and so on—is bad enough. But the declining number of boys who experience traditional religion leaves them with a spiritual vagueness that is inconclusive, impotent, and frustrating to boys who need spiritual depth. Traditional religion is not only more challenging and rigorous, it is more comforting because it is more certain; and it is certain because it spends more time on definitions, rules, and theology (or trying to understand the truth about God) than on self-exploration.

I say this not as a theologian myself, but as pediatrician, and base it on what I have seen in my clinical practice. Boys who adhere to a traditional religious practice are far more likely to be able to withstand the pressures of life, to have a sense of wholeness and purpose about themselves, than boys who have either been raised with no faith or with a formless self-directed faith. Structure is important for boys—and for many people. Traditional religion provides structure. It provides rules. And it provides authorities—pastors, priests, and rabbis—that a boy can turn to when he has questions.

Seventy-five percent of teens thirteen to seventeen years old in the United States identify themselves as either Protestant or

Catholic. One and a half percent identify themselves as Jewish.[9] They do so because most teens want to identify themselves with very specific religious practices. They are in this sense "religious" rather than, in today's amorphous use of the word, "spiritual." When we look at church attendance, the evidence for a desire for religious specificity becomes even more pronounced.

In the book *Soul Searching: The Religious and Spiritual Lives of American Teenagers* (Oxford University Press), by Dr. Christian Smith and Ph.D. candidate Melinda Lundquist-Denton, 52 percent of thirteen- to seventeen-year-old teens reported that they attend religious services at least twice a month. When asked how often they would *choose* to attend church or synagogue, 60 percent stated that they would attend *at least* twice a month.[10] Could it be that parents across America are in fact discouraging their sons from attending organized religious services? I believe so. Too many parents would rather strike church or synagogue off their to-do list, either because they're tired, or because they would rather spend that time doing something else, or because they are religiously disengaged or tepid themselves.

The result of this is religious ignorance among too many boys. They would like answers to life's biggest questions, but parents feel uncomfortable providing them. And many of those parents refuse to take their sons to the church or synagogue where they might find them. Again, I say this not as a proponent of one faith over another—though of course I have my own beliefs—but because as a doctor my own clinical experience confirms what all the research tells us: that religion is good for boys. And I think too many parents have been mislead about what their responsibilities are in this regard. We baby boomers who have read reams of child care books and psychology books replete with tips on how not to stifle our child's self-esteem and unique personality have faded quietly into the background of our kids' spiritual lives. We so eagerly don't want our children to be pushed by us in any direction educationally, psychologically, and spiritually that we hold back when we should lead. Many parents tell me that they want their kids to grow up to make their own decisions about God. They want their boys to make their own choices about which, if any, religion they want to believe. This is, in a way, noble. Our job as parents should be to educate and stimulate our boys to read and think on their own.

But the fatal flaw is that boys can't choose from an empty menu. Asking a child to choose his own faith is like flying him to Prague, taking him to the center of the city, and asking him to pick out where to stay and what to do. He doesn't have a clue because he doesn't know what his options are. He has never been there before and the city is expansive and overwhelming.

If parents really want to help their boys choose, then the responsible thing to do would be to give them an extensive education in the West's, if not the world's, religions. But frankly I don't believe that many parents who want their children to choose their own faith have the time, energy, resources, even the desire at the end of the day to do this. What really happens is that the boys receive nothing. And when this happens, be very, very careful, because having no frame of religious reference leaves boys completely vulnerable to involvement with cults and other "faiths" that no parent would want his child swept up in. The truth is, many of us withhold religious teaching because we have succumbed to parental peer pressure. It is the politically correct thing to do, to let our children choose, and the more choice the better, particularly when it comes to such sensitive and personal issues as faith.

But if you want to help your child, don't do this. Teach your boys about your faith. If you don't have one, figure out what you believe. And then figure out why you believe what you do about God. All the evidence about our sons tells us that not only do they *want* detailed, meticulous, well-thought out answers about

God, they need them. It makes their lives better. Church attendance keeps kids out of trouble. Fathers who take their sons to temple have better relationships with them. God is good for kids. So let's not create a barrier to God for our sons. There are many such barriers today, as has been made obvious by the recent spate of bestselling books promoting atheism. But such animosity towards religion is long-standing. In his *Pensées*, published posthumously in 1669, mathematician and philosopher Blaise Pascal addressed such animosity, saying, "Men despise religion; they hate it and fear it is true. To remedy this, we must begin by showing that religion is not contrary to reason; that it is venerable, to inspire respect for it; then we must make it loveable, to make good men hope it is true; finally, we must prove it is true.

"Venerable, because it has perfect knowledge of man; loveable because it promises the true good."[11]

Your sons need to know God and to be taught about him in the manner Pascal prescribed.

WHY BOYS NEED GOD

Reason #1—Hope

Chris Godfrey, a retired professional football player, has an enormous presence. Whether a room is filled with eighteen- or seventy-eight-year-old men, when Chris walks in, men stop talking. I have seen businessmen, teachers, and priests scurry when he enters. I even saw a prominent archbishop turn away from a conversation when Chris walked into a room. He is what many men want (or wanted) to be. He is the owner of a ring—a shiny, chunky Super Bowl ring.

But Chris's life didn't always feel so glamorous. As a young man playing defense for the Green Bay Packers, he received a phone call one day in his hotel room. It was his coach. Chris was being cut from the team. He felt devastated; it was his third cut in one year. Chris fell to his knees on his hotel room floor. He was a practicing Catholic, so the reflex felt natural. But this time, he recalls, he really needed help from God. He needed hope that his life wasn't over, even thought he felt like the bottom had fallen out.

Chris recalls, "I asked myself those important questions: 'Who am I?' and 'Where am I going?'" Football was his life. He had played on three Rose Bowl teams for the University of Michigan and had been offered a free agent contract with the Washington Redskins. Football was his past, and he thought it was going to be his future.

He told God that he would do whatever He wanted him to do and go wherever He wished. He gave up all control. The strapping, superbly fit football player, kneeling on his hotel room carpet, begged God for help. And Chris meant business.

He checked out of the hotel room and went to clean out his locker. Out of the blue, Chris remembers, Bart Starr approached him and apologized for having cut him from the team. He invited him to stay with the Packers. Chris was stunned. A year later, though, Chris separated his shoulder and the football league went on strike. Suddenly he found himself back in Detroit, unemployed and injured. His world stalled once again.

Another team formed in Michigan, in a new league, the U.S. Football League, and Chris joined the Panthers. He changed from defense to offense. His team won the USFL Championship and the following year he returned to the NFL, signing with the New York Giants as their starting right guard. Two years later, he helped lead the Giants to win Super Bowl XXI.

Chris insists that on that day in the hotel room, his life changed. He grew up. He saw God differently. He let God take charge. His troubles persisted, but ultimately, he succeeded. "God keeps His word, and if you do things God's way everything will work out well. Even though having a Super Bowl ring is great," says Godfrey, "having an identity as God's son is better."

God gave Chris hope on that dreary day he was cut from the Packers, when all other avenues of hope felt like they were exhausted. He had tried as hard as he could, and still he had been cut. Not once, but three times. Little did Chris know that the best was yet to come.

Hope is a critical element missing in the lives of hundreds of thousands of boys across America. It is a forward-thinking belief. When a boy hopes, he can sit in the midst of extraordinary hurt and grab hold of the belief that something better is yet to come. His pain will lessen. Or he will survive his parents' divorce. Perhaps he can still be somebody even if he fails to make the varsity football team in his junior and senior years. Without hope, boys who have suffered setbacks or been damaged by traumatic experiences, often feel that an enormous part of their life can never be restored.

Victor Frankl, a Jewish psychiatrist, was incarcerated in a Nazi concentration camp during World War II. He survived, and in his famous book *Man's Search for Meaning*, Frankl wrote that the men who were able to survive the camp did so because of one factor: hope. Those men who were able to focus on a positive future event, not only found meaning in their suffering, they were able to fall out of their filthy barracks and drag their emaciated bodies one more day to the work yard for another round of work.

In contrast, men who dwelt continuously in the present or who focused on life as it was before their imprisonment, fell into believing that life was meaningless. These men began on an inward journey of decay.

Frankl writes:

...the Latin word *finis* has two meanings: the end or the finish, and a goal to reach. A man who could not see the end of his "provisional existence" was not able to aim at an ultimate goal in life. He ceased living for the future, in contrast to a man in normal life. Therefore, the whole structure of his inner life changed; signs of decay set in which he knew from other areas of life....

Such people forgot that often it is just such an exceptionally difficult external situation which gives man the opportunity to grow spiritually beyond himself.... They preferred to close their eyes and to live in the past. Life for such people became meaningless.[12]

While the lives of American boys are not fraught with starvation, torture, or humiliation as those of the prisoners who lived with Frankl in the concentration camp were, many boys can still understand loneliness, meaninglessness, boredom, and emotional anguish because they feel it themselves.

But the answer for them—for all of our boys—is the same as it was for Frankl. It is living with palpable hope because without it, they will begin a process of inner decay.

Frankl wrote: "The prisoner who had lost faith in the future— his future—was doomed. With his loss of belief in the future, he also lost his spiritual hold; he let himself decline and become subject to mental and physical decay."[13]

Any boy who lives without hope cannot last long. Many of the boys who join gangs do not believe that they will live into their thirties. Many believe they will be murdered or die of a drug overdose. These are young men who have not been taught that their lives can be transformed. But they can escape their circumstances if they have parents, or other concerned adults, bold enough to teach them, to love them, and to persevere with them. But sadly, many of these boys can't find that caring adult, cannot imagine a life beyond ugliness, and cannot find hope.

Philosophy professor Dallas Willard wrote, "the only hope of humanity lives in the fact that, as our spiritual dimension has been formed, so it can also be transformed."[14] That transformation comes most readily to those boys who can turn to God, the ultimate father. This is where religion can provide the hope that so many boys lack. God has this advantage over any other provider of hope: He has no limitations; He will not die; He cannot fail. That is why for a boy, God is the best source of hope.

Reason #2—Love

Our boys live in a world that "squanders the sacred to protect the profane," writes Dr. Ravi Zacharias.[15] That's exactly what happens when we don't teach boys about God. This shows itself when boys develop ideas about love. For boys whose reference points are profane—as in popular culture—love is essentially sex, and it is transient and superficial. Boys who follow this path feel empty, because they have a fragmented notion of what love really is.

Boys with a strong, traditional religious belief, however, are much more likely to regard God as representing consummate love. So they see love in a broader, fuller picture. They know that love is not all about sex or even about romance, it is about caring and empathy and doing what is right. For some boys, God might not only represent love, He might be their only access to it, where parents are absent or drug-addicted. Certainly, traditional religious experience tells us that believers experience God's love as transcending all others. Everyone wants to experience a feeling of being loved without conditions. To be loved simply because he exists. The problem for boys, however, is that unconditional love is hard to come by. Many parents want to give it to their children but fail because it is hard and emotionally complicated. To extend unconditional love, one has to be emotionally sound oneself and expect nothing in return.

In other words, for a father to extend unconditional love to his son, he has to set aside any desire to be liked by his son, see his son succeed at something, or see his son respond to him in a certain way. These might all be good things, but a father who has to express that he will love his son no matter what. That's a hard thing to do. Most mothers and fathers shape their identity as parents around the responses they see from their children and from the "successes" they witness in their child. These parental needs can keep parents from extending complete unconditional love.

But all boys crave such love. When they seek it from parents and it fails to come, rather than realize that their parents are imperfect at loving, a boy finds fault within himself. He can't be perfectly loved, he deduces, because something is wrong with him. So, where is he to turn?

God is one place he can turn, because if unconditional love can exist, it most certainly can be found in God.

Boys need to know that they deserve such love. What might seem trite to some adults—"God loves you"—can be powerful to boys who believe it. Those who do believe it receive a great benefit. They have the validation of their self-worth that all of us seek.

Reason #3—Truth

All boys desire to find the truth. Young boys want to know what is right and what is wrong. Older boys want to know what is real and what is fake. More mature boys want to know what is true and what is false. Like love, knowing truth is a primal need. The biggest true or false question all humans face regards God. The struggle to decide truth regarding the existence of God has been probably the most broadly debated philosophical question in the history of man. Most people around the world and in the United States conclude that God does exist. But a significant minority in the United States and around the world believes that there is no God at all.

Dr. John Stewart of the Princeton University Theological Seminary summarized two primary reasons why men are tempted to renounce the idea of God's existence. These two, according to Stewart, are: first, human pain, and second, not wanting to hear what God would say to him if he believed.

In my experience, boys who struggle to discern the truth of God's existence struggle with these two points. The existence of human suffering is extremely difficult to reconcile with the idea of a benevolent God. I too have heard boys describe a personal fear of what God might say to them if they believed in Him. This last point leads boys away from searching for the truth, because they are afraid of what they might find. But something in a boy's spirit churns inside of him to figure out the truth of God. Blaise Pascal put it this way: "The heart has its reasons, which reason does not know. We feel it in a thousand things."[16] Pascal goes on to say that the human heart naturally loves God, but the human heart also loves itself, and at some point it hardens itself against the one or the other. "You have rejected the one and kept the other. It is by reason that you love yourself?"[17]Dr. Stewart refers to this internal churning as a human response to "echoes" in the universe, and says that there are four quests in every man's heart as he senses these universal whisperings.

First, men sense that there is a transcendent order, and this prompts a search for its Creator. Second, men have a natural, universal wonder about beauty, which prompts men to seek the meaning behind beauty. Third, a man's quest for a meaningful relationship (which every man needs in order to survive) leads him to conclude that such relationships are precious, because they offer a deeper sense of belonging, of "being home." This sense is universal, and leads men to wonder whether this sense of belonging isn't formed by God. Fourth, every man has a sense of right and wrong, of fairness and unfairness, and this leads man to wonder whether this universal moral law is not the law of God.

One of the most serious consequences for boys who are denied a religious education is that it blunts, or restricts, their search for truth. If a boy is taught that God's existence is not an important question, or if the question is closed by drumming into him that God does not exist, one of the most important, and maturing, intellectual quests a boy can have is cut off at its roots. Finding truth via wrestling over the existence of God opens a boy's mind like no other mental exercise. Too much of our secular world narrows a boy's mind by discounting, denying, or forbidding that exploration. We not only narrow a boy's mind, we stifle his deepest desires. We shouldn't.

Reason #4—Grace

As with hope, nothing affords a boy the opportunity to receive grace like the person of God. Every boy needs another chance. He needs to know that when he makes bad decisions and brings pain upon himself or others, regardless of his motives, that he can confront his mistakes, relinquish bad behaviors, and start again.

Only grace opens the door for a fresh start. And like love, grace is tough for parents to extend. It feels messy and emotionally sticky. We who love our boys want to be sure they understand their mistakes and learn from them. We want to ensure the mistakes aren't remade. We discipline and remind them of their failures as a means to keep mistakes at bay.

But whenever parents fail at extending grace, God succeeds. I know that on this point, and some of the others we've touched on, religions differ. But as most American boys are at least culturally Christian, it makes sense when we talk about religion in general to have Christianity's tenets foremost in mind, and one of the distinguishing beliefs of Christianity is this idea of grace, of having debts (sins, mistakes, all the anguished awful things adolescents do or think they have done) forgiven.

If American boys lack anything of significance in their lives it is grace. Many are keenly aware of their inabilities and failures.

They need reassurance that their errors can be put behind them. God can give them that.

Reason #5—Security

Every boy needs a way to find stability in his life, a way to find his footing. After his parents' divorce, his best friend's death in a car accident, his girlfriend's ditching him for the school quarterback, a boy who can turn to God has a great advantage over one who can't. He is secure in himself. He knows that not all is lost because God is with him always.

During the adolescent years many boys mentally begin to pull away from their parents. Because of this very healthy shift, most boys feel exquisitely vulnerable. And the vulnerability peaks when painful situations arise and because they are not fully mature men, boys can get knocked off their emotional feet much more easily. So what helps them stand up again? Who will grab their shoulders and place them upright as they challenge themselves not to go to a mother or father for help? Friends can get them up on their knees but an adult must be available to hoist them completely back up on their feet. For thousands of boys help from a mother, a father, or any older adult simply never comes. We are busy. Fathers often travel too much. Mothers are exhausted from long work days. Grandparents live hundreds of miles away. And some parents, frankly, are too self-absorbed to care.

Even if a parent does care, many times his love and support cannot be enough for a boy, because if he's a healthy, maturing adolescent, he knows he can't always be dependent on mom and dad; he knows he has to get beyond that dependence. As our boys grow older we realize that we can't be responsible for meeting all of their needs. But we need to have a backup plan, some other way to give our sons answers, support, and a sense of love. If we fail to give them God as the ultimate source of love, goodness, and wisdom where will they go? There are many possible wrong turns to take in an adolescent's life, and this is where many of them make that turn into things that can harm their lives forever.

When boys are fearful and confused they need answers—and failing to get them can lead to depression. And when they meet with inevitable setbacks in their adolescent years—social disaster, an academic failure, an athletic defeat—boys need a way to release the pressure building within them. Boys can be very good about hiding their self-doubts from their parents (they know they need to be "a man"), but this can make their inner selves feel abandoned and lonely. Boys who can turn to God at this point again have an advantage over those who can't. They will not feel alone. They know that they have a place in the universe despite every failure. They know that God cares and can understand their thoughts and fears when no one else can.

Resurrecting a boy's fallen spirit is a monumental task and every boy knows it. Giving a boy the security of God, the God that always sees him and always loves him, is the defense parents can offer their child. A father offers security, but when he gives his son God, he gives his son something greater. Dads make mistakes. God doesn't. Dad won't always be around. God will. And God loves them both. Every boy deserves the chance to know this.

CHAPTER ELEVEN

How Then Shall We
Teach Them to Live?

WE ALL HAVE A VISION of the sort of men we'd like our boys to become. Sometimes that picture is about securing a lucrative or prestigious profession, sometimes it is about having a successful marriage and the arrival of grandchildren, but deep down what most parents want to know is how can we raise our sons to be men, real men: the sort of men we respect when we meet them in our daily life—men of character. There are things that every parent can do to help raise boys who will become such men. It begins with teaching them, and living ourselves, the virtues we admire. But when it comes to that challenge, every one of us fears we won't be able to succeed.

Don't be afraid. Every parent can raise a son to be kind, truthful, and courageous.

Here's how we start. Create that mental picture of the man you want your son to be. You can plug in all the externals you want: you can make him a certain height and weight, choose his profession for him, even choose his bride. Finished? Good.

Now, strip all those superficial components away. Take away his job. Remove his spouse, home, car, and hobbies. What man do you have left?

Now go to work. Recreate his internal self. What do you want to find there?

Do you want a man who lives truthfully and works hard? Or do you see a man who is a scoundrel willing to crawl over anyone to get ahead? When we strip a man down to his character, we can see what he is made of. In a hard situation will he show courage or a lack of principle? If he has to make a choice between his children and himself, whom will he put first? Will he be respected by his friends as a man of character or will he be seen as a braggart and as someone who cuts moral corners?

If you want your son to become a courageous man, begin training him now. If you believe that he will live a happier life if he is honest, crush deceitfulness in him immediately. If you want him to be respected and honored for his character, teach him humility. And if you want him to use his masculinity constructively, teach him that strength, courtesy, and respect go together.

Every boy needs schooling in virtues in order to become a great man. And any parent can school him because at the heart of virtue is masculine intuition. Parents don't have to construct the virtues and then pour them into the heart of their son. The virtues are there, but in small fragments that must be cleared, shaped, and polished.

The great burden for parents is finding time. Haste is the enemy of virtue, because it gives us no time to discuss, think, wonder, or pray; it forces us to push our boys to perform when we should be working with them. Give time back to your son. Give him time to dream. Encourage him to question and to think. Boys must have time to think upon virtues before they embrace them. Otherwise, virtues become nothing more than a disposable outer layer of clothing. A man can put them on or off, depending on his mood. But real virtues are not so disposable—they become part of the boy.

At the outset, simplify your son's life. Give him space to be bored, to find ways to fill his time. When he does this, he will be forced to think. If you want to spur him on, give him a copy of Aristotle's *Ethics* or *Politics* or Plato's *Dialogues* or Pascal's *Pensées*—classics that will get him thinking about virtue and what it is and how to define it and live it.

To reflect on the big questions requires time to think; it requires leisure. Don't let haste deny you and your son the time to discuss the good things in life. Build time into his day for him to exercise truthfulness and for the two of you to discuss its importance. When you see your son exercise virtue, find time to praise him for it.

Boys will search for virtue, just as they will search for truth and self-worth, because in the heart of a developing boy is the desire to know the truth, to know what is good, and to know that he has some reason to do the right thing. This is why boys are famous for setting out rules, standards of conduct for themselves. They derive their moral code from those they admire (usually their parents). Once a boy sets out his rules, he holds them as the best and highest way a boy (himself) should behave. If a boy succeeds in following his code of conduct, he's able to respect himself, and he believes others will respect him as well. Respect and honor are important to boys (and men).

INTEGRITY

At the top of most lists of good behavior is honesty. Boys are keenly attuned to honesty in those around them. And they feel it immediately when people around them sway from it. If a boy has a strong conscience, his eyebrows, nostrils, hairline, and mouth will all betray him if he tries to lie, because he will know he is breaking the code of conduct. Boys consider honesty a masculine quality, so to betray it is to be less of a man. Heroes, in a boy's eyes, are deserving of honor because they stand for what is right and just, and what is right and just is honesty.

Living honestly feels better to boys than living with deception, even if that deception is meant to get them what they want. Boys like feeling strong and courageous, and telling the truth demands strength and honesty. Lying feels grungy. Lying makes boys fearful because they know it is a weakness. The liar is someone who is afraid of the truth.

This is why boys are so open to being trained to tell the truth. They know that if you teach them to be truth-tellers, you're teaching them to be strong. They know good boys, internally strong boys, tell the truth; wishy-washy boys lie. No one needs to tell them this; they know it.

So in teaching honesty you have a ready audience. Don't blow it by encouraging your son to tell white lies—even if they're well intentioned. Young boys think in black and white terms. A statement is either true or it is false. The younger the boy, the less gray he feels in his thinking. When a parent coaxes him to tell "white lies" he is confused. The term is an oxymoron. In order to accommodate his parents' wishes, he puts lies into the pool of acceptable speech. Beginning such ambiguous training so early on in life leads boys down a slippery path.

Even small lies tangle boys into knots. If Sam tells Bob he can't do a sleepover because he's going to his aunt's house (when he's really going over to his friend Ricky's house) it will inevitably backfire. When Bob finds out Sam lied (which he inevitably will), he receives a two-fold hurt: Sam stood him up for Ricky, and Sam lied to him. And Sam feels terrible too, because lying feels terrible. Don't train boys in acceptable lies, because lies make a boy miserable. Any boy who tells small lies at seven tells larger ones at seventeen and enormous ones by thirty-seven.

We all know that living truthfully is very hard and young boys need help to do it. Every boy wants to tell the truth, but actually doing it requires that someone—mom, dad, teacher, coach—help a boy put his intuition for honesty in practice, and not lead him astray by encouraging white lies or by padding the truth. You don't want to disturb your son's moral sense or make him think that living truthfully gets harder as you grow older. A boy should see his parents as models of honesty. Honesty is honorable. And honor is the self-consciousness of other virtues, the first layer of virtue-building in the mind of every boy.

A boy needs a sense of personal honor. Think of his daily life. Is there a boy in his tenth-grade history class who paid a classmate to write his paper for him? That paper got an A, while the paper your son struggled over got a B-. Why shouldn't he pay to have his papers written for him too? After all, the other boy didn't get caught.

Is there a girl in the eleventh-grade class who thinks your tenth-grade son is hot? And if so, what does she say to him via MySpace or Instant Messaging? Does she text him and suggest sexual fun? Why not respond to her overtures? She came onto him, after all?

Your son is a good kid. He knows it's wrong, it's dishonest, to have someone else write his papers for him. But he needs to have a sense of honor that denies temptation.

And what about the girl? Your son doesn't want a girlfriend; he doesn't think he's ready for that yet. In fact, he finds her messages a bit creepy. On the other hand, he doesn't want to hurt her feelings. He wants to be nice. Maybe there would be no harm going over to her house tonight to study?

Boys must be savvy and wise to the behaviors of their friends. Living honestly means seeing people—including himself—with his eyes wide open. Maintaining his integrity can be grueling, particularly during the teen years—but if he has a prayer at maintaining self respect, he must learn to know himself well. He must be honest about his desires and his goals and get help sticking to them. When he succeeds at this, he'll feel good because he'll feel honorable, honest, and strong.

COURAGE

Courage is the virtue that makes sure other virtues—like integrity, meekness, humility, and kindness—are put into action. Staying honest can be tough, so is placing another's needs before your own, and you won't learn kindness and humility from MTV. Boys who practice virtue are marching against the tide, and that requires courage.

The wonderful benefit of virtue, however, is that very often its rewards are immediate. A boy who shows courage can be proud of the fact. A boy who does the right thing under pressure knows he can control himself, which is a source of honor and self-respect. Every boy wants to have the courage to be daring—to throw caution to the wind and to race towards what is right. Every boy wants something that is worth risking his life for; every boy wants to know he has the courage to take that risk. To risk one's life for the sake of a friend, to act valiantly and courageously, is wholly masculine and that is why every boy wants to have it.

Modern day life doesn't often require boys to risk their lives for friends or to save girls from dragons, but it most certainly requires courage, just courage in different clothing.

We think of a courageous boy as one who walks into a room to find his friends smoking marijuana and walks out again, despite their pleas to try it with them. There is the honorable young man who refuses to take advantage of his date after she drinks too much. Instead, he drives her home and drops her off. These boys defend values that most of our culture doesn't pay attention to any longer. But he's your son—what would you want him to do? What sort of man do you want him to be? Courageous boys are all around us, even if the cowards get more attention. Help your son be one of the courageous ones.

HUMILITY

Watch a humble young man talk to his friends. Better yet, talk to him yourself. Humble boys and humble men are excellent at making anyone from the president of a university to an old woman checking groceries at a supermarket feel better about life and about who they are.

The reason for this is quite simple. Boys with an accurate perception of life and themselves spend little time worrying about themselves. They look outward, not inward. They not only enjoy a healthy respect for themselves but they respect others. They see their intrinsic humanity, their value, and they are not afraid of themselves or of life. They can embrace other's frailties, successes, and strains because their own sense of worth does not come from others, it comes from themselves.

We used to be better at training boys in humility than we are now. But it's time we focused on it again. It serves boys well. Humility teaches boys not to be arrogant—arrogant boys are miserable—and not to fall into a self-piteous sense of worthlessness. Humility is the virtue of balance.

Humble boys have a quiet strength. They know what gives a man infinite value (and it's not bragging or winning or accomplishing) and what does not. Boys with humility don't have to constantly worry about whether they're good enough or berate themselves about failure. They've checked their egotism at the door. In a word: they've matured. Humble boys pick up papers when a schoolmate drops them, they stand in the back of lines, they open doors for teachers. They don't try to be noticed but they often are because character always shines through. Humble young men are simply a delight to be around.

C. S. Lewis wrote, "If you meet a humble man he will not be what most people call 'humble' nowadays. He will not be a sort of greasy, smarmy person, who is always telling you that, of course, he is a nobody. Probably all you will think about him is that he seemed a cheerful, intelligent chap who took a real interest in what *you* said to *him*. If you dislike him it will be because you feel a little envious of anyone who seems to enjoy life so easily. He will not be thinking about himself: he will not be thinking about himself at all."[1] Maybe that's why every parent of a daughter wants her to marry a humble man. Fathers want their daughters to be loved by a man who places her worth and needs above his own, who will care for her and build her up and not crush her.

Humble boys usually emerge as life's winners. In contrast, boys who grow up believing they are better than others have such a skewed perception of their own worth that they crush others around them, particularly their closest loved ones. These are the men whose sense of superiority leaves them isolated, and they often lead lives of loneliness, anger, and self-destruction. And it's all because they miss a simple truth: no man is more valuable than another. Certainly every person has different talents, abilities, and traits, but every person is uniquely valuable. As we rush through our lives, which are full of competition, we forget this—and our sons aren't taught this unless we teach them. But teaching them about every human's infinite worth is a reminder to them of their own.

Humble boys enjoy longer and more meaningful friendships because they are true friends—not always focused on themselves. As a result they tend to win respect. And every parent wants a son who is respected by his peers.

We often make a critical mistake with our boys. In a well-intentioned effort to build their self-esteem, we teach them the

importance of doing better and performing better—all for the
sake of bettering themselves. We must teach them to better themselves in order to better the lives of others. Great men cannot be
great in a vacuum. The men we respect—who truly deserve our
respect—are the men who have accomplished great things in
pouring themselves out for others.

Teake was a humble young man. As a small child in China he
contracted polio and lost all significant function of his legs. He
moved to the United States with his parents when he was beginning elementary school. At a young age he decided that he
wouldn't live in a wheelchair. He learned to use metal crutches.
He'd thrust one crutch forward. Then he'd swivel his hips, swinging his floppy legs swung forward. Then he'd thrust the other
crutch forward and repeat the process. With remarkable determi-
nation he taught himself to walk, bowl, and play golf. On weekends, as a teenager, he competed in wheelchair road races. By his
young adult years, his muscular upper body formed a perfect V.

Teake went to medical school without a wheelchair. He preferred crutches to support his frail legs, because, he said, he liked
looking directly at peoples' faces. He was quiet, brilliant, and
kind. His demeanor served him well with sick children, particularly critically ill children. Perhaps he liked them best because
they never seemed to notice his silver crutches.

During his training, he became close with many of his patients.
Lilly was one of his favorites. She was an eleven-year-old girl
with cystic fibrosis. Her lungs often filled with thick mucous.
She'd contract pneumonia and have to be admitted to the hospital. Teake always volunteered to take care of her.

Lilly required hours of therapy for her chest. Every few hours, a
respiratory therapist would come to her bedside and fill breathing
machines with medicine for her to inhale. Then they would lay
her on her stomach and beat on her back, in order to loosen the
mucous in her lungs. It was very hard for Lilly to endure.

One week, the therapist became inundated with patients. The flu season hit and kids with asthma were admitted to the hospital in droves.

Lilly began missing a treatment here, another there. When Teake heard about her missed therapy, he went to a therapist and asked if he could watch him perform respiratory maneuvers on other patients with cystic fibrosis. He learned how to deliver the drug treatments and administer physical therapy, work that physicians never did.

When evening rounds finished and all physicians except those on call went home, Teake stayed behind. In fact, his roommate began to wonder where he'd gone. Teake's car was in the hospital parking garage, but no one in the building seemed to know where he was. His roommate scouted the halls for Teake.

He checked Lilly's room at 9:30pm. The television was on but it was muted. There he saw Teake. With his crutches leaning against the wall, he was seated on the side of Lilly's bed, his scant, dead legs dangling over the edge. His hands were pounding on Lilly's back to dislodge the mucous. Lilly was groaning. Teake continued to karate chop and bang away, telling her to hold on—it was almost over.

For one solid week the young doctor, exhausted from early mornings and staying awake all night on call nights, finished his rounds and quietly headed to the little girl's room. The metal crutches squeaked with every swing. Every night faithfully Lilly heard the creak and squeak of the metal crutches coming down the hall towards her room. Without fail.

Did the young man's work save the little girl's life? She had a terrible disease that killed her several years later. But on those days when he swung by, he most assuredly kept her lungs from becoming more infected: at least for one day, then for another. Before Lilly died she talked about Teake to her mother. He had cared for her as a doctor of course, but also, and more importantly, as a young man with humility; he had cared for her as he would have cared for his little sister.

When a boy learns to value the life of another as he values his own, people's lives around him change. Lilly's life—and the lives of Lilly's mother and father—was changed by the young man. That would not have happened had Teake had too much pride to do another man's job, a job lower down the hierarchy, and to do it after his own long, tiring shift was over.

Teach your son to cherish the common humanity of everyone he meets, and to always be willing to go the extra yard to help others. None of us is too important to do that.

MEEKNESS

Every boy must know meekness. The word means *constrained power*. Meekness is the state reached after a wild horse is broken. The animal, fierce with energy and strength, has been harnessed and brought under control.

Meekness is the antithesis of weakness. The word conjures in our mind the picture of a frail, balding man hunched over his cane who speaks so softly that one can hardly hear his words. This is most certainly not what meekness is.

It is the tall, fit stallion with well-defined muscle galloping steadily in a field—in total control—that should be our image of meekness. He can stop on a dime and catapult to a gallop. Every ounce of his energy is channeled in the proper form. Nothing is wasted throwing his head or bucking his hind legs into the air. Wouldn't you like your teenager to be like that?

While boys are most certainly not animals, the analogy fits. Every boy grows into puberty with escalating levels of testosterone, increased energy, thickening musculature, and an increasing sense of his power. He can yell louder—and he can actually intimidate people.

It is precisely during this sense of exploding power that a boy must learn meekness. Like the other virtues, he must be trained in it. It doesn't feel normal or even intuitive. If anything, it feels counterintuitive. He needs help learning to channel his energy and strength in a healthy direction.

The first step is to make sure your son understands that self-control is important. Many boys don't because their parents shy away from teaching discipline to teenagers. It should go without saying that undisciplined teens are a danger to themselves and to others. But unless a boy honestly believes that self-control is important, he will not exhibit meekness.

Second, before he's a teen you need to teach your son that when he uses his energy in a bad way—by acting inappropriately aggressive, by hurting others—he will run into a stronger force: you. If he is out of control, catch him, and turn him around quickly. Discipline him—consistently, fairly, and lovingly. This is his earliest training in meekness. Boys in elementary school need parental control because they are too immature to control themselves. In the teenage years, these early years of guidance can make your job a lot easier. So can your own behavior. Ideally, he's grown up watching you and learning about what living within control looks like. Teach him that having energy, strength, and excitement is wonderful but that he must learn to take it and use it for his benefit, not for his harm.

Active, energetic, rambunctious boys are not bad boys and should not be made to feel so. Boys are naturally active. They have energy to burn. That's why they need avenues where they can be active, burn up that energy, and test their strength. Boys need exercise. It is not a luxury, it is a necessity. Video games don't provide exercise. And neither do television or computers. All boys need to romp and learn that even in rambunctious play, there are rules and order. Through sports and exercise, they learn to control their muscles, control their bodies, and even control their emotions and their minds. As a boy grows older, he can transfer these skills he learns into other areas of his life. He can never learn to control his energy if he is not allowed to experience the fullness of its power.

Of course boys' needs are not just physical. Meekness is an intellectual virtue as well. As a gifted boy begins to recognize his potential, he quickly learns that he has abilities that his peers do not. He can read faster, multiply in his head, or memorize words more quickly. Bright boys feel explosions of intellectual curiosity and parents must be able to recognize this and provide outlets for them. And it is noteworthy that many such boys who are also highly creative might exhibit difficulty with concentration and attention because their minds are simply working too furiously. Give them books to read, instruments to play, projects to dive into; give your encouragement to their desire for knowledge and even their desire to daydream. But remember that bright boys are stunted if they're stuck in front of a television or lose themselves behind a computer screen or earphones. And these isolating electronic gadgets don't teach humility the way engagement with real people, or great books, or the challenge of playing an instrument does. Just as a boy's growing physical power can feel a bit frightening, so can his expanding mental power. Gifted children need to learn meekness to corral and focus their talents.

As with all efforts of self-control, adults have to show the way. Parents and teachers can help gifted children find the best way to direct and express their gifts. For many other boys, parents and coaches are the ones who can best teach self-control, or not. They can either encourage the healthy meekness of the trained show horse or they can encourage the behavior of the wild horse that kicks out its hooves at anyone who stands in its way. Any coach who teaches boys to win at all costs—including breaking rules—is destroying the character of the boys in his charge. Any coach that teaches his boys that self-control and self-discipline

will make them better players and a better team, that they need
to play hard but fair, and that they need to win or lose gracefully,
is doing a real coach's and a real man's work.

Joey was an extraordinary athlete. He was thirteen, in the
eighth grade, when the varsity soccer coach asked him if he
would like to be on his team. In a high school of 1,500 students,
the invitation was an exceptional honor. But Joey declined. He
didn't want to leave his buddies on the junior high team.

Every time he touched a ball, dived in a pool, or pedaled a
bike, he touched gold. Joey rarely lost a meet, a match, or a
game. By the time he was seven years old, his parents recognized
his talents. They had dreams for his future, but they didn't let
their dreams get in the way of making wise decisions. They determined to let him play what he wanted and when. No cajoling
him into sports or activities he didn't want, no private trainers or
Olympic development teams. They simply let him play sports for
the love of playing. I am convinced that their decisions helped
him excel more when he was a young adult.

When he began high school, he decided to play varsity soccer,
to his coach's delight. The community came to see Joey play. Usually his team won, but fans watched simply for the pleasure of
watching him. Every game he seemed to play better than the last.

One fall evening Joey's team played a team that was notoriously
rough. Joey's school was in a middle-class suburb. The opposing
team came from the inner-city and had a reputation for playing
soccer like hockey without pads. They charged into players, head-
butted them, slide tackled them, and learned how to cheat without
letting the referees see. Joey's team wasn't excited to play them.

Joey was the youngest on his team, but in spite of his age he had
an extraordinary build. As a freshman he was already six feet one
inch. He started as sweeper and, as always, played well. But after
the first half, Joey's team was demoralized. They were losing, and
one of Joey's teammates had to leave the game with an injury.

Joey was his team's highest scorer, and the opposing coach identified him as a major threat. He put in a tough kid to guard him. At one point in the second half, Joey raced across the field with the ball, running furiously toward the challenger's goal. A teammate broke free. Joey saw him, but also saw a defenseman running at his teammate. He realized the defenseman was out for blood.

Joey passed the ball but kept his eye on his opponent. His teammate was half the size of the defender. Joey feared he was going to be hurt. So he did something extraordinary. He ran at the defender to block him. Sure enough, the monstrous defender swung his cleats at Joey's teammate but missed and caught Joey full on the knee. Joey fell down, having taken the blow for his buddy. But more amazing, the defender kicked at Joey again after he fell. The referee blew the whistle and Joey simply somersaulted and landed on his feet. By the time he stood up, the giant defender himself had fallen and Joey had a perfect opportunity to strike back. The ref wasn't looking, the ball had moved past them, and as big as the defender was, he was smaller than Joey. Retaliating would be a cinch.

Joey stared down at the boy. He saw meanness on his face. But he simply grabbed his own ballooning knee, with its fractured kneecap, turned, and hopped off the field on one foot.

The spectators—even the parents on the opposite side of the field—erupted in applause. They whooped and clapped, not because a fight broke out, but because it didn't. In that tall, talented powerhouse that was Joey, they saw meekness.

KINDNESS

We live in a country inhabited by the highest percentage of kind boys and men in the world. We have men who are the heartbeat of international relief organizations bringing housing, food, clothing, and water supplies to millions trapped in poverty around the globe. We have soldiers in war-torn regions who do more than fight—they bring candy and soccer balls to children and build them schools and clinics. Unlike men in some other parts of the world, American men value girl babies as much as boy babies; we don't have a problem of "sex selection abortion." And unlike men in some other parts of the world, American men treat women courteously and with respect as fellow human beings. Every day we see acts of manly kindness, like the young man I saw in an airport, who gave up his seat on an overbooked plane so that a mother and child wouldn't have to spend the night at the airport in Detroit (he did instead). Or the teenage boy I know who met a nine-year-old orphan girl while on spring break in Jamaica; he spent the next two years trying to bring her back to the United States to give her a better life—and when he failed he broke down crying.

I have worked for years in a field dominated by men and I have seen them in action—their kindness, their compassion, their devotion. I have watched a seventy-two-year-old doctor from the States voluntarily performing operations in an indigent third world country in a makeshift hospital without electricity (or much else), week after week in sweltering conditions without complaining. I have seen obstetricians deliver new life. I have seen physicians at the bedsides of those who are dying. All of us, if we look around, can find kindly, heroic men at work.

American men are kind because they have been taught to be kind. It is a longstanding part of our culture that you can trace to our religious heritage, our founding political principles, the frontier tradition of helping each other, and probably a half dozen other sources. But the important thing to remember is that parents and families pass down this training from one generation to the next. Being considerate might not always be easy, but it makes for a healthy society. It also makes for better boys. Find a happy young man and you will find a kind one.

Contrary to what some people think, girls are not kinder than boys; they're just more expressive. Girls are empathetic, but boys see kindness as requiring action. They see a need and rather than talk about it, or talk to the person in need, they do something. Often they will attempt to do so without attracting attention to themselves.

Jordan was a boy like this. He lived in a neighborhood in the center of a small town where each home had a small back yard flanked by a detached garage. Behind the row of garages was an alley. After school, boys would meet in the alley to play street hockey. Some kids played with hockey sticks and roller blades, others with sneakers and brooms. Jordan was one of the boys with roller blades and a hockey stick. His parents were wealthier than some of the others on his street. About half the team had sticks and blades, half had sneakers and brooms.

Those with roller blades skated circles around the boys who ran. They consistently out-shot them and soon decided to play separately from the boys with brooms. Jordan didn't like the idea. He wanted to keep the group together. Jordan said that if the guys with sticks kicked out the guys with brooms, that he was out. Over the next few days, no one met in the alley to play hockey.

Then one of his friends came to him with an idea. Jordan thought it was a great idea, and he got all the boys together in the alley.

"We have new rules," he told them. "No blades, no broomsticks."

"Why should I give up my blades?" said one boy.

"That's stupid," said another. "How do you expect us to play without sticks? You want us to play with our hands?"

"No, dummy. We're each going to find five bucks, that way we can get a stick for everybody. Then we'll be even. It'll be a lot more fun."

Jordan's outward sportsmanship and problem-solving was disguised kindness. Sure, he selfishly wanted to keep eight on the team rather than shrink to a pack of four. But that's not what drove him to convince his roller blade buddies to put on sneakers. It was kindness towards those who didn't have roller blades. Boys have a wonderful humility. They won't boast about kindness or compassion. They'll even try to hide it, as Jordan did.

Alden had a similar story. When Alden was seven, he lived next to Mrs. Donovan. She was an eighty-three-year-old widow who looked like she was seventy-three. She drove, cooked, and spent hundreds of hours in her flower garden in the back yard. Sometimes after school, Alden ran into her yard and helped her weed. Mostly, he just sat and talked her ears off. Mrs. Donovan told Alden's mother that the boy liked to talk so much she had a hard time focusing on what he was saying. Once Alden even told her, "Mrs. Donovan, you know, I really want to keep on talking, but I'm just running out of words to say."

One afternoon Alden came home from school and learned that Mrs. Donovan was ill. She hadn't been outside in her garden all day.

Alden went to work. He needed to do something. What could he do? He had the perfect idea to make her feel better.

Alden cleaned a peanut butter jar, grabbed a ball of his mother's yarn and a pair of scissors. He headed to Mrs. Donovan's back yard.

For twenty minutes, the small boy snipped every single tulip he could find in her yard. He carefully bunched them and tied them with the yarn. He had so many tulips that he had to run home for more jars.

Carefully he placed the tulip-filled jars on her porch and rang the doorbell.

Mrs. Donovan appeared at the door in her bathrobe. When she saw Alden's face, she smiled. Then, she looked down at his feet and gasped. A long pause ensued.

"Alden! My tulips! How did you know they are my favorites?" she beamed. The young boy strode home with his chest puffed out like a rooster.

When his mother found out about the tulips, however, his posture changed immediately. Being much less quick to see his heart, she made him go to Mrs. Donovan and apologize immediately. He couldn't understand why.

Boys who are trained in kindness lead happier lives. They learn to be better friends, stronger spouses, and better businessmen because they think not always of themselves but of their customers. And they become more compassionate. Boys who are kind learn to take on the burdens of others, which makes them stronger men.

When boys are young, parents can begin developing their kindness by teaching them to speak well of others. Speech and behavior go together. Train a boy to speak well of others and over time he will treat those people better.

Disciplining a boy to talk differently will make him think differently. This technique works beautifully. If a parent insists that a boy stop talking negatively about a friend, for instance, over time he will either forget about the friend's bad habits or actually learn to like him. When boys are prohibited from complaining, they become happier. The way a boy talks about someone causes him to think about that person the same way. Boys think on what they say. If they complain, negative thoughts not only precede the complaint, they follow them. Then, a boy forms a very negative pattern of thinking. When this happens, he not only complains more but he begins to act unhappy. He wants to play less and go fewer places.

Many parents allow complaining because they feel that boys need to express their feelings. Boys do need to be encouraged to verbalize how they feel, but that's not what happens in complaining. More often than not, complaining erupts from a bad mood, malcontent, and boredom. Train verbal complaints out of your son. If you don't, he will mature into a miserable man and fail to see anything good past his own nose. Teach him, on the other hand, to say only positive things about others and he will act more kindly toward them. This can be simple to do.

Marci Billings picked up her four children after school and headed off to do errands. Each of the kids was in a bad mood and suffering from post-school irritation. I call it the school bus syndrome. It's hard to find pleasant kids the first half hour after school lets out.

Soon the kids began fighting. She had one boy and three girls in the car. Tears erupted and someone's drink spilled. At her first stop, all four went into the store with her. They piled back into the car and the bickering resumed even louder. Without saying a word, Marci pulled the car into a parking lot. When the car was stopped, she turned around and informed the children that the car wouldn't move until each child said something nice about the person sitting to their right.

They groaned. Two of the girls started hitting each other. The other two got mad at them because they wanted to go home. She waited and sipped her Diet Coke. She wasn't kidding.

Jimmy volunteered first. Being quite pragmatic, he realized that he needed to do what he was told in order to get out of there. His sisters fumed.

"Okay," he started. "Shelley. I like your braces. I think it's fun to see you smile after you eat egg salad."

Shelley burst into tears. Jimmy was serious. He thought that he was being kind.

After twenty minutes, Marci was able to drive away. Interestingly, she continued to demand one kind word a day toward a sibling from each of the four over the next few years. The result? The fighting amongst them dramatically declined.

In my experience, boys more easily adapt to changing their speech than girls do. Perhaps this is because they use fewer words, perhaps it stems from their orientation toward problem-solving. Once they identify what needs to be done, they do it with less concern about why or how.

Train a boy's tongue and you change his thinking. He can take his thinking into any direction simply by changing his choice of words or the tone of his words. Many men understand this and discipline their speech on their own. Successful men fully appreciate the power of words. Not just in their impact upon others but their profound impact on their own minds.

Once you've trained a boy to do this, watch his behavior. When a boy learns to discipline his speech, his thinking changes—and so do his actions. He studies harder, chooses different activities, and his interests change. He becomes a different boy.

Kindness, like integrity, meekness, courage, and humility must be harnessed. It is there—in every boy—just as the other virtues are there. But it will lie dormant, even die, if a boy isn't shown that it is there, that it exists as part of who he is as a boy, and that it will be a larger part of who he will become as a great man. Show him kindness yourself, and teach him in the responsibility of kindness.

Boys who grow up without being schooled in these virtues live vacuous lives. Boys who never learn to exercise courage never know what it feels like to live as a man. Boys who disregard truth and learn that lies are always a viable, even helpful, option never experience the fullness of masculinity, self-respect, honor, and truth.

Humility connects boys to others, offering them the keys to authentic and intimate living. When a boy appreciates the value of others, only then can he truly begin to honestly value himself. Humility brings freedom to work hard and to love well. And meekness requires all of these virtues. Meek men live courageously because they understand their power—and the strength required to control it. Meekness is authentically masculine; it is what we mean when we talk of a gentleman. When aggression is required for performance, they use it. When kindness is required to love others well, they have it.

Every boy deserves to be trained in these virtues: they are the gateway to authentic manhood. These are the virtues that will keep a boy on the right track.

There are only a handful of adults in your son's life who will teach him the great lessons in life. As his parent, seize the day. He won't learn these virtues from three hours of television, two hours of computer time, or even six hours in school. He needs to learn from you, and to see how you put them into practice. There's no time like the present to help your son become the man you want him to be. He is waiting.

CHAPTER TWELVE

Ten Tips for Making Sure You Get It Right

THE YOUNG BOY YOU LOVE is not in your life by accident. He is with you—his father, mother, teacher, or grandparent—because he needs something very specific from you. He doesn't want someone else's approval, affection, or admiration. He wants yours and yours alone. Without receiving what you have to give, his life feels empty and directionless—but when you begin to offer him kindness and affection, encouragement and love, his life changes.

If you have experienced a good relationship with your son, you know exactly what I mean. If you are a mother, you know that loving your son and being loved by him in return brings an indescribable richness to your life. If you are a father and you have been fortunate to have a strong relationship with your son, you see the best of yourself reflected in his character as he matures.

But perhaps you haven't been so fortunate. Perhaps your relationship with your son is broken or estranged and your energy has run out. Still, you should listen to that voice of conscience that tells you that reconciliation is still possible, that you can still make another effort, that you can succeed and the pain will go away—because you *can* succeed, and the pain *will* go away when you do. Your son, whether he's five or fifty, needs you. He will always crave the approval of his mother and father. And as the mature one, it's up to you to make the first step.

There is no more noble work than shaping a boy into a man. We need more good men, and you have the ability to do something about it. Raising good sons is a challenging task, but in my experience there are ten basic principles that all successful parents follow.

1) KNOW THAT YOU CHANGE HIS WORLD

From the time your son is an infant his relationship with you sets the template for his world. If you are trustworthy, he will trust others. If you are more critical than affectionate, he will guard himself from being too close to anyone. You become his emotional filter. All of his future relationships will be fitted into the framework of his relationship with you.

Fathers, you are larger than life to your sons. Mothers, you decide the comfort of his small world. If you are not available, someone must fill in for you or else his world will crumble. As a boy grows throughout elementary school, his feelings, experiences, and thoughts continue to evolve around his relationship with his parents. If the relationship is strong, his days at school will be more productive and enjoyable. If you had an argument before he left home, he may fail his math test or forget to hand in his homework. Your relationship influences every part of his day.

When he hits the adolescent years he scrutinizes his relationship with you. If your relationship is strong, he will find the process of maturing into a man easier. If you have a bad relationship, adolescence will be a tumultuous time of anger and rebellion, as he fights to strip himself of you, while suffering the psychological trauma of separation. In a healthy relationship there is little "undone business," so a teen's inevitable separation from his parents is far less traumatic. If a parent dies and the son has had a good relationship, he will grieve appropriately and then move forward. Boys who have business to finish or wounds that need healing can become stuck in grief after a parent's death. In some ways adolescence is a time of grieving. During the teen years, a boy purposes to leave behind his juvenile relationships and shifts into more adult ones.

Researchers at the University of Minnesota studied teen boys and girls to determine what most significantly affected the decisions they made about drinking, whether to take drugs and have sex, and so on.[1] If we polled 2,000 parents, the majority would probably say that teens are most influenced by peer pressure. And we would be wrong. *Parents* are the number one influence in a boy's life.[2] His relationship with his parents is the best indicator of the decisions he will make. Interestingly, looking more deeply at the study we see that what really influences boys' decisions isn't simply what parents say. It isn't just discipline. It is connectiveness—a deep sense that a son fits in the family—he belongs, if you will, with mom or dad. He feels appreciated, loved, and affirmed for who he is as a young man.

If you are feeling like an unnecessary, uninfluential appendage in your son's life, you are dead wrong. Change your perspective. Realize that no one matters more to him, and let him know that you will always be there to help him. Take the initiative. Stick with him. You will change the course of his life.

2) RAISE HIM FROM THE INSIDE OUT

Character counts more than performance in a young man's life. You can raise a superstar who plays four years of three varsity sports, scores a perfect ACT or SAT, and who can choose which Ivy League college to attend. But if he lies, doesn't value himself or other people, or is selfish, who cares what profession he ultimately chooses? He will be miserable.

Happiness in young men comes from solid character, not from being able to jump higher or to score better on standardized tests. Your son already knows how you feel about his performance. He has felt the tension in the car when you raced him to basketball practice after piano lessons. You might have given him the speech about how appreciative he should be for all the additional lessons, or coaching, or tutors you've given him to succeed. He knows that good grades are better than bad, that scoring a touchdown is better than fumbling the ball, that hitting the high note is better than missing it. But he needs to know what you think of him as a person. Do you like what you see beneath the stuff he does—his character, the deeper parts of who he is? The wonderful truth about boys is that they are not easily buffaloed. They realize why parents do what we do and pinpoint our motives quite easily—in fact they can do this from the age of five.

Far better that they see that what matters most to us is their character. We can shape this from an early age, when boys learn that good character means a good life. A successful parent will be rewarded by seeing that their son, age three, is aware that kindness to his sister counts. At five he feels proud when he tells the truth to his kindergarten teacher when he really wants to lie. At nine he feels good that he refused to be bullied into covering up a classmate's cheating (sure he was unpopular for a time, but feeling courageous is better than anything). At fourteen, he felt like a man for telling a pushy girl to stop sending him dirty text messages (sure he was tempted to respond in kind, but he has learned that his body is his, not hers, and he is learning to control it, and value that sense of self-mastery). When he is eighteen and a freshman in college and bails on a fraternity pledge because he wouldn't guzzle vodka until he vomited, he recognizes that he now appears a bit of a misfit, but he takes comfort that he's a courageous one. He doesn't feel a need to do stupid things in order to "fit in;" he takes pride and confidence in being his own man.

Boys want parents to see deeper into their lives. They want their character to be admired more than their performance because they know that their character is who they are; and if their character is solid they will get more satisfaction out of that than anything else.

If we have failed our boys, we have failed them here. We have focused on giving our boys opportunities to excel at sports, education, or the arts, at the expense of developing their character. Certainly boys develop character through competition and various academic feats. But happiness comes to boys the other way around. A "B" earned honestly is worth more to a boy than an "A" gained through cheating. A great performance that comes from his own dogged perseverance is worth more to a boy than one that comes after years of expensive lessons. The most important question for every parent should be: what will my son's character be like when he's twenty-five? Make that your focus, so that when he leaves home, you'll have a young man who is honest, courageous, considerate, and respectful of himself and others.

3) HELP HIS MASCULINITY EXPLODE

Boys want to know how to lead. Watch them play. Every boy wants to be the general of his boy army, or the first to score a touchdown. Leadership is a natural male instinct. So talk to your son about what it means to be a leader, about how he can show the qualities of a true leader, about the responsibility that comes with power, about how leadership is learning how to help, not hurt, others. Leadership is a sign of strength. But don't let it become a sign of conceit.

Leadership is important for boys not only because their masculine intuition drives them to it, but because it is necessary for them to mature. Many boys as they get older need to overcome self-doubt. They become terrified of rejection and failure so they hold back. They won't ask a great girl out for a date because they're afraid she might say no. Others won't try out for the wrestling team because they're afraid they might not be able to compete or will get cut from the squad and be humiliated.

Help your son expunge self-doubt. Don't tell him he is great at something he isn't, but teach him that trying and failing is part of becoming a strong male leader. Find examples in history of men who tried and failed repeatedly until they became great men (you'll find many examples, including Abraham Lincoln and Winston Churchill).

Boys are natural protectors. They intuitively want to exercise their own strengths, whether physical, intellectual, or emotional in order to preserve the well-being of another. Protectiveness is a wonderful attribute and sadly, many boys and men bury it because they have been told that it is unnecessary. No one needs it, they believe, so they shelve it and find themselves frustrated.

So teach your son to act on his instincts. If a classmate is struggling with math and your son is a math whiz, encourage him to help. If your son is gigantic, teach him to stand up for the skinny kid on the playground. If he is dating, teach him to honor his girlfriend by keeping her out of dangerous situations. If he takes her to a beach party and everyone is drunk, if he feels that he can "protect" her by taking her somewhere else, he is far more likely to leave the beach than if he felt he had no responsibility to protect her.

Let me tell you a secret about every girl and most adult women. The majority love to feel protected by men. They don't want to be controlled or manipulated, they want to feel that they are cherished, even that they are worth fighting for. So early in his life, encourage your son to exercise his masculine nature as a protector. He will love it, because it makes him feel strong and mature. It is also a way for him to help others and to lead himself to happiness.

Every boy needs to feel that he brings something significant to the table of every important relationship in his life. He wants to provide something that is entirely male and unique to him. He wants and needs to provide. So encourage him. What is he good at supplying that no one else can? Help him discover what he can give that will make another person's life better. By doing this and acting on these instincts, he begins to sense that he is exercising masculine power. This ability is extremely important to healthy masculinity. The reason men so often define themselves by how much they earn, how well they lead, or how effectively they protect their families is that men (and boys) really do need to feel that they are providing something useful. It is crucial to their self-respect. A boy's desire to provide, protect, and lead can make him a great husband, a great boss, a great dad. Help to him direct and fulfill these instincts.

4) HELP HIM FIND PURPOSE AND PASSION

Every single boy is born for a reason. And every boy needs to know this. He is no accident. He exists to do something and to be someone unique. We can't necessarily teach him what he should be, but we can teach him who he should be, and most important that he has a purpose, that he is here on earth to make a positive difference in the lives of others. Coming to this realization is profoundly freeing because a boy begins to see his life in a larger context. In this larger scheme, his actions are important, but he understands that if he was born to fulfill a purpose, then some higher power will be there to help along the way. This idea is simultaneously liberating, exciting, and comforting for boys.

If you want to guarantee a boy a healthy zest for life, lead him in this direction, because passion follows purpose. Parents can motivate boys only to a certain point. We can prod, cajole, bribe, and encourage boys to get good grades, not be rude, and to brush their teeth every night, but it is a boy's passion, his sense of having a personal mission, that is the greatest motivator. When a boy begins to experience the deep satisfaction of doing what he was born to do, he will want to exercise virtue, because he'll recognize that to achieve his purpose he needs to be courageous like never before, he needs integrity to keep true to his purpose, and he most certainly needs self-discipline to corral his power and energy in the necessary direction. Passion to achieve his life's purpose can weave virtue into his character.

Too few boys know why they are alive. Some believe there is no reason at all. They believe their lives have no purpose, no meaning. As a result they have no healthy passion, no drive, and no reason—in their minds—to exercise virtue; so they become destructive of themselves and others. Be certain that your son is not one of these lost boys. Make sure he knows he has a purpose, then help him discover, over the years, what that purpose is.

5) TEACH HIM TO SERVE

The primary objective of a successful parent is to take a boy from childhood to manhood, to give him the tools to love well and the heart to place others' needs before his own.

David is a junior at the University of Michigan and is in the top 5 percent of his class, which is even more impressive when you consider that his major is bioengineering. I had the privilege of watching David grow up and I can honestly say his obvious intelligence is not his greatest asset. His heart is.

When David was fourteen, he began working with a couple of other students at a soup kitchen one day a month. David was from a poor family. His mother was disabled because of a nervous breakdown. His father kept the family together, working fifty hours a week, packing lunches, and making sure everyone got safely on the bus for school every morning.

At first, David said, he began working in the soup kitchen just to get out of the house. Weekends were chaotic and stressful at home. But soon he became hooked. He found that he loved working with friends to haul food from local restaurants into church basements, and setting out plastic forks and knives and Gatorade. He couldn't describe specifically why he loved doing this, he just knew that he did. David learned the name of every needy person who came to the soup kitchen (including the drunk the police had to escort away) and where each one lived (whether it was in a cardboard shelter under a bridge or at the Goodwill Inn). And he expanded his volunteer work. He called friends, asking if they wanted to get rid of clutter—coats, boots, socks, anything. If they did, he'd pick it and bring the assorted clothes and other items to soup kitchen for those who needed more than food.

David came to see me before he left for college. He was visibly shaken. I asked what was wrong. "Randy died three days ago," he said. He dropped his head and began quietly crying into his palms. I waited. "Life just isn't fair," he started. "I really thought he was going to make it. He was working his meetings, going to Alcoholics Anonymous, he was delivering pizzas. The last time I saw him a few days before he died, we even talked about him helping me open another soup kitchen one day. He wasn't a loser, you know. He got it. He had it. He was almost there."

"What happened?"

"Something must have made him snap. He'd been sober six months. He was getting his act together. He got a room at a house and was paying rent. But then he walked out of his house at night, got a fifth or two, I guess, and fell over drunk. No one found him until the next morning. Dead—in a snow bank."

David spoke about Randy as if he were one of his best friends. Perhaps he was: an eighteen-year-old boy sobbing over a fifty-two-year-old man who froze in a snow bank.

After a time, I gently tried to change the subject. We talked about why he went to the soup kitchen in the first place. If his goal was to get away from the stress of living with a mother who cried all the time, why go to a place where all the people have severe problems of their own, why not hang out with friends or shoot baskets?

"You'll think I'm silly, but this is the truth. I go because of my dad."

"He makes you?"

"Oh no, no, no. I've watched him. My grandma lives next door. My mother's mother. You might know her. Anyway, every morning, even in the winter before we go to school, I see my dad leave our house and go over to hers. He snow blows her driveway and he shovels her walk. He lets himself into the house, stays there for a while and then he comes home. He does this ritualistically every morning. One day I asked him why. He told me he goes to make sure she's okay. He makes her peppermint tea and a piece of toast and then he comes home and gets us off to school. The amazing thing about my dad is that this isn't his mother. My mom actually complains constantly to my dad that he never does enough around the house, that he never pays enough attention to her, or to her mother. But he does, of course.

"Bottom line is, he's my hero. He just does what he knows he should do. He busts it. And I never hear him complain. I really think that he gets life and I want to know what my dad knows. The best way I figured I could do that was doing what he does. He helps people. So I help people."

David's life took on a profound simplicity. He imitated his father's service. He figured out what life is all about. He figured out his purpose. And it's helped make him not only an excellent student, but an outstanding, well-adjusted young man. He learned that the human spirit soars, that life becomes bigger and takes on more meaning when we draw close to others and serve them.

Boys who do this learn patience and compassion. They lose false pride, but gain real humility. They learn that love is work, but that it is worth loving without expecting a reward. They learn a deeper, more mature sense of themselves, of others, and of the world. They talk less about themselves and ask more questions. They look outward to see what needs repair and go about ways to bring change. Men who serve become better husbands and fathers because they have experienced the satisfaction that comes only through placing another's needs before their own.

If you want your son to have this gift, find a housing project and take him to pound nails. Skip the matinee or the trip to the mall and collect some winter coats and a few pair of shoes to distribute to the poor. Bring your son along with you to the soup kitchen and give a hungry man a sandwich and a word of encouragement. By doing so, you'll teach your son not to settle for simply being successful in life, but to truly do well in life.

6) INSIST ON SELF-RESPECT

Imagine you are a fifteen-year-old boy in tenth grade. You get up in the morning, hop on the school bus, and swing into a seat at the front because you're tired and don't want to be bothered by loud, rowdy boys in the back. But of course you can't avoid them, because they need to be heard and prove they are cool and macho by yelling out a new rap song.

You walk into class and groan because today is health education—a waste of time, you think. Your PE teacher, a woman in her mid-forties dressed in a purple jogging suit, talks to the class about sex. Some of the guys raise their fists and cheer (just to show off, of course). And the girls begin to laugh.

Here comes the banana. The teacher holds up five packets of condoms and wants to be sure that every boy knows what they are, how to use them, and to keep plenty in his wallet. If you're going to have sex, she says, you need to do it safely. And then she smiles and says, in a way that tells you she is indeed quite cool, that these "lifesavers" come in a variety of colors and flavors. More whooping from the boys and giggles from the girls.

You leave class feeling sticky and gross. The few who cheered in the back continue to whoop and laugh as class is dismissed but most of your buddies are quiet or staring at their shoes.

You go to your locker and grab some books. You pass by a couple who need to get a room somewhere. Geometry is next and when the teacher asks students to turn in their homework, only half of the class does. He scolds the rest but no one pays attention. The ones who didn't do their homework ask questions over and over, not because they don't know the answers, you realize, but because they are trying to kill time...and the teacher doesn't catch on.

After school you flip on MTV for an hour just to relax before you head off to football practice. Jay-Z has a new video out and you just want to catch a glimpse of it. After practice you come home, have dinner (maybe on a tray in front of the television) do a little homework, and then you chill-out by plugging in your iPod and listening to music until you go to bed.

That's the sort of life that many boys lead.

Where during your son's day does he learn that he is worthy of respect? Respect isn't found in grape-flavored condoms. It isn't found from his peers who have a lot of growing up to do (and might never make it). It doesn't come from sit-coms or rap music.

Every boy wants to know that he is respected. But finding self-respect is hard when his daily life is a continual round of people trying to tear down his modesty, his sensibilities, his intelligence, and his capabilities. He's right when he notices that adults expect bad intentions from teenage boys. And it's hard to rise above low expectations, especially when they come from parents, teachers, and coaches. He wishes they'd talk to him as a young adult who isn't always ready to drink, take drugs, or have sex, who might actually aspire to something more. Shouldn't adults set the tone and raise the bar not only for him but for his rowdy classmates? He wishes they would.

You can't control all the influences on his life, but you can certainly control yours, and yours is the most important to him. Your son is dying for someone—particularly you, his mother or father—to treat him as more than 160 pounds of mindless testosterone.

So teach him how to respect himself. Boys learn self-respect by extending respect to others. Fathers, don't let your boys walk through a door before a woman, even a small girl. Teach him how to speak well. Tell him it's important because his words matter. And they do. The word choices he makes will affect his own mood and the attitude of the person with whom he's speaking. He needs to think, and act, in a positive manner. When we train our boys to make courtesy a habit, they pay less attention to themselves and more attention to others—and in return, gain respect from their peers and the adults in their lives. Respect begets respect.

I am appalled at the way many adults speak to boys. Walk around a mall and listen to mothers call their young sons stupid, lazy, even worthless. Teachers, clerks, and coaches can demean boys in ways they would never do to girls. No one benefits from this.

If you are a parent who has difficulty controlling your temper and you find yourself taking it out on your son by throwing insults and constant criticism at him, face it. Do something about it. No young boy or man deserves to be called names, constantly criticized, or "put in his place" repeatedly. Boys who live with this spend their lives "proving" to others that they deserve respect after all and they make life miserable for themselves and their loved ones.

A word to fathers is necessary here. Sons learn self-respect primarily through their fathers. You are the epitome of masculinity in your son's eyes. If you respect him, the rest of the world can try to crush him, but they won't.

So fathers: be very, very careful how you speak to your boys. Choose your words carefully, your tone of voice wisely. Don't joke about him acting like a wimp or a girl. Your words will strike a blow to his self-respect that will be hard for him to regain. Don't berate him or criticize him, telling him to "be a man" when he is only eight. He can't be a man because he's only a boy. You can communicate any lesson you want, but you must always do it in a way that lets him know that you respect him as a boy. When it comes to his behavior, don't pay a wit of attention to what his friends' parents expect. Tell him what you expect. More important, be an example to him. Show him what self-respect, self-control, courtesy, and thoughtful conversation look like and sound like. It will change his life.

7) PERSEVERE

Sometimes the hardest part of raising boys is simply sticking with it when you've heard him slam his bedroom door once too often.

Parenting is exhausting. Teaching a classroom full of ninth-graders year after year can leave one hardened and distant. Certainly treating boys who are lonely, tattooed, pierced, and mad at the world leaves many physicians shaking their heads and restructuring their practices. Better to stick to healthy men and women than troublesome teens.

Loving our sons will take perseverance and a steeled will. But you must never stop loving them. Take a rest, if you have to. But never give up. Focus on one number—twenty-five—when he'll be the young man you want him to be. Young men are not "finished" until then. Some haven't even had complete brain development until they are twenty-three. So we can never give up.

Here's a challenge for you. Today, right now, make a commitment to double the amount of time you spend with your son. Think you don't have time? Sure you do. Take him with you on errands, turn off the evening news and help him with his homework, talk to him at breakfast, play catch with him after work, or take him fishing on the weekends. He needs to live life beside you.

When we treat troubled boys who have problems from drug abuse, alcoholism, and depression, we put them in a program where they spend almost all of their time with adults. The farther a boy has fallen, the more he needs a strong adult to reach down, pick him up, nurture him, discipline him, and order his life so that he can grow up from a boy to a man.

No son can spend too much time with his father. When teen years hit, quite often the two feel they may have too much of one another. But as an adult, don't you believe this. Stick with him. Be there. Keep your body under the same roof. Travel less from home (unless you go as a family), cut back your work hours until he is older, because once he leaves home, getting him back is much more challenging.

If your son is a good kid, enjoy him and let him know it. If he is troubled, know that you are a large part of the solution. So don't leave him. Take a deep breath and don't let him implode without a good fight from you. And the only way to accomplish this is by staying in his presence, at least until he is twenty-five.

8) BE HIS HERO

Boys look around for examples of heroism, because they want to be heroes themselves. A boys needs to see courage, integrity, and nobleness acted out. And to see these virtues, a boy turns first to his father. More than any athlete, rock star, or movie star, he wants you to be his hero. You don't have to earn the right to be his hero: you simply are, as long as you refrain from actions that will cost you the title (and you have to work hard to lose it).

A very successful lawyer recently remarked to me that every man aspires to meet or exceed his father's successes. Success is most easily measured professionally, but it carries deeper meaning in terms of character. Every boy wants to meet or exceed his father's integrity, courage, faithfulness, humility, or wisdom. The standards he tries to meet or exceed are the standards you set for him by your example; and he wants to meet or exceed them in order to acquire or solidify your affection and approval.

Many boys are not fortunate enough to have a father who has maintained his heroic status. Perhaps his father has left home and lives several states away. Their relationship is held together by infrequent phone calls, or a few e-mails, and both the calls and the letters feel strained. Often, boys absorb ill feelings towards their dads in the wake of a divorce. It's hard for him to construct a healthy picture of his dad as a hero if his dad has abandoned his mom. But maybe you didn't abandon her. Maybe she divorced you for her own reasons. If you are a dad separated from your son, you should know that he desperately wants you to be his hero. To do that you need to step up to the plate. Get to the boy. Write, call, and see him as frequently as you can. If you make the effort, he'll place you back up on the platform where he wants you to be. You will never regret it.

Perhaps you are a single mother and your son's father has no interest in him. Can you be his hero? Absolutely. He will transfer his expectations and wishes for a hero onto you. They'll be somewhat different expectation and wishes, but if you show him what love, integrity, courage, and fortitude look like, you'll be every bit of a hero to him.

What does a boy expect of a hero? Heroes are honest. They are courageous. They stand up for what it right. They don't cheat. They are selfless.

When a young boy sees an adult lie, he's bewildered, because he knows there is right and there is wrong. When a trusted adult cheats, a boy is crushed. When a mother has an affair—or a father gets caught in a business scandal—a boy feels his world crumble.

When boys think of heroes they don't think of those who amass millions or acquire notoriety. Boys are wiser than that. They cling to heroes who understand transcendence. But in today's world it can be hard for boys to find them, because the heroes offered to us by the media are so cheap and tawdry.

If you have doubts about your son's heroes, the men he imitates or reveres, and you want him to do better, find him a hero. Look around. What adult in his life is extraordinary? What man does he know who champions what is right and denounces what is wrong? Who sacrifices himself to benefit others?

When you open your eyes widely, you will find around you ordinary men and women who are remarkable. Talk about them in front of your son. Admire their attributes and tell their story. Don't wait until you find the perfect hero. Examples of courage, honesty, and self-control in people who grace his daily life are just as good when you admire those qualities in front of your son. Praise examples of such behavior often enough, reflect it in your own behavior, and you'll find that after a while your son will be emulating these virtues naturally.

A final word of caution is warranted. A boy needs a hero who is older than he is. There must be enough of an age difference that he can respect the hero as wiser and more seasoned. Boys never, ever benefit from being compared to their peers. Admiring a fellow teammate for the purpose of encouraging a boy how to live backfires. Regardless of how virtuous the other boy's behavior, your son will feel that you are comparing him to that boy. He will feel, since the other boy is successful, that he is a failure and resent what the other boy did right. Then he will flee from it.

Show him simple, heroic behavior and point to it in other adults. He won't be threatened as easily by others who are older than he is.

9) WATCH, THEN WATCH AGAIN

With the thousands of boys I have treated over the years, the answers to their problems are usually profoundly simple. We as parents miss the answers, because we don't pay enough attention to our sons.

Perhaps this is my mother's instinct, but I am impatient with adults who won't listen to their children. I know we have all been guilty of this—physicians, teachers, mothers, coaches, and fathers—but our kids pay a heavy price when we don't pay attention.

Colin first came to my practice when he was eleven. His mother brought him in because she was frustrated and confused. Colin was in the fifth grade at a private school and his grades were on a slow and steady decline. Since third grade she said his teachers had requested parent-teacher meetings to discuss his behavior and possible learning issues.

"His third-grade teacher first noticed his hyperactivity," she said. "That's when he started having to stay in for recess. His teacher told him that if he didn't behave he would lose his recess privileges."

(This is a common discipline enforced on boys—and it almost always backfires. Boys, particularly those with hyperactivity, need to move and teachers must find alternate ways to enforce discipline than bottling up his energy.)

As Colin's mother described how Colin's third-, fourth-, and fifth-grade teachers complained about him, Colin sat Indian-style on the exam room chair, his hat and coat on, absorbed in a Gameboy game.

"It was clear," she continued, "that he had ADHD. So I took him to his pediatrician and he gave him Adderall. I guess it worked. It quieted him down but he seemed like a different boy. He didn't want to eat; he didn't tell his ridiculous jokes. I felt like I lost a big part of him. His teachers noticed a big change too. They said he paid attention more. He raised his hand instead of interrupting. But something inside me was uncomfortable. I stopped his medicine. I know I shouldn't have, but I just wanted my Colin back." She looked at me a little pleadingly, acting guilty and confused.

Colin bent more tightly over his tiny computer screen, trying to disappear. He pulled his red knit ski cap over his ears.

"Colin," I asked, "what do you think about school?"

He didn't answer. His mother jabbed him with her elbow. "The doctor's talking to you; answer her."

"It's dumb," he said, without looking up.

"See," she said, "see what I mean. He's rude and when he's not sullen he's yelling or getting in trouble at school. The other day I knocked on his bedroom door, started to go in and before I got in the room he slammed the door on me. I tried to open it and he tied it shut. He's always making trouble!"

Colin didn't move.

I asked his mother more questions. What did Colin's father have to say? She told me that he was angry and thought Colin was acting spoiled. He would never have acted so badly as a kid, he told her. His own father wouldn't have stood for it.

During our first visit I learned that until second grade Colin was an easy, happy, rambunctious boy. Everyone at school loved him. During the summer between second and third grade his grandfather died suddenly of a stroke. Colin was staying overnight with him and his grandmother at the time. He went to bed one night, and when he woke the next morning his grandfather was gone.

Colin was crazy about his grandfather, she said. And because his grandfather was retired and always at home, Colin would often go to his house after school. They worked puzzles and he taught Colin to whittle spoons from a piece of wood.

After his grandfather died, Colin refused to visit his grandmother. The house was cursed, he said. He never spoke about his grandmother or his grandfather.

"We just left him alone," his mother said. "My husband and I would hear him crying in his room late at night. We didn't know what to say, we didn't know what to do so we just left him alone."

Colin's mother and father visited a family counselor several times at my request. His father didn't want to, saying that he didn't have a problem, his son did. I persuaded his father that he did have a problem—he had a problem with his son, and he, the dad, held the solution in his hands. When a child hurts, so do his parents, and there can be no resolution unless they're all involved.

The counselor was a quiet man in his mid-sixties. Colin's father said he reminded him of Colin's grandfather. The counselor gave Colin's dad tips on how to draw Colin out, especially how to make him more comfortable talking about his grandfather. Pay attention, he said, use a quieter tone of voice, ask a question and wait. If he answers, fine, but if he doesn't don't demand an answer.

Colin didn't have ADHD. He had unresolved grief over his grandfather's death. When his parents realized that his bad behavior reflected internal turmoil rather than defiance toward them, their attitude toward Colin changed.

His dad became more patient. He read to him at night and showed him more affection. He became the father to Colin that he had wanted his father to be to him when he was eleven years old: a bit less demanding, much more affectionate.

Within six months, Colin was a different boy. His grades sky-rocketed. He asked to take piano lessons. He told more ridiculous jokes and most important, he and his parents learned what really drove his "hyperactivity." It was sadness over losing a man he dearly loved.

10) GIVE HIM THE BEST OF YOURSELF

Boys are profoundly emotional creatures. In my experience many boys are more sensitive and more easily wounded than young girls. Sometimes we don't see it because boys guard their feelings more fiercely. No boy wants to be laughed at for crying in his fourth grade class. He will feel like a wimp. It's part of the "boy code"[1] not to let those emotions show. While bottling up deep emotions can sometimes be harmful to young boys, the truth is it can serve men well as they mature. Self-control is always a good thing. But there is a difference between manly self-control and boyish closure of his emotional self. Boys are not men. There is, or should be, an enormous difference between the way a man handles his emotions and the way a boy does. Our job is to watch our boys closely to ensure healthy transitions and emotional development.

It is fine for a boy to put on a brave face in front of his peers, but it is equally important that he feels he can sit down with his father in the study, or with his mom in the kitchen, and express his deep feelings, knowing he won't be ridiculed or rejected. Every boy needs this safety valve.

If Colin felt the comfort at home to cry in front of his father over his grandfather's death, nearly three years of school troubles could have been averted. Was his father negligent? No, not really. He just hadn't taken the time to really watch his son, and he didn't know how to address Colin's sadness.

Fathers, don't be afraid of your son's feelings. Yes, they are intense—and neither you nor he can successfully pretend that they're not. His bottled up feelings can actually make him behave and even move differently. He might punch, jump, or kick in unusual ways. His speech might change. His sleep habits could shift. He might pick new friends. That's how powerful his emotions are.

So teach him to acknowledge his feelings and understand them. Teach him that grief is natural. Teach him that feeling rejected when a girlfriend breaks up with him is normal. Be patient with him, but also teach him that the sense of grief and rejection are emotions to be acknowledged and moved beyond. Be ready to talk things through with him. Always keep your own questions simple and never force him to answer. Listen carefully to his responses. Watch his face as he talks, his body language. He is asking you to understand his message even though he doesn't quite understand what it is. The better a relationship you can build with your son, the more you are willing to sit down and give him your time, the better he will open up to you and ask permission to trust you. Say yes and mean it. When he divulges his deep thoughts or troubling feelings, don't ever criticize him. Listen. He will give you hints as to who he is and what he wants to be on the inside.

Boys who learn that their whole person—their abilities, behaviors, thoughts, and feelings—are taken seriously grow into confident, mature men. Every boy wants someone he loves and admires to look at him for more than a few moments out of every day. Because when he realizes that he is seen, he pays attention to what he is doing. He understands that in the eyes of the observer, if that observer is you, he is very important. Give this to the boy you love. Our sons deserve nothing more or less than the best of ourselves.

Raising a boy to be a man will be the toughest, most exasperating, painful work you will ever do. But the joy it brings is unmatched by anything else in your life. As I overheard a father say to his eighteen-year-old son when he tearfully dropped him off at college, "Let me tell you son. Seeing the man you have become at eighteen, well, for me, life just doesn't get any better than this."

Whether you are an asset manager, physician, teacher, or roofer, you know deep in your heart that success at work takes you only so far. It satisfies you; it makes you feel important. But you also know that at times it robs you from growing richer relationships with the ones you love. And for most of you, these relationships are the sources of real joy in your lives.

There is a boy who is waiting for you. Maybe he's two or perhaps he's twenty-two. He needs you to see him, to invest in him and then to teach him about life, work, and what his life is really all about. He needs you—his parent, grandparent, teacher, or mentor to take a risk for him. Love him fiercely because the world he sees is a confusing and painful one. It is his enemy and you are his ally. Show him that you are dangerous to that world because you take your responsibility for shaping his life very, very seriously. What are you waiting for?

Bibliography

"Adolescents are Key to Improving Sexual and Reproductive Health—the Lancet Adolescent Health Series." *Medical News Today*. March 27, 2007, October 30, 2007. Www.medical-newstoday.com.

"Boy Trouble." Editorial. *Boston Globe*. October 2, 2006, A10.

"Late-Breaking Father Facts." *Fatherhood Online*. National Fatherhood Initiative, 1994. November 7, 2005. Www.father-hood.org.

"Religiosity." Child Trends Databank. October 30, 2007. Www.childtrendsdatabank.org.

"Top Ten Father Facts." *Fatherhood Online*. National Fatherhood Initiative, 1994. November 7, 2005. Www.fatherhood.org.

—. "Effects of Violent Video Games on Aggressive Behavior, Aggressive Cognition, Aggressive Affect, Physiological Arousal, and Prosocial Behavior: A Meta-Analytic Review of the Scientific Literature." *Psychological Science* 12.5 (2001): 353-359.

—. "Inadvertent exposure to Pornography on the Internet: Implications of Peer-to-Peer File-Sharing Networks for Child Development and Families." *Applied Developmental Psychology* 25 (2004): 741-750.

—. *Boys Adrift* (New York: Basic Books, 2007).

—. *Driven to Distraction* (New York: Touchstone, 1995).

—. *The Hurried Child* (Cambridge: Da Capo, 2001).

—. *The Uses of Enchantment: The Meaning and Importance of Fairy Tales* (New York: Vintage, 1976).

—. *Why Gender Matters.* (New York: Broadway, 2005).

"Adolescent Alcohol Abuse, 10.4 Million Drinkers, USA." *Medical News Today,* August 15, 2005. Www.medicalnewstoday.com.

"Boys Will Be Men (For Parents & Teachers)," *Skipping Stones* 19.2 (March-April 2007): 32. Gale, Thomas, *General Reference Center Gold,* Hope College Library, July 3, 2007. Http://0-find.galegroup.com.lib.hope.edu.

"Involving Fathers In Children's ADHD Treatment Programs," *Medical News Today.* October 24, 2007. Www.medicalnewstoday.com.

"Juvenile Detention: Adolescents in Residential Placements," Child Trends Databank, October 30, 2007. Www.childtrendsdatabank.org.

"Pro-Social Activities and Attitudes." Child Trends Databank, October 30, 2007. Www.childtrendsdatabank.org.

"Psychological Bullying Hits Just As Hard," *Medical News Today,* May 28, 2007. Www.medicalnewstoday.com.

"Volunteering," Child Trends Databank, October 30, 2007. Www.childtrendsdatabank.org.

"Young Adults in Jail or Prison," Child Trends Databank, October 30, 2007. Www.childtrendsdatabank.org.

Allison, Paul D., and Frank F. Furstenberg, Jr., "How Marital Dissolution Affects Children: Variations by Age and Sex," *Developmental Psychology* 25.4 (1989): 540-549.

Almeida, David M., Elaine Wethington, and Daniel A. McDonald. "Daily Variation in Paternal Engagement and Negative Mood:

Implications for Emotionally Supportive and Conflictual Interactions," *Journal of Marriage and Family* 63 (2001): 417-429.

Anderson, Craig A., and Brad J. Bushman. "Effects of Violent
Video Games on Aggressive Behavior, Aggressive Cognition,
Aggressive Affect, Physiological Arousal, and Prosocial Behavior: A Meta-Analytic Review of the Scientific Literature." *Psychological Science* 12.5 (2001): 353-359.

Ashby, Sarah L., Christine M. Arcari, and M. Bruce Edmonson.
"Television Viewing and Risk of Sexual Initiation by Young
Adolescents." *Archives of Pediatric & Adolescent Medicine*
160.4 (2006): 375-380.

Ashtari, Manzar, Kelly L. Cervellione, Khader M. Hasan, Jinghui
Wu, Carolyn McIlree, Hana Kester, Babak A. Ardekani, David
Roofeh, Philip R. Szeszko, and Sanjiv Kumrad. "White Matter
Development during Late Adolescence in Healthy Males: A
Cross-Sectional Diffusion Tensor Imaging Study," *NeuroImage*
35.2 (2007): 501-510.

Ball, Marcia L., and Jennie A. Cerullo. *It Takes Courage!* (Har-
risonburg: Kerus, 2004).

Barber, Brian K., and Darwin L. Thomas. "Dimensions of Fathers'
and Mothers' Supportive Behavior: The Case for Physical
Affection," *Journal of Marriage and the Family* 48.4 (1986):
783-794.

Beaty, Lee A. "Effects of Paternal Absence on Male Adolescents'
Peer Relations and Self-Image," *Adolescence* 30.120 (1995):
873.

Bettelheim, Bruno. *A Good Enough Parent* (London: Thames,
1987).

Bettelheim, Bruno. *The Uses of Enchantment: The Meaning and
Importance of Fairytales* (New York: Vintage Books,1989).

Bickham, David S., and Michael Rich. "Is Television Viewing
Associated with Social Isolation?" *Archives of Pediatric and
Adolescent Medicine* 160 (2006): 387-392.

Biddulph, Steve. *Raising Boys* (Berkeley: Celestial, 1998).

Black, M. C., R. Noona, M. Legg, D. Eaton, and M.J. Breiding.
"Physical Dating Violence Among High School Students—

United States, 2003," *Morbidity and Mortality Weekly Report*
55.19 (2006):532-535.

Blakemore, Sarah-Jayne, and Suparna Choudhury. "Development
of the Adolescent Brain: Implications for Executive Function
and Social Cognition," *Journal of Child Psychology and Psychiatry* 47.3-4 (2006): 296-312.

Bradley, Robert H., Robert F. Corwyn, Margaret Burchinal, Harri-
ete Pipes McAdoo, and Cynthia Garcia Coll. "The Home
Environments of Children in the United States Part II: Relations with Behavioral Development through Age Thirteen,"
Child Development 72.6 (2001): 1868-1886.

Brown, Jane Delano, Kelly Ladin L'Engle, Carol J. Pardun, Guang
Guo, Kristin Kenneavy, and Christine Jackson. "Sexy Media
Matter: Exposure to Sexual Content in Music, Movies, Televi-
sion, and Magazines Predicts Black and White Adolescents'
Sexual Behavior," *Pediatrics* 117.4 (2006): 1018-1027.

Browne, Kevin D., and Catherine Hamilton-Giachritsis. "The
Influence of Violent Media on Children and Adolescents: A
Public-Health Approach," *Lancet* 365 (2005): 702-710.

Campbell, Andrew J., Steven R. Cumming, and Ian Hughes.
"Internet Use by the Socially Fearful: Addiction or Therapy?"
CyberPsychology and Behavior 9 (2006): 69-81.

Coles, Robert. *The Spiritual Life of Children.* (Boston: Houghton,
1990).

Committee on Adolescence. "Homosexuality and Adolescence,"
Pediatrics 92.4 (1993): 631-634.

Cotton, Sian, Elizabeth Larkin, Andrea Hoopes, Barbara A. Cromer,
and Susan L. Rosenthal. "The Impact of Adolescent Spirituality
on Depressive Symptoms and Health Risk Behaviors," *Journal
of Adolescent Health* 36.6 (2005): 529.e7-529.e14.

Coyne, Sarah M., Archer, John, and Mike Eslea. "'We're Not
Friends Anymore! Unless...': The Frequency and Harmfulness
of Indirect, Relational, and Social Aggression." *Aggressive
Behavior* 32.4 (2006): 294-307.

D'Angelo, Lori L., Daniel A. Weinberger, and S. Shirley Feldman.
"Like Father, Like Son? Predicting Male Adolescents' Adjust-

ment From Parents' Distress and Self-Restraint," *Developmental Psychology* 31.6 (1995): 883-896.

Dobson, James. *Bringing Up Boys* (Carol Stream, IL: Tyndale, 2001.

Dunn, Judy. "Annotation: Children's Relationships with their Nonresident Fathers," *Journal of Child Psychology and Psychiatry* 45.4 (2004): 659-671.

Eaton, Danice K., et. al. "Youth Risk Behavior Surveillance—United States, 2005," *Surveillance Summaries* 55.SS05 (2006): 1-108.

Eisenberg, Nancy, Qing Zhou, Sandra H. Losoya, Richard A. Fabes, Stephanie A. Shepard, Bridget C. Murphy, Mark Reiser, Ivanna K. Guthrie, and Amanda Cumberland. "The Relations of Parenting, Effortful Control, and Ego Control to Children's Emotional Expressivity," *Child Development* 74.3 (2003): 875-895.

Elkind, David. *All Grown Up and No Place to Go: Teenagers in Crisis*, Rev. ed. (Cambridge: Perseus, 1998).

Escobar-Chaves, S. Liliana, Susan R. Tortolero, Christine M. Markham, Barbara J. Low, Patricia Eitel, and Patricia Thickstun. "Impact of the Media on Adolescent Sexual Attitudes and Behaviors," *Pediatrics* 116 (2005).

Fagan, Patrick F. "Why Religion Matters Even More: the Impact of Religious Practice on Social Stability," *The Heritage Foundation Backgrounder* 1992 (2006). November 3, 2007, http://www.heritage.org/research/religion/bg1992.cfm.

Fairlie, Henry. *The Seven Deadly Sins Today* (Notre Dame, IN: University of Notre Dame Press, 1978).

Father Facts, Fifth Ed., National Fatherhood Initiative, 2007, www.fatherhood.org.

Feder, June, Ronald F. Levant, and James Dean. "Boys and Violence: A Gender Informed Study," *Professional Psychology: Research and Practice* 38.4 (2007): 385-391.

Feldman, Shirley S., and Kathryn R. Wentzel. "Relations of Marital Satisfaction to Peer Outcomes in Adolescent Boys: A Longitudinal Study," *The Journal of Early Adolescence* 15.2 (1995): 220-237.

Fergusson, David M., L. John Horwood, and Michael T. Lynskey. "Parental Separation, Adolescent Psychopathology, and Problem Behaviors," *Journal of the American Academy of Child and Adolescent Psychiatry* 33.8 (1994): 1122-1131.

Fleming, Douglas T., Geraldine M. McQuillan, Robert E. Johnson, Andre J. Nahmias, Sevgi O. Aral, Francis K. Lee, and Michael E. St. Louis. "Herpes Simplex Virus Type 2 in the United States, 1976 to 1994," *The New England Journal of Medicine* 337.16 (1997).

Fletcher, Anne C., Laurence Steinberg, and Meeshay Williams-Wheeler. "Parental Influences on Adolescent Problem Behavior: Revisiting Stattin and Kerr," *Child Development* 75.3 (2004): 781-796.

Forehand, Rex, Bryan Neighbors, and Michelle Wierson. "The Transition to Adolescence: the Role of Gender and Stress in Problem Behavior and Competence," *Journal of Child Psychology and Psychiatry* 32.6 (1991): 929-937.

Frankl, V. *Man's Search For Meaning* (Boston: Beacon Press, 2006).

Frosh, Stephen, Ann Phoenix, and Rob Pattman. "Struggling Towards Manhood: Narratives of Homophobia and Fathering," *British Journal of Psychotherapy* 22.1 (2005): 37-55.

Galambos, Nancy L., Erin T. Barker, and David M. Almeida. "Parents *Do* Matter: Trajectories of Change in Externalizing and Internalizing Problems in Early Adolescence," *Child Development* 74.2 (2003): 578-594.

Galvan, Adriana, et al. "Earlier Development of the Accumbens Relative to Orbitofrontal Cortex Might Underlie Risk-Taking Behavior in Adolescents," *The Journal of Neuroscience* 26.25 (2006): 6885-6892.

Galvan, Adriana, Todd A. Hare, Matthew Davidson, Julie Spicer, Gary Glover, and B. J. Casey. "The Role of Ventral Frontostriatal Circuitry in Reward-Based Learning in Humans," *The Journal of Neuroscience* 25.38 (2005): 8650-8656.

Gecas, Viktor, and Michael L. Schwalbe. "Parental Behavior and Adolescent Self-Esteem," *Journal of Marriage and the Family* 48.1 (1986): 37-46.

Giedd, Jay N., et al. "Puberty-Related Influences on Brain Development," *Molecular and Cellular Endocrinology* 254-255 (2006): 154-162.

Giedd, Jay N., Jonathan Blumenthal, Neal O. Jeffries, F. X. Castellanos, Hong Liu, Alex Zijdenbos, Tomás Paus, Alan C. Evans, and Judith L. Rapoport. "Brain Development during Childhood and Adolescence: A Longitudinal MRI Study," *Nature Neuroscience* 2.10 (1999): 861-863.

Giorgio, A., et al. "Changes in White Matter Microstructure during Adolescence," *NeuroImage* 39.1 (2007): 52-61.

Greenfield, Patricia M. "Inadvertent Exposure to pornography on the Internet: Implications of peer-to-peer file-sharing networks for child development and families," *Applied Developmental Psychology* 25 (2004), p.741-750

Greenfield, Patricia M. "Developmental Considerations for Determining Appropriate Internet Use Guidelines for Children and Adolescents," *Applied Developmental Psychology* 25 (2004): 751-762.

Grossman, Frances K., William S. Pollack, Ellen R. Golding, and Nicolina M. Fedele. "Affiliation and Autonomy in the Transition to Parenthood," *Family Relations* 36.3 (1987): 263-269.

Gurian, Michael. *The Wonder of Boys* (New York: Penguin, 2006).

Hall, Judith A. "Gender Effects in Decoding Nonverbal Cues," *Psychological Bulletin* 85.4 (1978): 845-857.

Hallfors, Denise D., Martha W. Waller, Daniel Bauer, Carol A. Ford, and Carolyn T. Halpern. "Which Comes First in Adolescence—Sex and Drugs or Depression?" *American Journal of Preventive Medicine* 29.3 (2005): 163-170.

Hallowell, Edward M., and John J. Ratey. *Delivered from Distraction* (New York: Ballantine, 2005).

Hardy, Sam A., and Marcela Raffaelli. "Adolescent Religiosity and Sexuality: An Investigation of Reciprocal Influences," *Journal of Adolescence* 26 (2003): 731-739.

Hartley-Brewer, Elizabeth. *Raising Confident Boys* (Cambridge: Fisher, 2001).

Hedges, Larry V., and Amy Nowell. "Sex Differences in Mental Test Scores, Variability, and Numbers of High-Scoring Individuals," *Science* 269.5220 (1995): 41-45.

Heintz-Knowles, Katharine, Meredith Li-Vollmer, Perry Chen, Tarana Harris, Adrienne Haufler, Joan Lapp, and Patti Miller. "Boys to Men: Entertainment Media Messages About Masculinity: a National Poll of Children, Focus Groups, and Content Analysis of Entertainment Media, *Children Now* (Oakland: Children Now, 1999), Fall 2007, www.childrennow. org.

Hofferth, Sandra L., and John F. Sandberg. "How American Children Spend Their Time," *Journal of Marriage and Family* 63 (2001): 295-308.

Holder, David W., Robert H. Durant, Treniece L. Harris, Jessica Henderson Daniel, Dawn Obeidallah, and Elizabeth Goodman. "The Association between Adolescent Spirituality and Voluntary Sexual Activity," *Journal of Adolescent Health* 26 (2000): 295-302.

Horn, Wade F. "U.S. Statement on Families." United Nations. 10th Anniversary of the International Year of the Family (New York: United Nations, December 6, 2004). Www.fatherhood.org.

Horn, Wade F., and Tom Sylvester. "Father Facts: Research Notes," *Fatherhood Online*, National Fatherhood Initiative, 1994, www.fatherhood.org.

Houston, Fiona. "The War on Boys (New Education Laws) (Special Men's Health Section)," *Men's Health* 9.8 (1994): 108.

Hymowitz, Kay S. "Parenting: The Lost Art," *American Educator* 25.1 (2001): 4-9. February 8, 2006. Www.aft.org/pubs-reports/american_educator/spring2001/parenting.html.

Jacklin, Carol Nagy. "Female and Male: Issues of Gender," *American Psychologist* 44.2 (1989): 127-133.

Jenkins, Henry. "Congressional Testimony on Media Violence," MIT Communications Forum. May 4, 1999, http://web.mit.edu/comm-forum/papers/jenkins_ct.html.

John P. Murray, Mario Liotti, Paul T. Ingmundson, Helen S. Mayberg, Yonglin Pu, Frank Zamarripa, Yijun Liu, Marty G.

Woldorff, Jia-Hong Gao, and Peter T. Fox. "Children's Brain Activations While Viewing Televised Violence Revealed by fMRI," *Media Psychology* 8.1 (2006): 25-37.

Johnson, Miriam M. "Heterosexuality, Male Dominance, and the Father Image," *Sociological Inquiry* 51.2 (1981): 129-139.

Johnston, Charlotte, Mandy Chen, and Jeneva Ohan. "Mothers' Attributions for Behavior in Nonproblem Boys, Boys with Attention Deficit Hyperactivity Disorder, and Boys with Attention Deficit Hyperactivity Disorder and Oppositional Defiant Behavior," *Journal of Clinical Child and Adolescent Psychology* 35.1 (2006): 60-71.

Johnston, Charlotte. "Parent Characteristics and Parent-Child Interactions in Families of Nonproblem Children and ADHD Children with Higher and Lower Levels of Oppositional-Defiant Behavior," *Journal of Abnormal Child Psychology* 24.1 (1996): 85-104.

Jones, Susanne M., and Kathryn Dindia. "A Meta-Analytic Perspective on Sex the Classroom," *Review of Educational Research* 74.4 (2004): 443-471.

Kagan, Jerome. "The Role of Parents in Children's Psychological Development," *Pediatrics* 104.1 (1999): 164-167.

Kaiser Family Foundation, "Sex On TV4 Executive Summary 2005,"1-15. Www.kff.org/entmedia/upload/sex-on-TV-4Executive-summary.pdf.

Kasen, Stephanie, Patricia Cohen, Judith S. Brook, and Claudia Hartmark. "A Multiple-Risk Interaction Model: Effects of Temperament and Divorce on Psychiatric Disorders in Children," *Journal of Abnormal Child Psychology 24.2 (1996): 121-150.*

Kendrick, Carleton. Interview. *Family Education*, Fall 2007, http://life.familyeducation.com.

Kessler, Ronald C., and James A. McRae, Jr. "Trends in the Relationship Between Sex and Psychological Distress: 1957-1976." *American Sociological Review* 46 (1981): 443-452.

Kindlon, Dan, and Michael Thompson. *Raising Cain: Protecting the Emotional Life of Boys* (New York: Ballantine, 2000).

Kleinfeld, Judith. *The Myth That Schools Shortchange Girls: Social Science in the Service of Deception*. Dept. of Psych., U of Alaska. Washington D.C.: The Women's Freedom Network, 1998.

Kraut, Robert E., Michael Patterson, Vicki Lundmark, Sara Kiesler, Tridas Mukophadhyay, and William Scherlis. "Internet Paradox: A Social Technology that Reduces Social Involvement and Psychological Well-Being?" *American Psychologist* 53.9 (1998): 1017-1031.

Kreeft, Peter. *Socrates Meets Jesus* (Downer's Grove, IL: Intervarsity Press),1987.

Kronenberger, W. G., V. P. Mathews, D. W. Dunn, Y. Wang, E. A. Wood, A. L. Giauque, J. J. Larsen, M. E. Rembusch, M. J. Lowe, and T. Li. "Media Violence Exposure and Executive Functioning in Aggressive and Control Adolescents," *Journal of Clinical Psychology* 61.6 (2005): 725-737.

Krosnick, Jon A., Sowmya Narayan Anand, and Scott P. Hartl. "Psychosocial Predictors of Heavy Television Viewing Among Preadolescents and Adolescents," *Basic and Applied Social Psychology* 25.2 (2003): 87-110.

Lenroot, Roshel K., and Jay N. Giedd. "Brain Development in Children and Adolescents: Insights from Anatomical Magnetic Resonance Imaging," *Neuroscience and Biobehavioral Reviews* 30 (2006): 718-729.

Lewin, Tamar. "Boys are No Match for Girls in Completing High Schooll," *New York Times*, April 19, 2006.

Lewis, C. S. *The Quotable Lewis*. Ed. Wayne Martindale and Jerry Root (Wheaton: Tyndale, 1990).

Lickona, Thomas. "Educating for Character in the Sexual Domain." State University of New York At Cortland. Second International Congress on Education in Love, Sex, and Life, Manila, Philippines, November 20, 2007, www.cortland.edu/character/sex_character/articles_sc.html.

Maccoby, Eleanor E. "Gender and Relationships: A Developmental Account," *American Psychologist* 45.4 (1990): 513-520.

Mahoney, Annette, Kenneth I. Pargament, Nalini Tarakeshwar, and Aaron B. Swank. "Religion in the Home in the 1980s and 1990s: A Meta-Analytic Review and Conceptual Analysis of

Links between Religion, Marriage, and Parenting," *Journal of Family Psychology* 15.4 (2001):559-596.

Mannuzza, Salvatore, Rachel G. Klein, Abrah Bessler, Patricia Malloy, and Mary E. Hynes. "Educational and Occupational Outcome of Hyperactive Boys Grown Up," *Journal of the American Academy of Child and Adolescent Psychiatry* 36.9 (1997): 1222-1227.

Mansfield, Harvey. *Manliness* (New Haven: Yale University Press, 2006).

Mansfield, Harvey. "The Manliness of Men," *The American Enterprise* 14.6 (2003): 32-34.

Markstrom, Carol A. "Religious Involvement and Adolescent Psychosocial Development," *Journal of Adolescence* 22 (1999): 205-221.

Mathur, Ravisha, and Thomas J. Berndt. "Relations of Friends' Activities to Friendship Quality," *The Journal of Early Adolescence* 26 (2006): 365-388.

Mead, Sara. "The Truth about Boys and Girls," *Education Sector*, June 27, 2006, www.educationsector.org.

Meeker, Meg. *Your Kids At Risk: How Teen Sex Threatens Our Sons and Daughters* (Washington, D.C.: Regnery Publishing, 2007).

Milevsky, Avidan, and Mary J. Levitt. "Intrinsic and extrinsic religiosity in preadolescence and adolescence: Effect on psychological adjustment," *Mental Health, Religion & Culture* 7.4 (2004): 307-321.

Murray, John P. "TV Violence and Brainmapping in Children," *Psychiatric Times* 18.10 (2001): 70-71.

Murray, John P., et al. "Children's Brain Activations While Viewing Televised Violence Revealed by fMRI," Mind Science Foundation, http://www.mindscience.org/murray_mediapsych.html.

National Fatherhood Initiative. *Father Facts 5*. Comp. Jamin Warren. 5th ed. National Fatherhood Initiative, 2007.

National Institute of Mental Health, National Institutes of Health, Department of Health and Human Services. "Teenage Brain: a Work in Progress," 2001, www.nimh.nih.gov/publicat/teen-brain.crm.

Nicholi, Armand M., Jr., ed. *The New Harvard Guide to Psychiatry* (Cambridge: Harvard University Press, 1988).

Nolen-Hoeksema, Susan, and Joan S. Girgus. "The Emergence of Gender Differences in Depression During Adolescence," *Psychological Bulletin* 115.3 (1994): 424-443.

O'Donnell, Lydia, Ann Stueve, Gail Agronick, Renee Wilson-Simmons, Richard Duran, and Varzi Jeanbaptiste. "Saving Sex for Later: An Evaluation of a Parent Education Intervention," *Perspectives on Sexual and Reproductive Health* 37.4 (2005): 166-173.

Olson, Cheryl K., Lawrence A. Kutner, Dorothy E. Warner, Jason B. Almerigi, Lee Baer, Armand M. Nicholi II, and Eugene V. Beresin. "Factors Correlated with Violent Video Game Use by Adolescent Boys and Girls," *Journal of Adolescent Health* 41 (2007): 77-83.

Ostrov, Jamie M., Douglas A. Gentile, and Nicki R. Crick. "Media Exposure, Aggression and Prosocial Behavior during Early Childhood: A Longitudinal Study," *Social Development* 15.4 (2006): 612-627.

Parmelee, Dean X., ed. *Child and Adolescent Psychiatry,* Mosby's Neurology Psychiatry Access Ser. (St. Louis: Mosby, 1996).

Peretti, Peter O., and Anthony DiVitorrio. "Effects of Loss of Father Through Divorce on Personality of the Preschool Child," *Social Behavior and Personality* 21.1 (1993): 33-38.

Perie, Marianne, Rebecca Moran, and Anthony D. Lutkus. *NAEP 2004 Trends in Academic Progress: Three Decades of Student Performance in Reading and Mathematics(NCES 2005-464).* U.S. Department of Education, Institute of Education Sciences, National Center for Education Statistics (Washington D.C.: Government Printing Office, 2005). Http://nces.ed.gov/Pubsearch/pubsinfo.asp?pubid=2005464.

Pollack, William S. "Male Adolescent Rites of Passage," *Annals New York Academy of Sciences* 1036 (2004): 141-150.

Pollack, William. *Real Boys* (New York: Owl, 1998).

Pruett, Kyle D. "Role of the Father," *Pediatrics* 102.5 (1998): 1253-1261.

Resnick, Michael, et. al. "Protecting Adolescents From Harm: Findings From the National Longitudinal Study on Adolescent Health," *Journal of the American Medical Association* 278.10 (1997): 823-831.

Richardson, Stacey, and Marita P. McCabe. "Parental Divorce During Adolescence and Adjustment in Early Adulthood," *Adolescence* 36.143 (2001): 467-489.

Rideout, Victoria, Donald F. Roberts, and Ulla G. Foehr. *Generation M: Media in the Lives of 8-18 Year-Olds*, Kaiser Family Foundation (Washington, D.C.: Kaiser Family Foundation, 2005) 1-40. Http://www.kff.org/entmedia/7250.cfm.

Rivers, Caryl, and Rosalind C. Barnett. "The Myth of 'The Boy Crisis,'" *Washington Post*, April 9, 2006, www.washington-post.com.

Roeser, Robert W., Jacquelynne S. Eccles, and Arnold J. Sameroff. "School as a Context of Early Adolescents' Academic and Social-Emotional Development: A Summary of Research Findings," *The Elementary School Journal* 100.5 (2000): 443-471.

Rohde, Paul, John R. Seeley, and David E. Mace. "Correlates of Suicidal Behavior in a Juvenile Detention Population," *Suicide and Life-Threatening Behavior* 27.2 (1997): 164-175.

Rostosky, Sharon Scales, Brian L. Wilcox, Margaret Laurie Comer Wright, and Brandy A. Randall. "The Impact of Religiosity on Adolescent Sexual Behavior: A Review of the Evidence," *Journal of Adolescent Research* 19 (2004): 677-697.

Sanders, Christopher E., Tiffany M. Field, Miguel Diego, and Michele Kaplan. "The Relationship of Internet Use to Depression and Social Isolation among Adolescents," *Adolescence* 35.138 (2000): 237-242.

Sax, Leonard. "The Boy Problem," *School Library Journal* (2007): 40-43. Fall 2007, www.slj.com.

Seipp, Carla M., and Charlotte Johnston. "Mother-Son Interactions in Families of Boys with Attention-Deficit/hyperactivity Disorder with and without Oppositional Behavior," *Journal of Abnormal Child Psychology* 33.1 (2005): 87-98.

Silveria, Marisa M., Michael L. Rohan, Patricia J. Pimentel, Staci
     A. Gruber, Isabelle M. Rosso, and Deborah A. Yurgelun-
     Todda. "Sex Differences in the Relationship between White
     Matter Microstructure and Impulsivity in Adolescents," *Mag-
     netic Resonance Imaging* 24 (2006): 833-841.
Sinha, Jill W., Ram A. Cnaan, and Richard J. Gelles. "Adolescent
     Risk Behaviors and Religion: Findings from a National Study,"
     Journal of Adolescence 30 (2007): 231-249.
Slater, Michael D., Kimberly L. Henry, Randall C. Swaim, and Joe
     M. Cardador. "Vulnerable Teens, Vulnerable Times: How Sen-
     sation Seeking, Alienation, and Victimization Moderate the
     Violent Media Content-Aggressiveness Relation," *Communica-
     tion Research* 31.6 (2004): 642-668.
Smalley, Gary, and John Trent. *The Blessing* (Nashville: Thomas
     Nelson, 1986).
Smith, Christian, and Melinda Lundquist Denton. *Soul Searching:
     The Religious and Spiritual Lives of American Teenagers* (New
     York: Oxford University Press, 2005).
Smith, Christian, and Robert Faris. *Religion and American Adoles-
     cent Delinquency, Risk Behaviors and Constructive Social
     Activities*, Department of Sociology, University of North Car-
     olina, Chapel Hill: National Study of Youth and Religion,
     2002, 1-65. Autumn 2007, www.youthandreligion.org.
Sommers, Christina Hoff. *The War Against Boys* (New York:
     Simon & Schuster, 2000).
Sowell, Elizabeth R., Paul M. Thompson, Colin J. Holmes, Terry
     L. Jernigan, and Arthur W. Toga. "In Vivo Evidence for Post-
     Adolescent Brain Maturation in Frontal and Striatal Regions,"
     Nature Neuroscience 2.10 (1999): 859-861.
Stahl, Lesley. "The Gender Gap: Boys Lagging, Girls Move
     Ahead," CBS News, May 25, 2003, www.CBSNews.com.
Steinberg, Laurence. "Cognitive and Affective Development in Ado-
     lescence," *TRENDS in Cognitive Sciences* 9.2 (2005): 69-74.
Stevenson, Michael R., and Kathryn N. Black. "Paternal Absence
     and Sex-Role Development: A Meta-Analysis," *Child Develop-
     ment* 59.3 (1988): 793-814.

Strasburger, Victor C., and Barbara J. Wilson. *Children, Adolescents, & the Media* (Thousand Oaks, CA: Sage, 2002).

Strasburger, Victor C., and Edward Donnerstein. "Children, Adolescents, and the Media: Issues and Solutions," *Pediatrics* 103.1 (1999): 129-139.

Subrahmanyam, Kaveri, Patricia Greenfield, Robert Kraut, and Elisheva Gross. "The Impact of Computer Use on Children's and Adolescents' Development," *Applied Developmental Psychology* 22 (2001): 7-30.

Subrahmanyam, Kaveri, Robert E. Kraut, Patricia M. Greenfield, and Elisheva F. Gross. "The Impact of Home Computer Use on Children's Activities and Development," *The Future of Children* 10.2 (2000): 123-144.

Teihard de Chardin, Pierre. *Toward the Future* (New York: Harcourt Brace, 1975).

Trends in Reportable Sexually Transmitted Diseases in the United States, 2005. U.S. Department of Health and Human Services, Center for Disease Control and Prevention (Washington, D.C.: Government Printing Office, 2006), http://www.cdc.gov/STD/stats05/trends2005.htm.

Tronick, Edward Z., and Jeffery F. Cohn. "Infant-Mother Face-to-Face Interaction: Age and Gender Differences in Coordination and the Occurrence of Miscoordination," *Child Development* 60 (1989):85-92.

Uhlmann, Eric, and Jane Swanson. "Exposure to Violent Video Games Increases Automatic Aggressiveness." *Journal of Adolescence* 27 (2004): 41-52.

United States. National Institutes of Mental Health. National Institutes of Health. *Let's Talk About Depression*, June 2001, www.nimh.nih.gov/publicat/letstalk.cfm.

United States. Surgeon General. Department of Health and Human Services. *Executive Summary Youth Violence: a Report of the Surgeon General,* October 30, 2007, www.surgeongeneral.gov/library/youthviolence/summary.htm.

Villani, Susan M. D. "Impact of Media on Children and Adolescents: A 10-Year Review of the Research," *Journal of the*

American Academy of Child and Adolescent Psychiatry 40.4 (2001): 392-401.

Walker, Lawrence J., Karl H. Hennig, and Tobias Krettenauer. "Parent and Peer Contexts for Children's Moral Reasoning Development," *Child Development* 71.4 (2000): 1033-1048.

Watts, Randolph H., Jr., and L. DiAnne Borders. "Boys' Perceptions of the Male Role: Understanding Gender Role Conflict in Adolescent Males," *The Journal of Men's Studies* 13.2 (2005): 267-280.

Wenk, DeeAnn, Constance L. Hardesty, Carolyn S. Morgan, and Sampson Lee Blair. "The Influence of Parental Involvement on the Well-Being of Sons and Daughters." *Journal of Marriage and the Family* 56.1 (1994): 229-234.

Werner, Nicole E., and Nicki R. Crick. "Maladaptive Peer Relationships and the Development of Relational and Physical Aggression during Middle Childhood," *Social Development* 13.4 (2004): 495-514.

Wolak, Janis, Kimberly J. Mitchell, and David Finkelhor. "Escaping or Connecting? Characteristics of Youth who Form Close Online Relationships," *Journal of Adolescence* 26.1 (2003): 105-119.

Youniss, James, Jeffrey A. McLellan, and Miranda Yates. "Religion, Community Service, and Identity in American Youth," *Journal of Adolescence* 22 (1999): 243-253.

Zacharias, Ravi. *Can Man Live Without God* (Dallas: Word, 1994).

Special Thanks

I WOULD LIKE TO EXTEND my deep appreciation to my wonderful family for your patience during my long hours of writing.

To my mother, Mary, thank you for your constant love, support and encouragement. You are a woman of great courage and fortitude.

To Marji Ross at Regnery, thank you for believing in my work. To Harry Crocker, thank you for your great ideas and editing. To Kate Frantz, I appreciate your editing as well and your patience with me.

Thank you Jeff Carneal for giving me another opportunity to write for an extraordinary company.

To my fabulous research assistants: Charlotte Meeker, Amy Pardini, Amber Wagner and Kara Francisco, thank you for your fastidious work.

Finally, thank you Anne Mann, for your loyalty and hard work, you are a great friend indeed.

Notes

Chapter One: Boyhood under Siege

1. "Trends In Education Equity of Girls and Women: 2004," *Education Statistics Quarterly*: Vol 6, Issue 4, 2004, 3.

2. Attention Deficit Hyperactivity Disorder, http//www.cdc.gov/ncbddd/adhd/dadabepi.htm.

3. Tamar Lewin, "Boys Are No Match for Girls In Completing High School," *New York Times*, April 19, 2006.

4. Sterling Lloyd, "Gender Gap In Graduation," *Education Week*, July 6, 2007. Http//www.edweek.org/rc/articles/2007/07/05/sow0705.h26.html.

5. "Trends In Education Equity of Girls and Women: 2004," *The Education Statistics Quarterly*: Vol 6, Issue 4, 2004, 9.

6. Ibid., 10.

7. Morbidity Mortality Weekly review, Surveillance Summaries June 2006/55(SS05); 1-108 "Youth Risk Behavior Surveillance",2005, 12.

8. Ibid., 7.

9. Ibid., 18.

10. Ibid., 23.

11. Ibid.,17.

12. Ibid., 22

13. Ibid., 8.

14. Ibid., 10.

15. Ibid., 8.

16. Ibid., 25.

17. Ibid., 26.

18. Ibid.

19. Ibid., 34.

20. Ibid., 32.

21. Fleming, D. "Herpes Simplex Virus Type 2 In the United States, 1976 to 1994," *The New England Journal of Medicine*, 1997;337:1105-1111.

22. Bonin, Liza. "Depression In Adolescents: Epidemiology, Clinical manifestations and diagnosis." UpToDate Online 15.3, http//www.utdol.com/utd/content/topic.do?topicKey=adol_med/3630&linkTitle=EPIDEMIOLOGY&source=preview&selectedTitle=4~40anchor=2#2.

23. National Fatherhood Initiative. *Father Facts 5*. Comp. Jamin Warren. 5th ed. National Fatherhood Initiative, 2007,114.

24. Smith, Christian and Faris, Robert. "Religion and American Adolescent Delinquency, Risk Behaviors and Constructive Social Activities," National Studies of Youth and Religion, 2002, 20.

25. Hardy, Sam A. and Raffaelli. "Adolescent Religiosity and Sexuality: an Investigation of reciprocal Influences," *Journal of Adolescence* 26(2003), 731.

26. Smith, Christian, and Melinda Lundquist Denton. *Soul Searching: The Religious and Spiritual Lives of American Teenagers*. (New York: Oxford University Press, 2005), 222.

27. Ibid., 241.

28. Ibid., 152.

29. Ibid., 153.

30. Ibid., 151.

31. Ibid., 152.

32. Ibid., 153.

33. Cotton, Sian, Elizabeth Larkin, Andrea Hoopes, Barbara A. Cromer, and Susan L. Rosenthal. "The Impact of Adolescent Spirituality on Depressive Symptoms and Health Risk Behaviors." *Journal of Adolescent Health* 36.6 (2005): 529e.

34. Smith, Christian, and Melinda Lundquist Denton. *Soul Searching: The Religious and Spiritual Lives of American Teenagers.* (New York: Oxford University Press, 2005), 151.

35. Ibid., 225.

36. Ibid., 243-245

Chapter Four: Electronic Matters

1. Victoria Rideout, Donald F. Roberts, and Ulla G. Foehr. *Generation M: Media in the Lives of 8-18 Year-Olds.* (Washington D.C.: Kaiser Family Foundation, 2005), 7. Http://www.kff.org/entmedia/7250.cfm.

2. Ibid., 6-7.

3. *Pediatrics*, Vol 120 No. 5 Nov 2007, 993-999.

4. Murray, John P., et al. "Children's Brain Activations While Viewing Televised Violence Revealed by fMRI," Mind Science Foundation, 1-2, http://www.mindscience.org/murray_mediapsych.html.

5. Kevin D. Browne and Catherine Hamilton-Giachritis. "The Influence of violent media on children and adolescents: a public-health approach," *Lancet*; 2005, 708.

6. Ibid., 14-15.

7. Anderson, Craig A., Bushman, Brad. "Effects of Violent Video Games on Aggressive Behavior, Aggressive Cognition, Aggressive Affect, Physiological Arousal, and Prosocial Behavior: A Meta-Analytic Review of the Scientific Literature" *Psychological Science*, Vol 12, No 5, September 2001, 357.

8. Ibid., 358.

9. Ibid.

10. Ibid.

11. Patricia Greenfield, "Developmental Considerations for determining appropriate Internet use guidelines for children and adolescents," *Applied Developmental Psychology*, 25 (2004), 755.

12. "Sex on TV 4," Executive Summary, Kaiser Family Foundation, 2005, 4. Www.kff.org/entmedia/upload/sex-on-TV-4Executive-summary.pdf.

13. Ibid., 4.

14. Ibid.

15. Ibid., 5.

16. Ibid., 2.

17. Ibid., 4-11

18. Ibid., 9.

19. Meg Meeker, *Your Kids At Risk: How Teen Sex Threatens Our Sons and Daughters* (Washington, D.C.: Regnery Publishing,) 2007, 31.

20. Patricia M. Greenfield, "Inadvertent Exposure to pornography on the Internet: Implications of peer-to-peer file-sharing networks for child development and families." *Applied Developmental Psychology* 25 (2004), 745.

21. Ibid., 745-746.

22. Ibid., 741.

23. Ibid., 744.

Chapter Five: Does Testosterone Drive Cars?

1. Armand M. Nicholi, Jr., ed. *The New Harvard Guide to Psychiatry* (Cambridge: Harvard University Press, 1988), 654.

2. Bruno Bettelheim, *A Good Enough* Parent (London: Thames, 1987), 312.

3. Lickona, Thomas. "Educating for Character in the Sexual Domain." State University of New York At Cortland. Second International Congress on Education in Love, Sex, and Life. Manila, Philippines. 20 Nov. 2007. Winter 2007, 25, www.cortland.edu/character/sex_character/articles_sc.html.

4. Nolen-Hoeksema, S and Girgus, Joan S. "The Emergence of Gender Differences in Depression During Adolescence," *Psychological Bulletin* 1994, Vol 115, No 3., 424.

5. Denise D. Hallfors, Martha W. Waller, Daniel Bauer, Carol A. Ford, and Carolyn T. Halpern. "Which Comes First in Adolescence—Sex and

Drugs or Depression?"*American Journal of Preventive Medicine* 29.3
(2005): 163.

6. Source: Depression in Adolescents: Epidemiology, Clinical
Manifestations, and Diagnosis, Liza Bonin, PhD. UptoDate Online 15.3.
http//www.utdol.com/utd/content/topic.do?topicKey=adol_med/3630&sel
ectedTitle=8~150&source=search_restt.

7. Ibid.

8. Parmelee, Dean X., ed. *Child and Adolescent Psychiatry.* Mosby's
Neurology Psychiatry Access Ser. St. Louis: Mosby, 1996, 215.

9. "Research Facts and Findings," *Adolescent Brain Development,* May
2002, 1. Http://www.human.cornell.edu/actforyouth.

Chapter Six: Encouragement, Mastery, and Competition

1. Bruno Bettelheim, *A Good Enough Parent* (London: Thames, 1987),
284.

2. Bruno Bettelheim, *The Uses of Enchantment: The Meaning and
Importance of Fairytales* (New York: Random House, 1989).

3. Bruno Bettelheim, *A Good Enough Parent,* 285.

Chapter Seven: A Mother's Son

1. Bruno Bettelheim, *A Good Enough Parent* (London: Thames, 1987),
294.

Chapter Eight: The Difference a Dad Makes

1. "Dimensions of Fathers' and Mothers' Supportive Behavior: the Case
for Physical Affection," *Journal of Marriage and Family* 48 (Nov 1986)
783–794. "Household Relationship and Living Arrangements of Children
Under 18 Years by Age, Sex, Race, Hispanic Origin: 2004; All Races,
White Only, Black only, and Hispanic only." U.S. Census Bureau. Current
Population Survey Reports Table C2. July 2005. Http//www.census.gov/
population/socdemo/hh-fam/cps2004/tabC2-all.csv.

2. Gallup, George."Report on Status of Fatherhood In the United
States." *Emerging Trends,* 20 (sept 1998): 3–5. Princeton Religion
Research Center, Princeton, NJ.

3. Kreider, Rose M and Jason Fields. Living Arrangements of Children: 2001. Current Population reports, 70-104. Table 1. Washington, D.C: US Census Bureau, 2005; Fields, Jason. The Living Arrangements of Children: Fall 1996. Current Population reports, p70-74. Internet Table 1. Washington, DC: US Census Bureau, 2001.

4. Report of Final Natality Statistics, 1996," monthly Vital Statistics Report 46, no.11, Supplement (Washington, D.C.: U.S. Dept. of Health and Human Services, June 30, 1998); see also,Father Facts, Fifth Ed, National Fatherhood Initiative, 2007 www.fatherhood.org.

5. Father Facts, Fifth Ed, National Fatherhood Initiative, 2007, 125. Www.fatherhood.org.

6. Ibid., 127.

7. Ibid., 129.

8. Ibid., 124–143.

9. Gary Smalley and John Trent. *The Blessing* (Nashville: Thomas Nelson, 1986).

10. Rebecca Gardyn, "Make Room for Daddy," *American Demographics* June 2000:34-35.

11. *Father Facts*, Fifth Ed, National Fatherhood Inititiative, 2007, 159-163.

12. William Pollack, *Real Boys* (New York: Owl, 1998), 115.

13. Ibid., 121.

14. Ibid.

15. Shawn Johnston, *The Pittsburgh Tribune Review*, March 29, 1998. See also: *Father Facts*, Fifth Ed., National Fatherhood Initiative, 2007, 127.

Chapter Nine: The Forgotten Step from Boyhood to Manhood

1. Rudyard Kipling, *If*. Http://www.everypoet.com/archive/poetry/Rudyard_Kipling/kipling_if.htm.

2. Ibid.

Chapter Ten: The God Factor

1. Robert Coles, *The Spiritual Life of* Children (Boston: Houghton,1990).

2. Sian Cotton, Elizabeth Larkin, Andrea Hoopes, Barbara A. Cromer, and Susan L. Rosenthal. "The Impact of Adolescent Spirituality on

Depressive Symptoms and Health Risk Behaviors." *Journal of Adolescent Health* 36.6 (2005): 529.e10.

3. Valerie King, "The Influence of Religion on Fathers' Relationships with Their Children," *Journal of Marriage and Family*, Vol. 65, No. 2 (May 2003).

4. Ibid.

5. Ibid.

6. Jill W. Sinha, Ram A. Canaan, and Richard J. Gelles. "Adolescent Risk Behaviors and Religion: Findings from a National Study." *Journal of Adolescence* 30 (2007): 246.

7. Ibid., 232.

8. Ibid.

9. Christian Smith and Melinda Lundquist Denton. *Soul Searching: The Religious and Spiritual Lives of American Teenagers.* (New York: Oxford University Press, 2005), 31.

10. Ibid., 37-39.

11. Blaise Pascal, *Pensées* (New York: Penguin, 1995).

12. Viktor E. Frankl, *Man's Search for Meaning* (Boston: Beacon Press, 2006, 70–72.

13. Ibid., 74.

14. Dallas Willard, *Renovation of the Heart: Putting on the Character of Christ* (Colorado Springs: NavPress Publishing Group, 2002).

15. Ravi Zacharias, *Can Man Live Without God* (Nashville: Thomas Nelson, 1996).

16. Pascal quoted in: *The Great Ideas, A Synopticon of Great Books of the Western World* Vol I, (Chicago: University of Chicago Press)1052.

17. Ibid.

Chapter Eleven: How Then Shall We Teach Them to Live?

1. C.S. Lewis, *Mere Christianity*, (New York: Macmillan, 1952), 114.

Chapter Twelve: Ten Tips for Making Sure You Get It Right

1. William Pollack, *Real Boys* (New York: Owl Books, 1998), 23–25.

2. Ibid.

Index

competence, learned, 16
competition: adolescence and, 101–3; mastery over emotions and, 97–98; mastery over energies and, 98–101; mastery over the body and, 96–97; power, understanding and, 49; winning and, 96. *See also* sports
complaining, 221–22
computer games, 54
Cooper, Gary, 59
coping skills, 16
courage, 2, 38, 204, 208–9, 223, 239, 241
crime: fathers, absence of and, 147; father's encouragement and, 93; God, belief in and, 188
Cruise, Tom, 173
cultural capital, 16
culture. *See* popular culture

D
dads. *See* fathers
The Dangerous Book for Boys (Iggulden and Iggulden), 1
Dateline, 64
daughters: father's protectiveness of, 122; mothers' affection for, 134; mother's love for, 122

daycare, 136
deadbeat dads, 8, 133
Dead Man Walking, 110
death, 178–79, 201, 243–44
deferred gratification skills, 146, 147, 176
depression, 8; adolescents and, 79–82; boyhood and, 11; clinical, 81; father's love and, 157; God, belief in and, 17, 188, 202; major depressive disorder and, 79–80; medication for, 81; peer pressure and, 77; post-partum, 128, 129; religion and, 16; sexual activity and, 79; STDs and, 12, 79; suicide and, 11, 81; unavailability and, 139
Dialogues (Plato), 205
discipline: balancing love and, 21–24; fathers and, 21, 93–94, 118; fear of, 118; listening and, 21–24; mothers and, 93, 118
divorce, 8, 46, 167; boyhood and, 7; estrangement and, 133, 134; over-dependence and, 135; parental relationships and, 15; religion and, 190
drinking. *See* alcohol use